Deadly Farce

Deadly Farce

*Harvey Matusow and the Informer System
in the McCarthy Era*

ROBERT M. LICHTMAN AND
RONALD D. COHEN

University of Illinois Press
URBANA AND CHICAGO

⊗ This book is printed on acid-free paper.

Library of Congress Cataloging-in-Publication Data
Lichtman, Robert M., 1933–
Deadly farce : Harvey Matusow and the informer system in the
McCarthy era / Robert M. Lichtman and Ronald D. Cohen.
p. cm.
Includes bibliographical references and index.
ISBN 0-252-02886-4 (cloth : alk. paper)
1. Matusow, Harvey, 1926– 2. Informers—United States—Biography.
3. Ex-communists—United States—Biography. 4. False testimony—
United States—History—20th century. 5. Anti-communist move-
ments—United States—History—20th century. 6. Communism—
United States—History—20th century. 7. United States—Politics
and government—1945–1953. I. Cohen, Ronald D., 1940– . II. Title.
E743.5.M36L53   2004
973.921'092—dc21   2003011714

Contents

Illustrations follow page 98

Preface

The McCarthy era, like the period of the civil rights movement and the Vietnam War that followed, often left an indelible mark on individuals whose formative years coincided with it. Young people of that era saw their parents' careers altered, their college professors lose jobs, their own futures jeopardized by reason of transient political affiliations. The very subject—"he's got a security problem"—was, like an illness, whispered about.

The unreality of the time was magnified by the public's celebration of the ex-Communist informer-witnesses who fueled the process. Political informing became for some of them a career path; its practitioners gained fame, wrote books, gave lectures. Harvey Matusow, while not the most famous of the class, was almost certainly the most flamboyant and had the most sensational career. His 1955 recantation abruptly ended the public's short-lived romance with the group.

There were practical reasons as well to write about Matusow. Primary materials documenting his career were abundant and available—FBI records, transcripts of trials, court hearings, and committee hearings, and countless newspaper articles. Matusow had given a large volume of papers to the University of Sussex, England; Albert Kahn, the copublisher of Matusow's book that accompanied his recantation, had left papers to the Wisconsin Historical Society; J. B. Matthews's papers collected at Duke University were an additional and important source. And Matusow was still very much alive, possessed of a good memory, and anxious to tell his story.

* * *

We owe a debt of gratitude to Harvey Matusow, who, prior to his death in 2002, repeatedly made himself available for interviews and to answer questions on details of fact. The archivists at the University of Sussex (Elizabeth Inglis and Dorothy Sheridan), the National Archives and Records Administration, the Wisconsin Historical Society, and the Duke University Special Collections Library were invaluable to us. Clinton Jencks, Bill Dufty, and John McTernan generously submitted to interviews, and Jenny Vincent sent a useful letter. Martin Matthews shared recollections of his father as well as some of his parents' papers. Kathleen Clifford and Gail Malmgreen helped produce a readable manuscript.

A special debt is owed David J. Garrow and Stanley I. Kutler, who graciously took the time to read our manuscript and to offer valued comment and encouragement. Dagmar and Robert Hamilton read the manuscript at a much earlier stage in the process. Joan Catapano of the University of Illinois Press gave firm and continuing support to our efforts.

To our families, friends, and our respective colleagues at the Banchero Law Firm and Indiana University Northwest, all of whom provided encouragement and listened patiently to extended accounts of arcane, half-century-old political events, we offer our profound appreciation.

Introduction:
The Informers' Era

"There were floodlights, banks of cameras, a battalion of newsmen, radio equipment and some 200 eager spectators lined up outside the hearing room," the *New York Times* reported. The time was Monday afternoon, February 21, 1955, and the place was the same vast, ornate Senate hearing room where the Army-McCarthy hearings had played out the preceding year.[1]

The new event was the opening day of public hearings in the Senate Internal Security Subcommittee's investigation of Harvey Matusow's recantation. Matusow, a glib twenty-eight-year-old ex-Communist and former undercover FBI informant, had in the preceding four years built a considerable reputation as an informer-witness. He made frequent appearances as a government witness in various "Communist" cases, and as a "friendly" witness he had named names before the House Committee on Un-American Activities (HUAC), the Senate Permanent Subcommittee on Investigations (better known as Joe McCarthy's subcommittee), and, not least, SISS, the subcommittee now conducting the hearings.

But a few weeks earlier, to great fanfare, Matusow had announced that much of his testimony, including that in two major criminal prosecutions, had been false and that he had written a book telling all, soon to be published by a tiny publishing house whose principals were reputedly Communists. Defendants in the two criminal cases, including Communist Party officials, had already moved for new trials, seeking to overturn their prison sentences. Apart from the subcommittee's inquiry, the Department of Justice had instituted multiple federal grand jury investigations. The government, of course, suspected a Communist plot.[2]

The sense of theater was heightened by the subcommittee's selection of

Matusow himself as its first witness. Seated before the microphones and cameras, waiting for the hearings to begin, the stocky witness, "[l]ooking dark-eyed and sallow," the *Times* said, chatted easily with photographers. He knew some of them from prior committee appearances. When one called out, "Tell us a lie," Matusow grinned.[3]

The subcommittee's demeanor, however, was grim, and its questions hostile. "Haven't you called yourself 'leader of the Kremlin's Youth Movement in this country'?" its counsel asked. "I lied," Matusow responded. "Is one of your book publishers a Communist?" "I have accused him of being so, but I told a falsehood." "Were you 'lying for money' when you were paid for a 1952 election speech accusing a Democratic congressman of Communist ties?" "Yes sir; I was."[4]

He had in the past been "a perpetual and habitual liar," Matusow conceded. But no longer, he assured Republican senator William E. Jenner:

> Senator JENNER: You are telling the truth now?
> Mr. MATUSOW: Yes, sir.
> Senator JENNER: You are not a habitual liar?
> Mr. MATUSOW: No, sir.
> Senator JENNER: You are not a perpetual liar?
> Mr. MATUSOW: I am not a perpetual liar now.[5]

Matusow attributed his transformation to religion. "Sir, I believe in God, very strongly. . . . I believe in God and Christian charity, and I understand the meaning of it, sir." A Bronx native, the son of Russian-Jewish immigrants, he had been baptized in the Mormon faith the preceding fall.[6]

Matusow would spend five more days on the subcommittee's witness stand. The subcommittee in its report would attribute his recantation to a Communist plan to discredit government witnesses.[7]

Murray Kempton, writing in the *New York Post*, expressed the view of many Americans. "What is undisputed fact," he wrote, "is that [Matusow] was either a liar then or is a liar now." But, Kempton added, "[y]ou and I didn't offer him as a trustworthy man; the United States government did."[8]

Informers and Informers

While only a handful of McCarthy-era informers recanted their testimony, the class of ex-Communist informers was substantial in size. In the 1952–54 period, the Department of Justice had on its payroll, under contract and paid on a per diem basis, at least eighty-three ex-Communists of whom, it said, thirty were "regularly used as witnesses" and fifty-three were "occasionally used." Hired as "expert consultants" under a statute intended to enable the government to retain eminent scientists and educators on a part-time basis, their prevailing rate of compensation was thirty-four dollars per day (twenty-five dollars plus nine dollars "in lieu of expenses"), a not insignificant sum at the time. The Department of Justice list—it was leaked—almost certainly was not exhaustive, because congressional committees and state and local agencies separately retained ex-Communist informers.[9]

The government's practice of maintaining a stable of political informer-witnesses on its payroll was peculiar to the McCarthy era. "It is a novel arrangement," Richard Rovere wrote in 1955, "this hiring of people to take a solemn oath and testify favorably to the government. American history offers no precedent for it." The informers' "usefulness," he said, "derives from their ability and readiness to identify people as Communists, to describe Communist activities for the enlightenment of judges, juries, and security panels."[10]

The impact of the informers' voices, their accusations and warnings of domestic subversion by American Communists, repeated on countless occasions, was indisputably significant. A *New York Times* editor's insight was by no means unique when he wrote in 1951, apropos of informer Elizabeth Bentley, that "what many of the ex-Communists have been saying these past few years has succeeded in genuinely frightening large numbers of Americans, in influencing legislation and in profoundly altering many lives. They form an inescapable part of the social and political history of this generation."[11]

The August 1948 testimony before HUAC of the two most renowned ex-Communist informers, Whittaker Chambers and Elizabeth Bentley, as much as any single event, triggered "the McCarthy era." Their revelations that American Communists employed in federal departments and agencies had cooperated in Soviet espionage—the individuals they named included Alger Hiss, a former State Department official who accompanied President Franklin Roosevelt to Yalta, and Harry Dexter White, a former assistant secretary of the treasury—amplified by antiadministration politicians and media, right-wing clergy, veterans' and patriotic groups, among others, shaped the American political scene for the succeeding decade.[12]

Neither Chambers's nor Bentley's 1948 disclosures were news to the authorities. The essence of Chambers's testimony had been revealed in September 1939 to Assistant Secretary of State A. A. Berle. Bentley defected from the Soviets in 1945, and her disclosures to the FBI, which resulted in almost immediate reports to the Truman White House, were made in November of that year.[13]

In the summer of 1948, however, FBI director J. Edgar Hoover, angered by what he considered the Truman administration's failure to take more decisive action against Communists and left-wingers in government, and motivated by an intense personal dislike of Truman, decided to go public with Bentley's and Chambers's revelations. He handed the two to HUAC and to a counterpart Senate committee, which rushed them to the witness stand. Hoover's timing was influenced not by security considerations but by the fact that 1948 was a presidential election year and Truman a candidate.[14]

The Bentley-Chambers disclosures created a sensation. Bentley's accusations related to 1941–44, wartime years during which the Soviet Union and the United States were allies in the crusade against Nazi Germany. While Chambers had split with the Communists much earlier, in the late 1930s, the confrontation between the rumpled and psychologically troubled Chambers, who claimed a close personal relationship with Hiss, and the elegant and accomplished Hiss, who initially denied even knowing Chambers, was pure drama.[15]

The Bentley-Chambers testimony, which was immediately challenged and for decades sharply controverted, has in recent years received strong confirmation. KGB archives in the former Soviet Union, which were opened (albeit selectively) in the early 1990s, and VENONA project messages (nearly three thousand wholly or partially decrypted cables dispatched by Soviet agents in the United States during World War II and intercepted by U.S. Army intelligence), declassified starting in 1995, indicate that a number of the individuals named by Bentley and Chambers did assist Soviet espionage. Bentley's defection in November 1945, these sources show, resulted in the virtual destruction of the KGB's spy networks in the United States for years to come.[16]

* * *

But espionage by its nature is a covert activity, known only to a limited number of trusted individuals. The testimony of most ex-Communist informers in the McCarthy era, unlike that of Bentley, Chambers, and a very few others, had little or nothing to do with spying. The Department of Justice's stable of eighty-plus informers—Harvey Matusow among them—rarely testified about espionage. What they did inform about were political affiliations and activities.

The Communist Party of the U.S.A. (CPUSA), despite the existence of a party underground in which a tiny percentage of American Communists assisted Soviet intelligence, was primarily a political organization, which took positions on public issues and entered candidates in elections for public office. The grist for the informers' mills was testimony about membership or, more likely, past membership in the "open" party or in one of dozens of "front" organizations. In most cases, the individuals about whom the informers were queried and whom they named never had access to sensitive information; most had never worked for the government.[17]

The use of informers in a wide variety of situations having no connection to spying reflected the sweep of the measures that federal, state, and local governments and some private businesses took in the name of responding to the Soviet espionage threat. It is these measures that characterize or define "the McCarthy era."

The Scope of "Antisubversive" Measures

The federal "loyalty" program, instituted by the Truman administration under a 1947 executive order and reorganized and termed a "security" program by the Eisenhower administration when it took office in 1953, was applied to almost all federal employees and to every applicant for a federal job.[18]

Determinations in loyalty-security cases usually turned on the employee's present or past membership in a proscribed political organization. To this end, in 1947 Attorney General Tom C. Clark compiled a list of "subversive" organizations, by 1950 numbering 197, some existing but in many cases long defunct. The list, of course, included the CPUSA. But most of the listed groups were "fronts," that is, organizations set up and often controlled by the Communist Party but intended to attract non-Communists as members (e.g., groups whose stated goal was opposing fascism or supporting the civil rights of black Americans). Informers often supplied evidence of an employee's membership in a listed organization.[19]

The federal government's program to deport resident aliens who were or had once been Communist Party members did not involve government personnel. But a 1940 federal statute made even past membership in an organization advocating the violent overthrow of the government an automatic ground for deportation. In 1950, in order to save the Immigration and Naturalization Service (INS) the task of trying to prove it in every case, Congress enacted a statute specifically identifying the CPUSA as an organization advocating the violent overthrow of the government. To establish deportability after 1950, nothing more needed to be shown than a person's alien status and membership in the party at some time after entering the United States.[20]

The Justice Department customarily drew from its stable of informers to prove past membership in the Communist Party. Matusow's testimony in 1953, for example, contributed to the deportation of Goldie Davidoff, a Canadian alien married to an American and employed by the party's newspaper, the *Daily Worker*.[21]

The government also sought to prevent American citizens from going abroad. The State Department, until restrained by the Supreme Court in the late 1950s, routinely denied passports to hundreds of persons believed to be Communists or members of proscribed groups. The impact of this practice fell most heavily on left-wing entertainers, blacklisted at home but employable abroad (singer-actor Paul Robeson, for example), and scientists invited to teach or lecture abroad (such as Linus Pauling, a Nobel Prize–winning chemist). Informers often supplied the information on which the government based passport refusals.[22]

Ex-Communist informers played an essential role in criminal prosecutions of Communist Party officials under the Smith Act for conspiring to teach or advocate the forcible overthrow of the government. In these cases, the informers were not used to prove party membership on the part of the defendants, who openly identified themselves as party officials, but rather to tie each defendant to advocacy of forcible overthrow. This frequently took the form of testimony that a defendant had endorsed an inflammatory passage in a Marxist text. Some of the testimony Matusow later recanted, given in a 1952 Smith Act trial in New York City, was of this character, intended to tie Alexander Trachtenberg, a party warhorse, to a passage in a book by Andrei Vishinsky, a Soviet official.[23]

The idea of forcing Communists to register with the government was one of the panaceas of the period, and in 1950 Congress enacted legislation creating an administrative agency, the Subversive Activities Control Board, which was empowered to force Communist organizations to register, and in the case of the CPUSA, to identify all of its members. Informer testimony became a staple in proceedings before the SACB.[24]

In succeeding years, the SACB held protracted hearings directed not only at the CPUSA but also at a large number of alleged front organizations. Shortly before he recanted, Matusow appeared as a government witness at SACB hearings to compel registration by Veterans of the Abraham Lincoln Brigade and the National Council for American-Soviet Friendship, both on the attorney general's list.[25]

Hearings of congressional investigating committees provided the most visible and desirable forum for informers. Before the committees, notably HUAC, SISS and, in 1953–54, the McCarthy subcommittee, informers were invited guests, treated with respect and not subjected to cross-examination, as they were in criminal trials and at deportation or SACB hearings. Often their testimony at committee hearings received favorable attention in the press.

HUAC, the most prominent of the committees (until its abolition in 1975), conducted a nearly continuous series of hearings investigating Communist influences in government, labor, and industry—particularly the high-profile motion picture industry, to which it returned without fail every few years. SISS, headed by the powerful Senator Pat McCarran of Nevada, was perhaps best known for its relentless pursuit of Owen Lattimore, a Johns Hopkins professor and China expert, whom informer Louis Budenz named as a Communist Party member (in the face of persuasive contrary evidence) and against whom Matusow also testified (testimony he later recanted).[26]

America's states and cities, not content with the umbrella of protection against Communist "subversion" provided by the federal government, took independent action. State legislatures organized "little HUAC" commissions—Matusow was employed by the one in Ohio. State and local governments subjected 80 percent of the roughly one million American public-school teachers in the 1950s to some form of loyalty screening. Matusow was hired as a "consultant" by the New York City public school system to identify Communist teachers.[27]

Informers played a central role in the blacklisting of alleged Communists in the motion picture and radio-TV industries. The radio-TV industry boycott utilized *Red Channels,* published in 1950, a list of industry names substantially distilled from "Appendix IX," a huge and indiscriminate listing of many thousands of alleged Communists and Communist sympathizers published by the Dies committee, HUAC's immediate predecessor, in 1945. *Counterattack,* a periodical for which Matusow worked in the early 1950s, promoted and added to the blacklist.[28]

"Antisubversive" Politics

The enthusiasm of legislators and public officials for sweeping programs of this kind did not reflect a belief that such measures were a necessary means of uncovering or forestalling Soviet espionage. Rather, politicians correctly perceived strong popular support for "antisubversive" measures—the more sweeping, the better.

The public by the early 1950s had adopted a punitive and unforgiving attitude toward American Communists. A carefully executed 1954 public opinion poll of nearly five thousand persons in all parts of the country showed that 89 percent believed that an admitted Communist should be fired from a college teaching job; 68 percent that one should be fired from a clerk's job at a store; and 63 percent that one should be fired as a radio singer. When asked whether admitted Communists should be stripped of their American citizenship, 77 percent thought they should; 51 percent believed they should "be put in jail."[29]

Republicans, after twenty years of the New Deal and the Fair Deal, captured the presidency and both houses of Congress in 1952, making effective use of the "Communist" issue. Their vice presidential candidate, Richard M. Nixon, as a HUAC member had built a national reputation on his role in the Hiss-Chambers case. Shortly before election day, Senator Joe McCarthy appeared on national television to attack the Democratic presidential candidate, Governor Adlai E. Stevenson of Illinois, attempting to tie him to the convicted Hiss—McCarthy's famous "Alger—I mean Adlai" speech. Matusow, more versatile than most informers, campaigned for the election of McCarthy and other right-wing Republicans in Senate races, charging that Communists supported their Democratic opponents.[30]

The era also brought to prominence a loose but politically powerful confederation of right-wing politicians, journalists, authors, informers, officials of veterans' organizations, clergy, businesspeople, and World War II–style isolationists, whose nearly exclusive focus was on the exposure and punishment of left-wingers, on whom they were quick to pin a "Communist" label. Richard Gid Powers in 1995 termed this group "countersubversive anticommunists"; liberals at the time called them "professional anti-Communists" or "red-baiters." McCarthy was their hero.[31]

Leading "countersubversives" included Hearst columnists George Sokolsky and Westbrook Pegler as well as Alfred Kohlberg, leader of the pro–Chiang Kai-shek "China lobby" and a source of funding for numerous "countersubversive" causes. J. B. Matthews, the former top staffer and brains of the Dies committee, was a linchpin of the "countersubversives" by virtue of his massive files on left-wing groups and individuals. Matusow, when he gained prominence as an informer, sought out the "countersubversive" elite and became an acolyte in their circle.[32]

While Joe McCarthy, the pugnacious and rough-hewn junior senator from Wisconsin, gave the era its name and tone, FBI director Hoover, more than anyone else, determined its politics. Hoover had a long-standing hatred of the "poison of foreign isms" and Communism in particular ("the most evil, monstrous conspiracy against man since time began"). At the absolute command of a large and well-financed federal police organization, and in possession of files detailing the political activities and personal behavior of tens of millions of Americans, not least virtually every politician in Washington, Hoover in the 1950s was an immensely powerful official, essentially immune from criticism.[33]

Plainly, prudence counseled politicians and public officials, if they did not affirmatively support antisubversive measures, at least to go along or to remain silent.

The Role and Rewards of Informers

The types of issues in McCarthy-era "Communist" cases cried out for informers: the political character of long-defunct organizations, the extent of an individual's knowledge of or participation in an organization, and, most important, whether he or she had ever been a *member* of the Communist Party or other "subversive" organization. Because witnesses on these kinds of issues were frequently unavailable, unwilling to testify, or hostile to the government's position, government agencies sought evidence from "professional" informers.

The sheer volume of employee-loyalty cases, deportation proceedings, Smith Act prosecutions, SACB proceedings, and congressional and state investigative committee hearings created a large market for informers. While ad hoc witnesses could testify in a single proceeding, the most valuable and frequently used witnesses were those who could testify against a significant number of individuals. Prosecutors and investigators sought out informers who had been members of the Communist Party, often able to name hundreds of their former associates. The Justice Department's stable of paid informer-witnesses consisted entirely of ex-Communists. "[A]n accident of history," Richard Rovere wrote, "puts the ex-Communist, whether his faith was feigned or authentic, in possession of an extraordinarily negotiable thing—his past."[34]

Informers often acquired a facility as witnesses by dint of repetition and experience. When testifying at a well-publicized congressional committee hearing, in Joseph Alsop's view, informers were required to become entertainers: "They must pose; they must attitudinize; they must be portentous; they are also strongly driven to embroider and elaborate and invent something new to say—all in order to give satisfaction to their audiences."[35]

Those who succeeded were in great demand. Matthew Cvetic, a former undercover FBI informant from Pittsburgh, testified sixty-three times in various types of "Communist" proceedings. Louis Budenz testified an estimated twenty-five times before six different congressional committees, seven times in court trials, at least four times in administrative proceedings, and in an undetermined number of deportation hearings. John Lautner, an expelled Communist Party official, became a key prosecution witness in Smith Act trials after 1950, and between 1952 and 1956 he was a witness in twenty-five proceedings.[36]

Informers named prodigious numbers of alleged Communists, past and present. Barbara Hartle, a West Coast party official who turned informer following her conviction in a Smith Act prosecution, accused over 400 (including her ex-husband and ex-common-law husband); Matusow named 216. Among those who joined the party to work undercover for the FBI, Cvetic gave 411 names to HUAC, and Mary Markward 318. Detective Mildred Blauvelt of the New York City police department's "Red Squad" named 450 names in only four days of testimony before HUAC in 1955.[37]

Significant economic incentives encouraged these witnesses. Lautner, who after 1951 earned his living supplying information about the Communist Party, received a total of $22,000 from the Department of Justice between 1952 and 1956; in 1958 he went on HUAC's payroll as a consultant. Cvetic received, apart from witness compensation, $12,500 for the motion picture rights to his story (*I Was a Communist for the FBI*), $6,500 for a ghost-written magazine series, and additional income from lectures. Cvetic's aggregate income from these activities during his glory years ranged from $10,000 to $15,000 annually—a substantial income in the 1950s.[38]

Louis Budenz earned even more. *Collier's* paid him $20,000 for a series of articles in 1948; royalties from his first book, *This Is My Story*, by 1952 reached $9,000. In addition to witness fees and his salary as a professor at Fordham University, Budenz earned over $60,000 from magazine articles, book royalties, and lecture fees between 1945 (when he defected from the Communist Party) and 1954. As an editor of the *Daily Worker*, he had earned about $90 a week.[39]

Leading informers also enjoyed the perquisites of fame. For example, when the film *I Was a Communist for the FBI*, recounting Cvetic's exploits, received its premiere in his hometown of Pittsburgh in April 1951, a parade was held marking "Matt Cvetic Day." In 1952 Cvetic received an Americanism award from the Pennsylvania Legionnaires' convention, presented to him by Governor John S. Fine of Pennsylvania and Bebe Shopp, the reigning Miss America.[40]

Many achieved renown as authors. By 1952, Budenz had published *This Is My Story*, *Men without Faces: The Communist Conspiracy in the U.S.A.*, and *The Cry Is Peace*. Angela Calomiris, an FBI undercover informant who surfaced at the 1949 Foley Square Smith Act trial, wrote *Red Masquerade: Undercover for the FBI*, published in 1950. *Out of Bondage* by Elizabeth Bentley and *This Deception* by Hede Massing (like Bentley, a self-confessed ex-Communist spy) were published in 1951. By far the most important (and best written) of this genre was Whittaker Chambers's *Witness*, a Book-of-the-Month Club selection in 1952, serialized in the *Saturday Evening Post*. Herbert Philbrick's successful *I Led Three Lives: Citizen, "Communist," Counter-*

spy, also published in 1952, became (like the accounts of Cvetic's activities) both a motion picture and a successful TV series.[41]

The celebrity of ex-Communist informers in a nation that despises "stool pigeons," "rats," "canaries," and "squealers" is not easily explained. It was, in part, a consequence of the leading roles assigned them by congressional committee chairmen and prosecutors and of the extensive and often highly favorable press coverage their testimony received. The informers also gave a simple explanation for America's perplexing cold war problems, one that absolved it of responsibility. And their celebrity, of course, was greatest among those who agreed most ardently with their anti-Communist message.

Whatever the reason, "the political informer," Frank J. Donner observed in 1954, "is coming to be regarded as a social hero, as an exalted being endowed with special authority, insight, and reliability."[42]

Professional informer-witnesses fell into two main categories: apostates and undercover police informants. Most of the former group had moved from one end to the other of the political spectrum. Whittaker Chambers, who made this journey, believed that "'[i]n our time, informing is a duty.'"[43]

The second category consisted of individuals who had joined the Communist Party not out of conviction but because they were recruited to do so by the FBI or a local police "Red squad." They came from various backgrounds. Herbert Philbrick worked as advertising manager for a group of movie theaters when he joined the party under the bureau's auspices. Matthew Cvetic, a low-level federal employee when the FBI hired him, had earlier tried unsuccessfully to join U.S. Army intelligence.[44]

The Credibility Issue

A timing factor affected the credibility of informers. An FBI informant working undercover inside the Communist Party, whose allegations might well be tested against reports by others, had reason to be accurate. So also did the apostates in their initial and exhaustive debriefings by the FBI, unaware of what the bureau knew and with their futures still in doubt. But after an undercover FBI informant surfaced or an apostate had finished telling his or her story to the bureau and the person became a professional informer-witness, a new set of influences came into play.[45]

Continuing appearances before HUAC and other congressional investigating committees required, if the committee were to receive new publicity, that new names be named. Similarly, there was pressure to meet the needs of prosecutors in criminal or deportation cases for testimony showing this or that new individual to have been a Communist. Whatever the motive, informers in later testimony began to identify as important Communists individuals whom they had never mentioned in earlier, exhaustive FBI interviews. "On a nod from prosecutors," David Caute wrote, informers "sold hunches or guesses as inside knowledge, supporting their claims with bogus reports of conversations and encounters."[46]

There was little risk that informers would be prosecuted for perjury, because they provided an invaluable service for the Justice Department, the FBI, and congressional investigating committees. Moreover, after using an informer as a witness in judicial or administrative proceedings, the government had a vested interest in sustaining that person's credibility, for otherwise the cases might have to be retried and the government's past efforts wasted. If a head-on credibility conflict developed, the accused Communist, not the informer, was thus likely to be indicted for perjury. The Hiss-Chambers and Lattimore-Budenz cases and the case of William W. Remington, a young government official who denied Elizabeth Bentley's accusations under oath and was convicted of perjury, are examples.[47]

The FBI, upon learning that one of its informers had publicly named an individual not mentioned in earlier interview reports, was likely immediately to reinterview the informer and to update its files to include this new accusation, not to reevaluate the informer's credibility. The bureau's primary concern was that it might be criticized for being unaware of the informer's new evidence.[48]

There were, to be sure, instances in which the bureau concluded that an informer was unreliable or had committed perjury—Matusow and Cvetic are examples—and in such cases it advised the attorney general or the heads of the Justice Department's Criminal or Internal Security divisions. But having thus insulated itself against future criticism, the FBI did not interfere with the department's continued use of the informer as a witness in later cases.[49]

The attorney general and his subordinates in the Justice Department bore the ultimate responsibility for the selection of government witnesses. Under the settled principles that should have guided their exercise of judgment, the government's interest in a criminal case was "not that it shall win a case, but that justice shall be done"; a prosecutor's knowing use of perjured testimony was not only unethical but a violation of due process of law. But in the McCarthy era, Justice Department lawyers repeatedly used witnesses whose credibility they had every reason to doubt, sometimes in the face of express warnings from the FBI.[50]

Over time, an increasing number of instances of perjury by informers became manifest. An early example, in 1948, involved a Washington state legislative committee that imported informer George Hewitt to testify in its investigation of alleged Communist activities at the University of Washington. When Hewitt's false accusations against Melvin Rader, an English professor at the university, gave rise to perjury charges against him, he fled to New York City, where (with the assistance of the Justice Department) he successfully resisted extradition to Washington state and continued to testify in deportation cases against alleged Communists.[51]

Paul Crouch, who became a professional witness after seventeen years as a Communist Party member, committed a series of egregious perjuries. He testified, for example, at one of the many trials of Harry Bridges, the militant West Coast waterfront union leader, that Bridges had been present at a party convention on June 28, 1936, in New York City. Bridges responded with witnesses, newspaper reports, and other documentary evidence proving his attendance at a union meeting in Stockton, California, at a time that made it impossible for him to have been in New York City on the day in question.[52]

At the Bridges trial, Crouch also testified that he "had no knowledge of the existence" of a party official named David Davis. But several years later, at a 1954 Smith Act trial in which Davis was a defendant, Crouch testified to having had a long acquaintance with him, beginning in 1928 and including frequent attendance with him at party meetings.[53]

Manning Johnson, a black ex-Communist who left the party in 1940 after ten years' membership and became an informer-witness, admitted in a 1950 sedition case against Steve Nelson, a party official, that he had falsely denied being an FBI informant in a 1948 deportation proceeding. Johnson stated that he would tell a lie "[i]f the interests of my Government are at stake," and that if it were necessary for "maintaining secrecy of the techniques and methods of operation of the FBI, who have the responsibility of the protection of our people, I say I will do it, and I will do it a thousand times." In 1957, the INS was still using Johnson as a witness in deportation cases.[54]

Perjuries by Joseph Mazzei, a former FBI undercover informant, resulted in a 1956 Supreme Court reversal of the convictions of Communist Party officials in a Pittsburgh Smith Act prosecution. By the Justice Department's own admission, Mazzei testified falsely before the McCarthy subcommittee that a party "hit" man, one Louis Bortz, had been chosen "to do a job in the liquidation of" Senator McCarthy. He also perjured himself, the department disclosed, in a bastardy proceeding in a Pennsylvania court.[55]

Although sometimes compelled to admit that its informers had at times given perjured testimony, the government consistently opposed efforts in the courts to vacate criminal convictions or administrative determinations on that ground. Nor did it prosecute Crouch, Johnson, Mazzei, or other perjurious informers.

Recanting informers were another story. In these cases, there was the element of double cross and usually also a claim that government lawyers had suborned the informers' perjuries. The government brought perjury prosecutions against two informers who disavowed under oath their earlier testimony, Harvey Matusow and Marie Natvig—not for their earlier testimony but for their disavowals.

Natvig's recantation came in a Federal Communications Commission case that featured a near epidemic of recanting government witnesses. In this unusual proceeding, brought by the Republican-controlled FCC, whose chairman, John C. Doerfer, was a close McCarthy associate, the agency sought to deny renewal of valuable broadcast licenses held by Edward Lamb because of his alleged Communist ties. Lamb, a former left-wing union lawyer from Toledo, had become a wealthy businessman as well as a prominent Democrat. The witnesses presented against him included Natvig, who claimed to have been a Communist Party member for twelve years and to have known Lamb well; Lowell Watson, who had testified for the government in a series of deportation and denaturalization cases; and the ubiquitous Louis Budenz.[56]

Due in no small part to the investigative effort that Lamb had the financial resources to mount, Natvig, Watson, and a third witness, Clark Wideman, all finally disavowed their testimony against him. Prosecuted for perjury, Natvig was convicted and sentenced to eight months in prison.[57]

Matusow's recantation, by virtue of his flamboyance and prominence as an informer, created a louder public furor and had farther reaching consequences.

Matusow's Case

Until his recantation in early 1955, Matusow had been in many respects a typical informer, more versatile than most, active in every aspect of the informer's trade—undercover FBI informant; government witness in criminal, SACB, and deportation proceedings; namer of names before congressional and state committees; and participant in entertainment industry blacklisting and "clearing." He was a friend to Joe McCarthy and the "countersubversive" elite. When Matusow recanted, Murray Kempton termed him "the fifties' witness against the fifties."[58]

Matusow's motives and the events surrounding his recantation, even now, are less than clear. He left his job with McCarthy but continued to testify for the government; he admitted perjury to a Methodist bishop but denied to HUAC that he had done so. Although Matusow placed himself in the hands of a pro-Communist book publisher, ideology seemingly was not his motive; no other publisher would touch his book. Nor, contrary to the government's claim, could the modest publisher's advance he received adequately explain his drastic action.[59]

Matusow's recantation triggered a wide-open national debate concerning the government's use of professional informers. For the first time, the issues posed by the government's maintenance on its payroll of a small army of ex-Communist informers, used to testify against political dissidents, received close public scrutiny. In response to the Matusow case, the Justice Department dismantled its stable of informers. Because, moreover, informers had been used in so wide a variety of cases, Matusow's recantation served to discredit the government's entire antisubversive program.[60]

Novelist John Steinbeck, writing in the *Saturday Review,* commented: "I suspect that Government informers, even if they have told the truth, can't survive Matusow's testimony. He has said that it was a good racket. Well, Matusow has ruined the racket. It will never be so good again."[61]

An angered Justice Department prosecuted Matusow for perjury—for testifying falsely that prosecutor Roy Cohn induced him to commit perjury in the Smith Act trial. Upon his conviction, he served three and one-half years in a federal prison.[62]

Still a young man at the time of his release from prison, Matusow in the ensuing years underwent something of a change in character. The last four decades of his life, during which he became a practicing Mormon, were characterized by accomplishment and not insignificant good works. He lived at various times in England, New England, and the American West—residing for years in a tiny Mormon community in Utah, active in public-access cable television. He died in Claremont, New Hampshire, in January 2002, at age seventy-five, following an automobile accident.[63]

1   Birth of a Party Member

Harvey Marshall Matusow was born October 3, 1926, into a distinctly mid-dle-class Bronx neighborhood. Not long before, the borough had been largely rural, and the apartment houses in the neighborhood were comparatively new, often boasting large courtyards and wrought iron decoration. The Bronx had attractive parks, two universities, a fine zoo and botanical garden, and in the New York Yankees of the time arguably the best baseball team ever.[1]

Matusow's family lived in an apartment just off the Grand Concourse, a wide boulevard constructed in the early years of the century and now lined with solid, imposing buildings. Largely Jewish and, at least before the Depres-sion, reasonably prosperous, the residents of the neighborhood were better off than the working-class Jews in nearby Hunts Point. "After the Jewish High Holy Day services," a Bronx historian wrote, "men would promenade along the wide tree-lined Grand Concourse wearing their expensive suits, escort-ing their ladies who were dressed in the latest fashions and furs." Yiddish was commonly spoken, reflecting the immigration wave of central and eastern European Jews around the turn of the century. Matusow's parents, both immigrants from czarist Russia, had reason to be proud of where they lived.[2]

His mother, Sylvia, nicknamed "Kitty," and his father, Herman, had arrived separately in the United States in the same year, 1906. Each had an immi-grant's tale about the journey. Kitty told how her grandfather, with whom she was traveling, purchased passage to New York from a port on the Euro-pean continent, only to find that he had been cheated and the ship was bound for Liverpool. Herman had a more harrowing story. Only twelve and travel-ing without family members, he met an older man on the ship who agreed to pose as his uncle. When they reached Ellis Island, however, the man got cold feet and told immigration officials, "I never saw the kid until he got on the ship in Danzig." Refused entry, Herman spent almost a year returning to his hometown in Russia; but after a few months, he emigrated again to the United States, this time successfully.[3]

The two shared a frugal nature and an instinct for survival but differed in other respects. Kitty was an observant Orthodox Jew who lit Sabbath candles, kept a kosher home, and sent her sons to Hebrew school. She was quiet and direct in her manner. The eldest of ten children, all of whom eventually lived in New York or New Jersey, her family name was Stolpensky—in America, Stolpin. Herman, who also came from a large family, one that included two medical doctors in New York City, was not religious at all. A short, well-dressed man, he possessed a hair-trigger temper, a good sense of humor, and a passion for playing cards. Although he understood well the operations of the Bronx Democratic machine of Boss Ed Flynn, which exercised an important influence in the lives of residents, he was, like his wife, apolitical. Years later, they could not comprehend their son's political about-faces and the anger he stirred.[4]

After entering the United States, Herman displayed energy and ingenuity. He worked as a singing waiter in Coney Island and, during World War I, served as a quartermaster sergeant in the U.S. Army. During the 1920s, he built a chain of cigar stores in good Manhattan locations, including two stores near Times Square. But he lost almost everything in the 1929 crash. "During the depression," Harvey recalled, Herman's "card earnings kept us alive."[5]

Harvey had one sibling, his brother Danny, three-and-a-half years older, his best friend, protector, and hero, with whom he shared a bedroom. Danny was a fine athlete and a good student, with a naturally warm and easy way with people—attributes that incited mixed feelings in his kid brother. "I wanted to be him," Harvey later wrote, "and I couldn't." To compensate, he said, "I tried too hard, and I pushed, bluffing my way through, being loud and glib, pretending that I could do but not proving it."[6]

As a boy, Harvey sometimes assisted his father at one of his stores, located in the Manhattan theater district, obtaining rolls of nickels from the box office of a nearby theater for use in the store's pinball machines. He liked to recall the nickname he gained, "Kid Nickels." He was a Boy Scout for two years.[7]

Both brothers attended Bronx public schools. But Harvey, despite his quick intelligence, proved a consistently poor student, a circumstance he later attributed to dyslexia (a condition largely unknown at the time). "I couldn't write an English composition that made any sense grammatically," he recalled. "I could fix most things, but I couldn't read a diagram or a blueprint."[8]

He did develop "street smarts." At age twelve, he went to work in the neighborhood for Phil the Bookie. As a messenger and gofer, he saw bribes given to police officers and drew the lesson that government was corrupt. As a teenager, he worked as a stockroom clerk for a clothing store in Manhattan. Along with other neighborhood kids, he attended a lot of Yankee games, sometimes cutting school to do so.[9]

* * *

World War II changed everything. In August 1942, Danny enlisted in the Army Air Force and, called to active duty in March 1943, was sent to England. Harvey, bored by his studies at William Howard Taft High School, could hardly wait until he was seventeen, the minimum enlistment age. In November 1943, barely a month after his seventeenth birthday, he joined the army. His enlistment had an immediate side benefit, a high school diploma, awarded to students who enlisted while in their senior year. As he was flunking some of the subjects he needed to graduate, Harvey would not have received his diploma otherwise.[10]

In September 1944, less than two months before Harvey's active-duty call, the family received a telegram advising that Danny was missing in action. His B-17 aircraft had been lost in a daylight bombing raid over Nuremberg. The next day, Harvey, who had selected the air force branch, requested and received a transfer to the infantry.[11]

Called to active duty on October 31, 1944, four weeks after his eighteenth birthday, he was trained as a rifleman and assigned to the European theater.[12]

* * *

Matusow's military service abroad was in many ways broadening and liberating. From a parochial Bronx neighborhood, his stomping ground became end-of-the-war France and Germany.

He saw a minimum of combat, largely the mopping up of bedraggled German soldiers bypassed by Patton's Third Army in its rapid advance. Viewing scores of bombed-out houses, he was struck by the personal items—photo albums, letters, and diaries—strewn about. In April 1945, after he reported spells of headaches and dizziness, army doctors diagnosed him as having a "[p]sychoneurosis, anxiety state, mild, acute"—a condition that, an interviewing psychiatrist speculated, might be associated with his brother's death.[13]

On V-E Day, in the spring of 1945, Matusow, on a three-day pass in Paris, experienced the exhilaration of the war's end. People were "floating, smiling, everyone was smiling," he recalled. He sat in Paris cafés and heard remarkable war stories, some told by French Communists who had served in the Resistance.[14]

Matusow got a break when he was ordered to enroll at a U.S.-sponsored college in Biarritz. This opportunity came about because the military, seeking to reduce the pressure on it to bring all the troops home at once, tried to create some pleasant duty assignments for American soldiers in Europe. Matusow's Biarritz assignment, although it stemmed from his possession of a high school diploma, was hardly an academic experience. He worked as a photographer for an army public relations unit, receiving frequent weekend passes to Paris.[15]

A transfer to an assignment in Germany followed. In 1946, stationed in Mainz and interrogating German prisoners, Matusow gained information from a prisoner who had kept a detailed diary and map, enabling him to locate his brother's burial site in a church cemetery in a Nuremberg suburb. He informed his parents, and two years later the army confirmed his findings and moved the remains to a U.S. military cemetery in France.[16]

In July 1946, Matusow received orders to return to the United States. Wise by that time in the ways of the army, he selected the manner of his return, as part of an armed guard for hospitalized court-martial prisoners. The group boarded a comfortable hospital ship in Bremerhaven, and Matusow spent the ten-day journey to New York playing cards. His ship docked in Staten Island, and the group proceeded by ambulance to a military hospital, where the prisoners were delivered to local MPs. Hailing a cab, Matusow headed home to the Bronx for thirty days' leave.[17]

The army discharged him on August 3.[18]

* * *

After life as an American serviceman in postwar Europe, Matusow found the Bronx a considerable letdown. Not only was the Grand Concourse not the Champs Elysee but also the army had given him a job, a position in life. As a civilian, although barely twenty years old, his prospects were unpromising. While millions of returning veterans attended college under the G.I. Bill, Matusow was a poor student who had gained his high school diploma via a loophole. Uncertain of his future, he worked briefly at his uncle's cigar store in Manhattan and then went on unemployment insurance, at twenty dollars a week for former servicemen, a program referred to as the "G.I. 52-20 Club."[19]

He tried further schooling, for which the G.I. Bill paid a stipend, but without success. Enrolling in a technical school that offered training in architecture and engineering, Matusow lasted about five weeks. He registered for free night classes at City College of New York's downtown facility at 23rd Street.

These classes, he later said, "didn't mean education to me." Rather, they killed time and, more important, quieted his mother's complaints. An added dividend was their downtown location, close to Greenwich Village. Matusow liked the Bohemian atmosphere and diversity of the Village, and he frequented the bars on MacDougal Street.[20]

Mostly, however, he hung out in the Bronx with a half dozen or so childhood friends. They played cards, shot pool, went to the bowling alley, saw an occasional movie, pitched coins at cracks on the sidewalk, and, for hours on end, stood on the same street corner and talked about nothing of consequence.[21]

His father's car, a well-cared-for 1937 Chevy, gave Matusow an occasional means of escape. But the car also tied him to his parents' home, and as the only surviving child he became increasingly the focus of their concern and their questions, both as to his plans for the day and for the long term.[22]

* * *

Matusow's invitation from the political left came unexpectedly in November 1946, as he killed time on his street corner tossing a rubber ball against a wall. A neighborhood friend of his brother named Julie Sheik, whom Matusow had not seen since his return, came by and greeted him. Julie asked the usual questions: how he'd been, what the army had been like, and what his plans were. Presented with a sympathetic and safe ear, Matusow poured out his frustrations, his lack of direction, his boredom. Julie mentioned that he was active in the local chapter of American Youth for Democracy and invited Matusow to a party in the neighborhood that Saturday night, an invitation gratefully accepted.[23]

Matusow understood that AYD was a left-wing group—a year later, it would be listed by the attorney general as a Communist front—but he was not put off. America, after all, had just fought a war in alliance with the Soviet Union; in any case, a Saturday night party entailed no strings. The party turned out to be an AYD fund-raiser, with a one dollar charge at the door. He paid and had a fine time, enjoying, he later explained, "an echo of the comaraderie" that had existed in the army in Europe. About twenty-five young people, mostly from the neighborhood, attended; they drank wine and sang songs (folk, union, and protest songs he had never heard before); the conversations concerned serious issues; the women were intelligent and attractive. Before the party ended, he was invited to a local AYD meeting the following Friday.[24]

When he didn't show up that night (three of his street-corner friends persuaded him to go barhopping in Greenwich Village instead), Julie suggested that he attend the following Friday's meeting. Matusow came to the meeting, held upstairs in a neighborhood movie theater, and was warmly received. The evening consisted of three hours of talk, most of it about opposition to Universal Military Training and saving the Office of Price Administration, the wartime agency that administered price controls. Discussion focused on the nuts and bolts of political action—slogans, letters to members of Congress, setting up folding tables on sidewalks to pass out literature or to gain signatures on petitions. He was impressed; here were young people doing something worthwhile, not just playing cards or talking aimlessly on street corners. Asked to join AYD, he did; asked to subscribe to the *Daily Worker,* he did that also.[25]

In the succeeding months, AYD activities began to dominate Matusow's life—going to meetings, circulating petitions, distributing literature, working on programs for the club's weekly meetings, and, on the social side, attending parties. He became the club's education director and social director.[26]

He did continue, on and off, to attend CCNY classes, mostly those with a business focus, and worked at a couple of jobs. In March 1947, he became a trainee at the Grey Advertising Agency in Manhattan; but after he took part in an unsuccessful effort to organize a union at the agency, he lost his job. In October, he tried working as a theatrical agent, helping to manage performers, find bookings, and plug songs, but he tired of it after a few months.[27]

Matusow spent ten days during the summer of 1947 at Camp Unity, a Communist Party–run summer camp in upstate New York, about eighty miles from New York City, where he participated in AYD Week, a fund-raising effort. Among other activities, he observed young campers engaged in outdoor lovemaking at "Lenin's Rock," a place in the woods where a rock had been sculpted into a portrait of Lenin. His description would become, four-and-a-half years later, part of his initial and highly successful performance before HUAC.[28]

In AYD Matusow came to realize that with his gift of gab and quick-wittedness, he might be good at political activity. He began, he later wrote, "to find excitement and fulfillment in organized political activity" and experienced "a pride of accomplishment" in the use of his "organizational talents." But he found "frustrating" the variety of political viewpoints within his AYD club—liberals, Zionists, socialists, and Communists (about 35 to 40 percent of the membership). He was "more attracted" to the Communists because they seemed to have "the strength of purpose" he had felt as a soldier, and they also ran the club. "By not being a Communist," he recalled, "I felt left out of things—inferior again."[29]

At Camp Unity, Julie Sheik had attempted to recruit him for the Communist Party, and in the fall, Matusow, just twenty-one, joined. "[A]t a social gathering of the JOE YORK YOUTH CLUB of the Communist Party, Mt. Eden Section," he later told the FBI, "he stepped forward and requested that his name be added to the Communist Party's roster."[30]

Matusow ascribed joining the party to his search for an "identity." Murray Kempton, writing in 1955, while less charitable, did not disagree. Matusow, he said, "joined the Communist Party in 1947 after a year's post-Army idleness, chiefly, it appears, as an alternative to standing on street corners."[31]

* * *

Matusow's service in the Communist Party (until he betrayed it) was unremarkable. Issued a "[d]irt brown, peasant-looking membership card," he attended his first party meeting in the Bronx in October 1947. Initially he was distressed that, like AYD meetings, it consisted of "talk, talk, more talk." But he found an important difference: "here everyone was committed, no fence sitters—this was the real thing."[32]

His first assigned task was to obtain signatures on a petition in support of Eugene Dennis, the party's general secretary, who had been convicted of contempt of Congress for refusing to appear before HUAC. When Matusow received the petition forms, Dennis's case was on appeal, on the ground that a Communist Party official could not receive a fair trial from a Washington, D.C., jury largely composed of federal employees subject to loyalty screening in their jobs. In 1950, a divided Supreme Court would decide the issue, adversely to Dennis.[33]

Enthusiastic in his new role as a Communist Party member, Matusow immediately took the petition forms to his father's pinochle game, where he quickly obtained four signatures, along with small contributions to the Dennis defense fund, from the amused card players. The following day, he went to a Bronx shopping street and, focusing on middle-aged and elderly women shoppers, soon filled two petition forms with signatures and gained eighteen dollars in contributions.[34]

However, when he hurried that evening to the local party office to turn in the petitions and money, he found no one there to receive them. After an hour's wait, someone finally did arrive; but he told Matusow that the petitions were not needed now and to "come back next week." Only four or five other persons, it turned out, bothered to submit petition forms.[35]

As the 1947 Christmas season arrived, Matusow had little to occupy his time. He usually slept during the day in his room at his parents' apartment, arising at dusk. He tried his hand at stream-of-consciousness diary entries and filled his room with unread books on Marxism and Leninism. His Com-

munist activities were largely limited to his local AYD club. Talk that the party
would go underground in response to mounting FBI and HUAC pressure
depressed him.[36]

But with the coming of the new year, his spirits rose. He registered at the
party's Jefferson School of Social Science to take courses in Marxism-
Leninism. Then, in a significant step, he moved from his parents' Bronx apartment to lower Manhattan, at which time, he wrote, his party activities "took
on new meaning." He became a paid employee of the party, spending virtually all of his time on party causes.[37]

That summer he worked at the Jefferson School bookstore at its summer
camp, Camp Sherwood, near Monticello in upstate New York—"a great
twelve-week working holiday," he termed it. There, he sold ice cream and soft
drinks along with left-wing books and was paid twenty-five dollars per week,
plus room and board. He became the camp's square-dance caller, played a
bit part in its production of Clifford Odets's *Waiting for Lefty*, and pursued
an active social life.[38]

In the fall of 1948, Matusow went to work for People's Songs, an organization that promoted and performed folk music and also had close ties to
the third-party presidential campaign of former vice president Henry Wallace. He worked at the organization's tiny office in Manhattan, ordering and
selling songbooks, records, and pamphlets and earning thirty-five dollars per
week. A musician associated with People's Songs, Pete Seeger, would soon
help organize the Weavers, a vocal group that for a brief period achieved
mainstream commercial success singing folk songs—success that would end
abruptly, in no small part because Matusow in 1952 named Seeger and other
members of the group as Communists in testimony before HUAC.[39]

* * *

Matusow could not help but be aware of the rapidly increasing hostility toward American Communists that accompanied the worsening cold war. The
year 1947 saw the inauguration of the federal-employee loyalty program and
the start of HUAC's Hollywood hearings. These hearings, "a gala premiere,"
as Walter Goodman termed them, included as witnesses, "friendly" and
unfriendly, many well-known film-industry names. In the summer of 1948,
a presidential election year, HUAC presented the Hiss-Chambers drama,
along with Elizabeth Bentley's testimony naming Communist spies in federal agencies. And in an apparent response to Communist Party support for
Henry Wallace's candidacy, which appeared to jeopardize President Truman's
election bid, the Justice Department indicted Eugene Dennis and eleven other
top party officials under the Smith Act.[40]

At Camp Sherwood, when news of the Smith Act indictment broke, Matusow phoned the *Daily Worker* in New York City to order two hundred extra copies of its special edition. He sold copies at the camp and tried to distribute the newspaper to often startled vacationers in the area.[41]

Back in New York City after Labor Day, Matusow worked long hours for the Wallace campaign. He stuffed envelopes, canvassed voters in Lower East Side tenements, and gained experience in street-corner campaign oratory. When the votes were counted, however, Wallace's Progressive Party ticket, which Democrats feared would appeal broadly to working-class and liberal voters at the core of FDR's New Deal coalition, drew only a little over a million votes, mostly in New York, about 2.3 percent of the national total, and President Truman was elected. Matusow stood among the crowd of Wallace supporters, a few feet from the candidate, as he made his concession speech.[42]

The voters' massive rejection of the Wallace candidacy stirred fears of government repression against American Communists. Although Matusow found less concern among working-class Communists on the Lower East Side than among their middle-class brethren in the Bronx, he believed that the fear and apprehension of party members was "growing stronger daily."[43]

Fear was evidently greatest among top party leaders, who foresaw a period of overt American fascism, during which the Communist Party would be outlawed and party officials and members would be constantly at risk of sudden arrest and detention. In early 1949, the party stopped issuing membership cards and destroyed its central membership list. A portion of the party's apparatus soon went "underground" to a clandestine existence. Four of the eleven Smith Act defendants jumped bail and disappeared from view. Other party officials, not charged with any crime, left their homes, took assumed names, and changed their appearances.[44]

All of this was anathema to Matusow, who had not joined the Communist Party to hide his light under a bushel. The party's new attitude permeated the most mundane activities of its members. When party members met, they would look over their shoulders to see if they were being observed; they were careful not to say anything of substance on the phone, which might be tapped. Matusow, one of whose jobs was switchboard operator at party headquarters in New York City, could not avoid this pervasive fear. His party activities continued, but "the texture," he found, "was different."[45]

One activity, however, was definitely to his liking. The party published a Sunday edition of the *Daily Worker* called simply *The Worker.* Faced with plummeting circulation, *The Worker* began a contest to sell reduced-rate subscriptions (one dollar for a six-month subscription), with first prize being a trip to Puerto Rico as the guest of the Puerto Rican Communist Party.

Matusow ended up selling 326 subscriptions in less than three months and winning the contest.[46]

His nearly two-week trip, accompanied by Ted Bassett, a New York County party official, took place in May 1949. The head of Puerto Rico's Communist Party, Juan Santo Rivera, traveled with them on the island, where they visited sugar plantations and small factories. Matusow described the trip in idyllic terms: workers broke into song and lifted party officials to their shoulders. Despite evidence of FBI surveillance of their movements, he found none of the fear that paralyzed the party on the mainland. "[I]n Puerto Rico," he wrote, "I found the real Communist Party."[47]

Back in New York City, he found a tougher reality. Immediately upon his return, a party member of Puerto Rican descent, Balmes Hidalgo Jr., greeted him and asked about his trip. The next day, working the switchboard at party headquarters, he learned that Hidalgo was an FBI undercover informant who just that day had begun testifying as a government witness in the ongoing Smith Act trial.[48]

Asked to hurry to the Foley Square courthouse to tell defense counsel whatever he knew about the witness, Matusow recalled that upon entering the courtroom he had a strong emotional reaction, feeling hatred for J. Edgar Hoover and for the hostile trial judge, Harold R. Medina. But his reaction to the informer-witness, he wrote, was oddly different: "I just wanted to reach out and somehow touch and pacify his fear, as a mother with a child who's just fallen—relax his fear so that he stopped lying."[49]

Three years later, when another set of Communist Party officials went on trial in a second Foley Square Smith Act prosecution, the FBI undercover informant who testified for the government was Matusow.

* * *

Matusow's summer of 1949 was again substantially a paid vacation, spent operating the bookshop at Camp Unity. He also participated in daily poetry readings (Carl Sandburg and Langston Hughes being prominent among the poets) and in the weekly performances of left-wing plays. "Here at Unity," he recalled, "I was mixing my revolutionary 'zeal' with art, and it made me feel whole."[50]

However, his summer was marred, shortly before Labor Day, by a defining event of the period, the Peekskill riots. The Harlem chapter of the pro-Communist Civil Rights Congress had scheduled an August 27 fund-raising concert by Paul Robeson, to be held on picnic grounds near Peekskill, a small town forty miles up the Hudson River from New York City. The conservative local citizenry, viewing the event as an invasion by black and Jewish

Communists from New York City, was outraged, and a mob of veterans and vigilantes turned out to assault early-arriving concertgoers with clubs and rocks, overturning cars, burning a display of books, and injuring thirteen persons. Robeson never made it to the picnic grounds, and the concert was not held.[51]

But after an angry public meeting in Harlem, the event was rescheduled for the following weekend, on September 4, and more than fifteen thousand attended, including hundreds of union members (many who were veterans), armed with baseball bats and tire irons, serving as security guards. The concert itself was peaceful, and Robeson, by all accounts, sang superbly. Leaving the grounds, however, the concertgoers' buses and cars were ambushed by a mob that had stationed itself along several miles of exit roads and hurled rocks through the windshields of the slow-moving vehicles; 150 persons were injured. Westchester County police reportedly fraternized with the mob, although a local grand jury would find them blameless. Matusow recalled that he drove Robeson's son, Paul Jr., a young man he had met at Camp Unity, from the concert in the back seat of his 1941 Plymouth convertible, hidden from the mob by a blanket.[52]

In the fall, Matusow became "state literature director" for the Labor Youth League, a newly formed, party-controlled youth organization. His tenure in that position, however, was short-lived. In early 1950, he was demoted, he later told the FBI, after he took a job with a Harlem collection agency requiring the collection of installment debt from blacks and Puerto Ricans. The party's term for his offense, he said, was "white chauvinism."[53]

More important to Matusow, in the fall of 1949 he fell in love and moved in with Kay Kerby, an African American divorcee in her mid-twenties. Light-skinned with long black hair, raised in southern California, she worked as a journalist for the *Amsterdam News,* New York's leading newspaper for black readers. The couple had met at a New York City performance of "Unity Theater," an offshoot of the Camp Unity drama group. Matusow was, he wrote, attracted by Kerby's "broad smile" and "quiet intensity." Initially, they lived in her basement apartment in Harlem but soon moved to an apartment on the West Side. She helped him find a job in the advertising department of the *Amsterdam News.* Their relationship, however, did not survive the following summer.[54]

* * *

In February 1950, Senator Joe McCarthy exploded on the national scene with his Wheeling, West Virginia, speech. The story is now familiar. An undistinguished Midwest Republican during his first three years in the Senate, notable largely for his devotion to the interests of large corporations, McCarthy needed an issue upon which to improve his uncertain chances for reelection in 1952. Trying out, in a Lincoln Day speech in an obscure city, an adviser's suggestion that he make Communists-in-government his issue, he gave it his own spin and hit pay dirt.

What McCarthy evidently said at Wheeling (there was dispute later) was, "I have here in my hand a list of 205—a list of names that were made known to the Secretary of State as being members of the Communist Party and who nevertheless are still working and shaping policy in the State Department." He had no such list. On February 10, in Salt Lake City, he placed the number at "57 card-carrying Communists"; on February 20, on the Senate floor, he said that he had 81 documented cases (but he later went back to 57). McCarthy never remotely proved the charges.[55]

The senator did run successfully for reelection in 1952, and Matusow was present in Wisconsin, campaigning for him.[56]

* * *

About the time of the Wheeling speech, Matusow began seriously to consider becoming an FBI informant inside the Communist Party. Before he and Kay Kerby separated, he had already made his decision and was, unknown to her, an undercover informant—reporting to the FBI the names and activities of his associates at a time when party membership entailed substantial risk.

Over the years, Matusow has offered varying rationales for his decision. In *False Witness*, published in 1955, contemporaneously with the recantation of his testimony as an informer, he cited both his own disillusionment with, and increasing public antagonism toward, the Communist Party. As to the first, he criticized "[t]he mechanical approach toward me that I found in many party leaders, their absolutist attitude." Unspecified criticism by party members rankled: "I took on a feeling of hurt and envy toward those who were criticizing me." Presumably, he was referring to events surrounding his demotion from his Labor Youth League position, only weeks before he approached the FBI.[57]

As to the second reason, he wrote: "I found myself agreeing more and more with the growing antagonism toward the Communist Party in the United States. The Cold War was not a factor when I joined the Communist Party in 1946, but in 1949 it was in full swing. The first Smith Act trial of Communist leaders had resulted in a conviction. Apprehension in me was now added to disillusionment." He was more plainspoken in his testimony before SISS: "When I went to the FBI in 1950, I was afraid that I might be prosecuted and convicted as a Communist. . . . It was partly fear, partly confusion, but more fear than anything else, that sent me to the FBI."[58]

There was an added element to this calculus: Matusow's fascination with the public attention lavished on ex-Communist informers. "[F]or the first time in our history," he wrote in *False Witness,* "the informer was a hero." He cited Herbert Philbrick, Elizabeth Bentley, Paul Crouch, and Louis Budenz, "all hailed as heroes." He explained in blunt terms his response to this phenomenon: "I climbed on that bandwagon. It was the easy way up—to let the world know that I was not just another guy."[59]

In more recent years, Matusow has presented an alternative scenario in which he turned informer not for his own benefit but for the intended purpose of later recanting and discrediting J. Edgar Hoover and the McCarthyites. He gave this scenario to *Rolling Stone* magazine in 1972, stating that shortly before he approached the FBI in 1950 he prepared an affidavit explaining his intention, which he then had notarized, unread, by his father and placed in a safe-deposit box, to be revealed "in the event of my death." He repeated this version to Victor S. Navasky in 1979 and then twice in the 1990s, in an oral history and in unpublished memoirs. There was no one at the time, he wrote, to whom he could reveal his hidden intention. "Couldn't talk to anyone in the Party, for you never knew if the person you were talking to wasn't in contact with the FBI."[60]

A one-page, typed document in affidavit form, dated January 21, 1950, and signed by Matusow, can be found in the collection of papers he gave to the University of Sussex, England, in 1968. Headed "TRUE COPY" (the words are repeated three times across the top of the page) and typed on onionskin paper, it bears the notarial stamp of Herman Matusow, who died in 1957, but not his signature. The document states that Matusow intends to offer his "services as an informer" to the FBI in order "to collect . . . information on their operation, . . . so that at some future date I may be able to publish whatever facts I might obtain, with the hope of helping end the climate of fear and opression [*sic*] which now exists in the country." It adds that Matusow "WILL NOT OFFER NEW INFORMATION" to the bureau.[61]

But neither in *False Witness* nor in more than two weeks of intensive cross-examination at new-trial hearings in the Jencks and Smith Act cases and at SISS's hearings—all in 1955, after he recanted—did Matusow even hint at the existence of the 1950 affidavit or the strategy it outlines. The zeal, moreover, with which he would embrace his informer role—he gave a great deal of new information—and the halting and gradual manner of his withdrawal from it, belie his supposed strategy.[62]

Observers had another, more persuasive, opinion about what motivated him. Murray Kempton wrote in 1955: "It is not difficult to understand what drove Matusow: his every ism has been an affectation born of a morbid love of admiration." Judge Edward J. Dimock, the trial judge in the Smith Act case, who observed him for days on the witness stand, cited his "craving for a role in the center of the stage." In this view, Matusow abandoned the Communist Party because, headed underground, it could not, and in any case would not, give him "a role in the center of the stage."[63]

His action, of course, had two distinct facets. The decision to break with the Communist Party is easily explained, for thousands of others were doing it at the same time. But unlike virtually all of the others, Matusow stayed in the party as an FBI informant. Certainly, he did not conclude, as Whittaker Chambers did, that an ex-Communist had a moral or religious "duty to inform." For Matusow, the party's flaws were that it was losing the political battle in the United States and, perhaps worse, failed to appreciate the value of his services. "Nobody paid me much attention," he said later. He saw, moreover, inviting career opportunities for ex-Communist informers.[64]

His first step on his new path took place in late March 1950, when he phoned the FBI's New York City office.[65]

2   The Making of an Informer

Matusow, in his phone call on March 27, 1950, told an FBI agent that he was a Communist Party member in good standing but "has always been anti-Communist." He wanted to discuss "working with the Bureau" in connection with party matters. They arranged a meeting for the following day at the bureau's office in the Foley Square federal courthouse.[1]

There, interviewed by two agents, Matusow was startled to see his personal FBI file placed on the desk in front of him. But his immediate fear of being too late in offering his services proved unjustified. The slender file contained not much more than a report of the party event held at St. Nicholas Arena in Manhattan fourteen months earlier, at which he was awarded first prize in the *Worker* subscription contest, and an article in the *Worker* relating to his subsequent Puerto Rico trip.[2]

Matusow's interview, however, was not cursory. The agents first elicited a detailed personal history, with emphasis on his American Youth for Democracy (AYD), Communist Party, and Labor Youth League (LYL) activities and the names of his associates. They scrutinized his relationship with Kay Kerby, who he said was "close to" the party. Reflecting his assessment of the FBI's biases, Matusow told the agents that Kerby was white, "of Danish extraction."[3]

Asked why he contacted the FBI, Matusow gave varied answers, summarized in the agents' report to the director's office. First, he "hated" Communists and had joined the party "so as to prepare himself to work as an informant with some agency like the FBI." Second, he "always could have been classified as a liberal" and had joined the party "to study its social program from the inside." Lastly, he "did not come in for any patriotic motive," and "possibly opportunism had something to do with his action."[4]

But Matusow explained precisely what he wanted from the bureau. He expected reimbursement for contributions he was required to make to Communist Party causes "while rendering service to the FBI." (Two days after the interview, he phoned to say he had been "taxed" $150 in a current party fund drive, would probably be able to get the amount reduced to $100, and wanted the FBI to "loan him" $50.) He wanted help in obtaining an increase in his VA disability allowance for his wartime back injury, in regaining his status in the army reserve, and in obtaining cortisone treatments for Kerby, who suffered from arthritis.[5]

The interviewing agents judged Matusow "a vain, egotistical and self-centered individual" with "a 'know it all' attitude" who would be difficult "to keep in check"; but they nonetheless sought permission to "maintain contact" with him "looking toward his possible development as a Confidential Informant." Their April 7 report concluded that Matusow "will enjoy the confidence of the comrades with whom he comes in contact, and thereby more readily have access to information of possible value to the Bureau." "[H]is future in the Communist Party," the agents predicted, "is a bright one."[6]

To be sure, their report added, his motives in coming to the FBI were "completely opportunistic," and "his prime motivating factor" was "financial remuneration for his services." But this they viewed as a plus: "[B]ecause of his financial interest in the success of our relationship with him, it is felt that his services could be quite valuable." The agents conceded that he gave inconsistent explanations on a number of matters, but they offered assurance that "[i]f future contact with MATUSOW is authorized, an attempt will be made to clarify these points." They asked permission to offer him "an initial payment of $25.00 in order to keep him 'on the string.'"[7]

In the days following his March 28 interview, Matusow sought to persuade the FBI that he would indeed be a valuable informant. In a March 30 phone call, he mentioned his membership, since the summer of 1947, in the United Office and Professional Workers of America, a Communist-dominated union. He was considered a "fair haired boy" at Locals 16 and 18, he said, and could identify the officers of those locals as Communist Party members. On April 4, he called to advise that he and Kerby had been "offered the opportunity of taking over the book shop at Camp Unity" during the summer of 1950. The agents included the added information in their report.[8]

On April 14, Matusow phoned with another inviting morsel, one that prompted a separate message by wire to headquarters. He "SUGGESTED," the New York office reported, "THAT THE FBI MIGHT BE INTERESTED IN EXAMINING HIS LIBRARY," eleven hundred books on Marxism-Leninism and "MANY HUNDREDS OF PAMPHLETS ISSUED BY THE CPUSA DURING PAST THREE

YEARS WHICH WERE NOT FOR PUBLIC DISSEMINATION." The agents sought authorization "TO EXAMINE THIS LIBRARY." Their message was marked "URGENT" because Kerby, identified as Matusow's "PARAMOUR WITH WHOM HE RESIDES," was then in the hospital and was expected to be absent from their apartment for only another week.[9]

The reply to the agents' requests, in the form of a wire marked "URGENT" and signed "HOOVER," arrived three days later. "IN VIEW INFORMATION [YOUR LETTER] APRIL SEVENTH AUTHORITY *NOT* GRANTED UTILIZE MATUSOW AS [CONFIDENTIAL INFORMANT]" (emphasis added), it read. The instructions were unambiguous: "MAINTAIN CONTACT WITH HIM AND ACCEPT ANY INFORMATION HE VOLUNTEERS. SPECIFICALLY YOU MAY EXAMINE HIS ALLEGED LIBRARY AND ADVISE BUREAU CONTENTS THEREOF. CHECK MATUSOW'S ARMY RECORD."[10]

Matusow and the New York office worked together in the succeeding weeks to persuade headquarters to change its mind about informant status for Matusow. On April 24, the agents came to his home and took inventory of his "library"—"approximately eleven hundred volumes [books by Marx, Engels, Lenin, Stalin, and Gorky were prominent], not counting miscellaneous pamphlets and magazines," they confirmed. Matusow communicated with the New York office "at least twice weekly," "furnishing oral reports on Labor Youth League meetings and identifying those present, known to him." He took pictures of marchers in the Communist Party's 1950 May Day parade and gave them to the agents (although his snapshots turned out to be "of such poor quality" that the marchers "could not be identified"). Matusow later described his May Day effort: "Each of the 144 clicks of my shutter caught the face of a friend. Most of them recognized me and waved as I took their pictures. 'Send us a copy,' some of them shouted."[11]

The agents prepared a twenty-one-page letter to the director's office, sent on June 7, stating the case for retaining Matusow. "He has proved extremely cooperative," they wrote, and "[i]n no instance where he has furnished information which could be verified, has his information proved inaccurate." His military record was unflawed. His earlier, imprudent monetary demands had been abandoned—"MATUSOW has in no way mentioned money during the past two months." "In view of MATUSOW's evident willingness to cooperate with this office," the letter concluded, "permission is requested . . . to utilize his services as a confidential informant" and to "reimburse" him "at the rate of $40 a month, plus expenses not to exceed $20 per month for the next six months."[12]

This time the New York office got the authorization it wanted. The reply from headquarters on June 22 concluded that "[u]ndoubtedly, Matusow is of considerable value to the Bureau."[13]

Even so, there were reservations. The authorization to pay Matusow a monthly stipend was limited to an initial three-month period, and the New York office was instructed "to corroborate all information furnished by Matusow if at all possible to be certain he is not a plant by the Communist Party." Headquarters expressed concern that the relationship might be disclosed to the press, cautioning that "the informant is being supported for the most part" by Kerby, a journalist for the *Amsterdam News,* and that Matusow also had a part-time job with the newspaper. "Close control should be maintained over Matusow and his activities," the reply emphasized, "and he must be impressed with the fact that his relationship with the Bureau is strictly confidential."[14]

* * *

Three days later, North Korean forces invaded South Korea, and President Truman committed American troops to the conflict. The CPUSA opposed Truman's decision, becoming even more unpopular and politically isolated than before. The extent of the party's alienation from even the most sympathetic elements of the non-Communist left was underscored by the resignation of Henry Wallace, who supported the American effort in Korea, from the Progressive Party, whose standard bearer he had been less than two years earlier.[15]

With American troops suffering casualties at the hands of a Communist army, many Americans became more willing than ever to support summary action against domestic Communists. Party member Matusow, however, had secured a shield against anti-Communist anger.[16]

* * *

As an informant, Matusow's reports to the FBI described Communist Party and Labor Youth League meetings, supplying names, addresses, phone numbers, and job descriptions. He provided diagrams of the interior of party headquarters in New York City. When the bureau asked for physical descriptions of individuals, he took photographs of his party colleagues as they participated in strikes or demonstrations. He passed the film to FBI agents in street-corner meetings and later identified each individual at the FBI office.[17]

He developed a mind-set to deal with the continuous betrayal of friends that his role entailed. "As I reported on a friend," Matusow later wrote, "he was no longer my friend. I began to distrust and hate him. I stopped trusting people by knowing myself untrustworthy. I grew to hate people because I had injured them."[18]

His informant work in New York City, however, was of short duration; in July 1950 he departed for the West Coast. Matusow's decision to leave the city in which he had lived his entire life (except for military service) was triggered primarily by the breakup of his relationship with Kay Kerby. The strain of informing on friends whom he continued to see was also a factor. He told the FBI that he planned to obtain permanent employment in Los Angeles, selling air-conditioning equipment for a firm he had worked for in New York, and since the party would transfer him to a unit in the Los Angeles area, he hoped to continue informing on party activities. The bureau advised that "his pay would be discontinued until he established himself as an informant in the Los Angeles area to the satisfaction of the Los Angeles office."[19]

Matusow complicated his trip by taking with him his entire library of Communist literature to sell to a San Francisco bookstore, Books on Telegraph Hill, owned by Mel Brown, a friend. He hoped to realize as much as a thousand dollars from the sale, substantially more than he could expect on the East Coast. To provide the needed transport capacity, he traded the 1950 Ford that he and Kerby owned for a Jeep station wagon and a small trailer. On July 23, he left New York City, hauling a sizable load of books, and headed west.[20]

When the overloaded Jeep suffered a broken axle in Missouri, Matusow traded it and the trailer for a Dodge pickup truck. He then proceeded to Taos in the northern New Mexico mountains, known for its artists' colony, where Craig and Jenny Wells Vincent, whom (he would later testify) he had met as Communists in New York, ran the San Cristobal Valley Ranch, a vacation resort for left-wingers. Matusow intended to stay at the ranch only a week; but "his back which was previously hurt in the Army, is giving him serious trouble," the FBI reported, and "he will be forced to stop over at Taos for at least a month before proceeding to California." He ended up staying in Taos more than five months.[21]

* * *

Matusow continued to supply information to the FBI, virtually without interruption, through its Albuquerque office. Within a few days of his arrival, he furnished the names and thumbnail biographies of some twenty guests at the San Cristobal Valley Ranch, nearly all identified as Communist Party members or "apparently" members. One was a New York City school teacher; another "a teacher of music or voice at UCLA"; a third employed by a New York state antidiscrimination agency. Still another guest, "not believed to be" a party member, was a Progressive Party official in New Mexico who "described himself as an anarchist."[22]

Matusow also met Clinton Jencks, a young organizer for the left-wing International Union of Mine, Mill, and Smelter Workers, against whom he would later provide, and then recant, damaging courtroom testimony. Jencks came with his family to vacation at the ranch because he knew Jenny Vincent, who sang folk songs at Mine-Mill conventions. In Matusow's report, he described Jencks, who was active in organizing Mexican American copper-mine workers, as "a CP member from Silver City, New Mexico." He reported that Jencks led an evening discussion group at the ranch and talked about planned slowdown tactics by the union at Silver City to obstruct the Korean War effort. For his part, Jencks recalled that the Vincents had cautioned him about Matusow and that their conversation was guarded and lasted no more than "a minute or two."[23]

In the following weeks, Matusow showered the FBI with additional data on guests at the ranch. On August 24, he furnished information on fifty-five guests and the license numbers of eleven automobiles. In a September 3 report, he identified twelve persons "who were either guests at the San Cristobal Valley Ranch, or believed to be favorable to the Communist Party." Two days later, he gave the names of thirty more individuals and three license numbers. On September 15, he furnished information on fifteen persons, and less than two weeks later, another twenty. He also handed over three volumes of photographs. In addition, he made oral reports, meeting an FBI agent weekly in a room at a Taos hotel; occasionally, they met in the agent's automobile on the outskirts of town or in Santa Fe, when Matusow wished to communicate something he deemed important. A grateful Albuquerque office paid him $115 for his services from September 15 to November 1 and obtained authorization from Washington to raise his pay to $75 per month.[24]

When not informing, Matusow supplemented his income and enjoyed the Taos scene. He rented an apartment and enrolled under the G.I. Bill as an art student at the Taos Valley Art School. He sold some of his books and took jobs driving a taxi, managing a pool hall, and working as a night hotel clerk. A group of D. H. Lawrence devotees lived in Taos, and Matusow served as a gofer for the author's widow, Frieda, and Mabel Dodge Luhan, a noted writer and Bohemian, who together presided over the group. "[S]itting at the feet of the outer circle of the Lawrence legend," he termed it. Doughbelly Price, a colorful real estate broker and one-time candidate for local office, whose business was called "Doughbelly's Clip Joint," became his friend. When the weather turned cold and summer residents departed, Matusow boarded their cats.[25]

* * *

Events in the headlines, far removed from Taos, could only confirm Matusow in his decision to turn informer. During the spring of 1950, the Tydings committee, a special subcommittee of the Senate Foreign Relations Committee, held highly publicized and contentious hearings marking a last-ditch Democratic effort to discredit McCarthy by forcing the senator to put up or shut up on his charge that card-carrying Communists were on the State Department payroll. Informer Louis Budenz stepped into the public spotlight as McCarthy's "rescuer-in-chief," testifying that Owen Lattimore, an occasional adviser to the State Department on China, was a secret Communist. McCarthy not only survived politically but his influence and reputation among conservatives as leader of the anti-Communist crusade was enhanced.[26]

The public's hostility toward American Communists, a potent factor in Matusow's decision, was increasing. In July and August 1950, the Justice Department arrested Julius and Ethel Rosenberg and charged them with conspiring to steal America's atomic secrets for the Soviets. In September, the Congress enacted, over President Truman's veto, the Internal Security Act of 1950, creating legal machinery to compel the Communist Party, its members, and all Communist-front organizations to register with the government. At the end of November, Chinese Communist troops entered the Korean War in force, inflicting large numbers of American casualties.[27]

* * *

In October, Matusow had "received information that he is in trouble as far as his Communist Party membership is concerned," and according to the FBI's report, he might have to return to New York City to avoid expulsion from the party. A few days later, however, he got word that the difficulty "had been cleared up and that he was in no danger of being expelled." Relieved, Matusow made plans to form an active party group in Taos from among former and inactive members. During November, he continued to supply information to the bureau, including data on "five persons believed to have Communist sympathies in the Taos area." But after receiving further word that he was still in trouble with the party, Matusow left Taos on November 30 and returned to New York City.[28]

On December 20, Jesse Wallach, a local Communist Party official, summoned Matusow to a meeting attended by two other party members, at which he was advised of the charges against him. There were three: possession of a *Political Affairs* magazine with "OSS" (the initials of the government's Office of Strategic Services) stamped on the inside cover; theft of books and money from the Workers Book Shop (where he was employed briefly in 1949); and fraud in *The Worker* subscription contest (individuals to whom he sold subscriptions began receiving four or five copies). Matusow denied all of the charges. He had purchased the magazine, he said, from a used-magazine dealer; he took books from the bookstore, when he was LYL's state literature director, to use at meetings; and it was common practice to put subscriptions at a single address under one name to avoid disclosing unnecessarily the names of the other subscribers—all to no avail.[29]

After the meeting, Matusow advised the FBI that he was being kicked out and had been told "to disassociate himself" from the Communist Party. The bureau wasted little time in cutting him loose. On January 10, 1951, headquarters instructed the New York and Albuquerque offices that in view of "the fact that [Matusow] has stated he is no longer a member of the CP and will no longer associate himself with the CP, no additional contacts should be had with him in a confidential capacity." It was permissible, the message explained, to contact him to "verify or amplify information previously submitted by him, but you should have no contacts with him to obtain information of current value."[30]

Adding insult to injury, on January 18, the CPUSA publicly announced Matusow's expulsion. The announcement, printed in the next day's *Daily Worker,* minced no words. The party had expelled Matusow, it read, "for being an enemy agent." He was "also found to have engaged in irregularities and misrepresentations during a press drive." The announcement concluded with a detailed description (not unlike an FBI most-wanted description) to enable party members to recognize and avoid him in the future: "His main contacts were among the youth and he is now operating in New York City since his recent return from the Southwest. Matusow is in his middle twenties, medium height, plump, white, has a round face, black hair and eyes."[31]

* * *

The Communist Party and the FBI, in quite different ways, had provided Matusow with financial and psychological support. With both sources of support suddenly stripped away, he quickly sought out a third, the U.S. Air Force. His military service at the end of World War II had been a positive experience, with camaraderie, travel, and secure employment.

On November 21, 1950, in Taos, shortly before returning to New York and his anticipated expulsion from the party, Matusow enlisted in the air force reserve as a staff sergeant, his prior military rank, signing up for a three-year period. After the January announcement of his expulsion, choosing not to face party friends in New York, he went back to New Mexico and asked the air force to call him promptly to active duty.[32]

Waiting for his call, Matusow first stayed in Taos, finding little to do, and then, fleeing the forbidding Taos winter, moved south to Albuquerque, where he found work driving a taxi and lived in a cheap hotel. With the Korean War in progress, his call to active duty came promptly, in late February 1951. Assigned to Brooks Air Force Base in San Antonio, Texas, he hurried to inform the FBI of his new military address, stating he would keep the bureau "advised of his whereabouts in the event the FBI were interested in questioning him re his past CP activities."[33]

Matusow quickly made himself a headache for the air force. Required to fill out a personal history questionnaire that called for all organizational memberships, he listed the Communist Party and a few dozen Communist-front organizations. "I hadn't belonged to all those organizations," he later wrote, "but if I had ever signed a petition or attended a mass rally given by one of them, I put it down. Just to be cute." When two FBI agents came to the base shortly afterward, on a routine inquiry about an individual he had known in the party, the rumor spread that he was a Communist spy.[34]

The air force instituted an agency check, to which the FBI responded on March 13. The bureau's "blind memorandum" described Matusow's Communist Party membership, his contacts with the FBI, and his expulsion from the party, including each of the party's charges against him. During 1950, the memorandum acknowledged, he "furnished this Bureau with information of value."[35]

On April 11, Matusow attempted to resume his informant role with the FBI, showing up at its San Antonio office. The agents' report of his visit stated, "MATUSOW indicated his desire to become acquainted and possibly affiliated with the Communist Party in San Antonio, Texas, and to furnish regular written reports regarding their activities." As to his expulsion from the party less than three months earlier, he had a ready answer: "MATUSOW stated that he did not think that anyone in this area of the country would know that he had been expelled and further that if they did find out, he felt sure he could explain to them that it had been a mistake."[36]

Moreover, "in an effort to be of service to the FBI," Matusow had already done some volunteer investigative work—at the Jewish Community Center USO in San Antonio. He "there met one MAX HALPERIN," the bureau's report stated, who, in the course of a conversation about books, "suggested that he (MATUSOW) attend the Little Theater production of 'The Mad Woman of Chillot' [sic] in San Antonio, which he did." After attending the performance, Matusow again saw Halperin, who suggested he contact "a collector of books and records" named Elya Bresler. Matusow visited Bresler at his home, the evening before he came to the San Antonio office, and elicited from him an account of his service with the Communist-led Abraham Lincoln Brigade during the Spanish Civil War—the unrepentant Bresler wore the brigade's "lapel pin" as he talked with Matusow.[37]

The reply from headquarters, however, did not mention Matusow's new information, and it gave short shrift to his request to become an FBI informant inside the Communist Party in San Antonio. "For your information," the San Antonio office was advised, "Matusow's expulsion was published not once but twice in the 'Daily Worker' and the second time, his picture was also displayed." The message instructed that "no steps should be taken by your office to develop Matusow in a confidential capacity nor should any payments for information be made to him."[38]

* * *

Matusow's assignment at Brooks AFB, during which he performed office work for a personnel unit, lasted less than three months. In mid-May 1951, the air force transferred him to Wright-Patterson AFB near Dayton, Ohio. His phone call to advise the FBI triggered a warning to the nearby Cincinnati office that "MATUSOW is in the habit of building up his own importance, and any dealings that the Cincinnati Office may have with him should be most circumspect."[39]

At Wright-Patterson the air force, surprisingly, placed Matusow in a highly sensitive intelligence personnel unit, located behind wire fences in a remote part of the base. Fearful that, with his background, he could easily be framed on an espionage charge, Matusow told his superior officer he was a former Communist Party member and would refuse access to classified documents. He was then assigned to the base personnel office to help enlisted men fill out forms for G.I. insurance. Thereafter, the air force, distrustful of Matusow and aware of the potential for criticism in handling his case, assigned Office of Special Investigations (OSI) agents to report on his activities and denied him promotion.[40]

Matusow tried to escape his air force limbo by volunteering to serve in Korea, but he was unsuccessful. He next tried a "cute" ploy—sending an anonymous letter to HUAC, mailed from New York, that stated, in substance: "Do you know that Harvey Matusow, a Communist youth leader, is now in the Air Force at Wright-Patterson Air Force Base, etc.?" His goal, he later said, was either to get out of the air force or to be called to testify before HUAC. HUAC did not respond.[41]

In August, reaching a breaking point, Matusow turned himself in to the base hospital for psychiatric observation. A notation in his military medical records confirms, "nervous breakdown, 1951, Ohio."[42]

But then he had a stroke of good fortune. Pursuing a time-honored practice of soldiers in distress, Matusow sought out the base chaplain, Major William Coolidge Hart, a Catholic. He told the chaplain a compelling story: he had once been a Communist Party member but now wanted to fight

Communism and clear his name; the air force wouldn't give him a chance to fight overseas and instead assigned OSI agents to watch him; but he understood what the Communists were trying to do and wanted to expose them; he wanted a chance to instruct young people on the dangers of communism. Sympathetic, Chaplain Hart advised Matusow he would need clearance to speak to youth groups on communism and suggested he consult the base Public Information Office.[43]

With the chaplain as his reference, Matusow took his story to the public information officer, Captain Howard Hensley, who asked Martha Edmiston, chief of the office's Press Section, to join them. Edmiston inquired whether Matusow had ever sought to clear his name by testifying before HUAC or one of the other congressional committees. He answered no and eagerly sought her assistance. She said that her husband, John J. ("Ed") Edmiston, a reporter for the *Dayton Journal-Herald*, might be willing to help. Matusow phoned that evening and met Ed the next day at a Dayton bar frequented by newspaper reporters.[44]

The Edmistons greatly impressed Matusow. Martha was, he wrote, an "attractive woman in her early forties" who "had that perpetually youthful look, short haircut, fresh outdoor ruddy complexion, brisk walk and pleasant mannerisms." Ed was a "tall, thin graying man with strong features [who] worked on the financial page of the paper and carried himself in such a way as to fit his type of reporting." Only later did Matusow discover that Ed had an alcohol problem.[45]

The Edmistons invited Matusow to their home in Waynesville, about twenty miles from Dayton. "Their home was a two-story log cabin on a seven-acre tract of land. The house reflected the folk traditions of the area and had a quiet serenity. I needed it at that time," he recalled. As an added fillip for Matusow, a cat fancier, Martha had filled the house with cats.[46]

* * *

The Edmistons were almost uniquely qualified to tutor a former Communist Party member and FBI informant who wished to testify as a "friendly" witness before HUAC. During 1940 and 1941, they had been undercover FBI informants in Communist Party units in Columbus and Cincinnati, having joined the party at the bureau's request. In July 1950 they had testified before HUAC concerning party activities in southern Ohio in the early 1940s, and they now received frequent invitations to speak to civic and church groups in their community. They were professionals in the fields of journalism and public relations.[47]

Seeing in the youthful and articulate ex-Communist their return ticket to the top rung of the informer scene, the Edmistons took Matusow under their wing. Later, after his recantation, a chagrined Martha put it differently, explaining that he had "impressed her as a humble, appealing young man" whom she assisted "in what appeared to her to be a worthy and patriotic undertaking." From Matusow's standpoint, the Edmistons were nothing less than a godsend.[48]

In the following weeks, he became a regular weekend guest in their home. They asked him to prepare notes of his Communist Party experiences, which they closely reviewed with him. By September, the Edmistons had found, Matusow said, "what I had missed—the importance of youth in relation to Communism." This aspect of the Communist effort, moreover, "had been completely overlooked" by HUAC in its hearings. "Youth" was to become Matusow's area of expertise as a witness, his shtick. He was delighted: "It seemed that in my naivete I had underestimated my importance as a witness."[49]

The Edmistons worked with Matusow on his "deportment." As they sourly stated, after his recantation, "they strove to correct some of MATUSOW's crude mannerisms, which appeared to them to be 'hangovers' from his several years of Communist Party training and association, notabl[y] bad table manners, overbearing treatment of waiters and other service employees, constant nervous interruption of the conversation of others and insistence on being the center of attention of all persons present."[50]

With Matusow thus groomed, the Edmistons contacted Donald Appell, a HUAC investigator and friend, who had worked with them in preparing their own testimony before HUAC in 1950. No mere anonymous gumshoe, Appell had been at the center of events in the 1948 Hiss-Chambers saga. A tall, baby-faced ex-marine (Chambers would describe him in *Witness* as a "brisk, pleasant young man"), Appell had been present at Chambers's farm and was handed the microfilm that would doom Hiss when Chambers removed it from its temporary hiding place in a pumpkin. When the Edmistons telephoned at the end of September 1951, Appell agreed to come to Dayton to interview Matusow.[51]

He arrived in early October. Martha Edmiston drove him to Wright-Patterson, where they arranged with the air force to make Matusow available to Appell in his room at the Biltmore Hotel in Dayton. HUAC's cachet was such that the air force provided a staff car and driver to transport Matusow to and from the hotel for each of two days of interviews. Arriving at the hotel, Matusow found Appell more interested in watching the World Series on television than in commencing the interview, although he did ask Matusow a few questions between innings. But after a dinner with the Edmistons, the two men commenced their discussions in earnest in Appell's hotel room.[52]

Appell soon pronounced himself satisfied that Matusow would be a useful witness for HUAC. Before departing Dayton, he left a HUAC subpoena making Matusow "subject to call" by the committee.[53]

For Matusow, the receipt of a HUAC subpoena was a triumph. It enabled him "to thumb [his] nose at the Air Force investigators" who observed his daily activities, for he now "had the power of Congress behind" him. If he required any justification for becoming a HUAC witness, Matusow later wrote, "[t]he lack of trust the Air Force had shown me was the straw that broke the camel's back in justifying my role as a witness."[54]

At the end of October, HUAC sent Matusow a letter directing him to appear in Washington on November 26.[55]

* * *

Observing the political scene during 1951, Matusow could only conclude that, despite his air force detour, it was by no means too late in the day for him to become a successful informer-witness.

Throughout the summer, Senator Pat McCarran's Internal Security Subcommittee conducted hearings in a second high-profile investigation centered on Owen Lattimore. SISS's extended inquiry, intended to prove that China had been "lost" to the Communists because of State Department policies fostered by American Communists, put Louis Budenz, Lattimore's accuser, prominently in the news once more.[56]

In June, the Supreme Court affirmed the convictions of the eleven top Communists tried in the 1949 Foley Square Smith Act trial, holding that the Smith Act provision making it a crime to conspire to teach or advocate forceful overthrow of the government did not contravene the First Amendment's freedom of speech guarantee. The speech issue was sharply posed because the government's evidence consisted primarily of passages from books, many of them venerable Marxist texts, and testimony that the defendants had taught the views stated. Evidence that Communist dogma was about to be put into action was absent.[57]

The Court's decision, *Dennis v. United States,* opened the door for the Justice Department to institute a wave of new Smith Act prosecutions in cities across the country, against hundreds of lesser Communist Party officials—"second-string" and then "third-string" Communists. These prosecutions would rely heavily on the testimony of ex-Communist informers, including Budenz, Paul Crouch, John Lautner, Joseph Mazzei, and, less than a year later, Matusow.[58]

* * *

In October and November 1951, Matusow and the Edmistons still had work to do to prepare for his maiden appearance as a HUAC witness, including strategic instruction. He should name as Communists, they advised, only individuals whom he had met at a party function or who had been identified to him as Communists by other Communists (which left him considerable leeway). They told him, Matusow recalled, to "play my big cards one at a time. For if I didn't do it that way my life as a witness would be short."[59]

Even before Matusow came in contact with HUAC, he had, at the Edmistons' urging, been preparing "an autobiography of sorts, a complete chronological list of events of my activities in the Communist Party, and in front groups, starting in 1946." This document, he later testified, went through "about six drafts," two of which he gave to HUAC. While prepared with "some care," he said, "a lot of it was editorial on my part and put a lot of what you might say 'window dressing' in it." The Edmistons described the paper, which was dated October 19, 1951, as "a typewritten memorandum, containing more than 70 pages, which purported to sketch his early life and to give a narrative account of his experiences in the Communist Party." Matusow doubtless impressed HUAC by the detail of his account, as well as the very large number of names provided.[60]

Matusow also produced a second, shorter paper, which the Edmistons described as "a typewritten list of names of persons he identified as members of the Communist Party, containing more than 30 pages." He accompanied each name on this list with the specific party unit to which the individual belonged, plus whatever other biographical data he could recall.[61]

Although Matusow and the Edmistons prepared the two documents primarily to promote his forthcoming appearance before HUAC, they took care to furnish copies to the FBI. The documents may in fact have been intended as a form of "final report" to the bureau on Matusow's activities, because termination of his FBI relationship, following his expulsion from the Communist Party, had been abrupt and without the slightest formality.[62]

Matusow completed the shorter document first and on October 1 personally delivered it to an FBI agent in Dayton. "[M]uch of this information," the agent reported Matusow told him, "had previously been furnished by him to the New York Office," but "he had never prepared such a list in this form." Also, Matusow said he expected to complete in two weeks "a paper in which he will relate his entire experiences with the CP and in which he will reveal other individuals" mentioned in his list by name only. A copy of that paper, he promised, would be furnished to the Cincinnati office.[63]

On October 20, the Dayton agent sent Matusow's list to headquarters and to nine local FBI offices. The agent included in his report a new list of twenty-seven names, derived from Matusow's paper and broken down by the individual's local FBI office.[64]

* * *

With their preliminaries complete, Matusow and his coach, Ed Edmiston, piled into Ed's automobile and began their long drive to Washington for Matusow's HUAC debut, scheduled for November 26. Matusow had no second thoughts. "I was frightened," he recalled, "but I was cocky. This was to be my big test."[65]

3 Hitting the Big Time

Matusow's Washington trip was a quiet success. He testified before HUAC on November 27 and 28, 1951, but in executive session, a dress rehearsal behind closed doors for a later public performance. If disappointed by the absence of press coverage and a live audience, he handled the situation well. He concentrated on being courteous to committee members and staff, many of them southerners, including John S. Wood of Georgia, HUAC's chairman.[1]

Wearing a new air force uniform, Matusow gave the HUAC members, seated slightly above him at a large horseshoe-shaped table, polite "yes, sir" and "no, sir" answers. As his stage fright dissipated, he began to gesture with his hands and to speak more confidently. He told how as a young man, recently returned from wartime military service, he joined the Communist Party, making sure to mention the name of virtually every person with whom he had associated. When finished, he basked in the praise of committee members and staff. "I accepted the compliments," he recalled, "and searched for more." His public debut would come about two months later.[2]

Returning to Dayton with Ed Edmiston, Matusow was jubilant, certain that his career as a witness had been successfully launched. After his Washington trip, the Edmistons said later, he became "an overbearing individual who seemed suddenly to have been overcome by a sense of his importance as a public figure" and caused complaints by air force personnel at the base that he "was 'throwing his weight' and boasting he was a 'national figure.'"[3]

A December 9 broadcast by columnist Drew Pearson did not improve this situation. Pearson, the recipient of leaked information, predicted HUAC would soon investigate Communist youth activities in the New York City area and that its key witness would be Sergeant Harvey Matusow.[4]

But the air force had no place in his future. Matusow asked to be released from active duty—a request the air force happily granted, on December 11, 1951.[5]

* * *

Although Matusow had been telling his story to the FBI since March 1950, the bureau carefully parsed his executive-session testimony, particularly the scores of names he gave. Headquarters sent copies of the hearing transcript, obtained in December 1951, to the New York, Albuquerque, and San Juan offices to determine whether Matusow had disclosed new information and to direct them to take action in the light of his testimony. When the field offices failed to respond promptly, they were instructed, "EXPEDITE REVIEW OF MATUSOW'S TESTIMONY."[6]

The New York office reported that "MATUSOW identified 181 individuals and 26 organizations" and that a memorandum concerning his testimony "has been placed in the case file of each individual and organization where such case file exists." Case files existed, the report continued, for 72 of the individuals; files for 87 others had not yet been located; and the files of 3 persons "have been reopened on the basis of information given by MATUSOW." Headquarters, however, spotted a discrepancy. Matusow identified 181 individuals, it pointed out, but the 72 for whom a file was found and the 87 for whom a file was not found "total 159 rather than 181." "This discrepancy should be clarified in your next communication to the Bureau."[7]

The bureau also followed up on Matusow's inclusion of Clinton Jencks's name on the list he gave the Dayton FBI agent in October. The Justice Department and the FBI had already initiated what would be a more than decade-long campaign against Jencks's union, the Mine, Mill, and Smelter Workers, which had been expelled from the Congress of Industrial Organizations (CIO) as Communist-dominated in early 1950.[8]

The bureau inquired about Jencks in an interview with Matusow in Dayton in late December 1951, leading to a contradiction in Matusow's account. In his October paper, he had written: "I was told by a known Party member who had worked with Jenks [sic], that Jenks was a member of the party. Jenks himself told me so before I left the [San Cristobal Valley] ranch." But in a signed statement given to the bureau on December 29, he said: "I have never been told by Jencks that he is a member of the Communist Party, and I have never seen any direct evidence to prove that he is a member of the Communist Party. However, there is no question in my mind but that Jencks is a member of the Communist Party."[9]

The Justice Department would later prosecute Jencks for falsely denying party membership, using Matusow as its key witness.[10]

* * *

Contemporaneously with his FBI interview, Matusow's career took another leap forward when the Justice Department decided to use him as a witness in the Smith Act prosecution of sixteen "second-string" Communist Party officials in New York City—a decision made without the bureau's endorsement.

FBI headquarters, which disliked any tendency to self-promotion in its confidential informants, had mistrusted Matusow from the outset. It initially rejected him as an informant and, after being persuaded by the New York office to change its decision, voiced repeated cautions. It had unhesitatingly terminated Matusow when his expulsion from the party provided the opportunity. But in December, when Justice Department prosecutors considered using him as a witness, the FBI expressed no opinion. Headquarters simply wired its New York office on December 20: "THE COMPLETE BACKGROUND OF THIS INDIVIDUAL SHOULD BE MADE AVAILABLE TO THE US [ATTORNEY] SO THAT HE WILL BE FULLY APPRISED OF THIS INDIVIDUAL'S CHARACTER AND PARTY OPERATIONS, PRIOR TO FINAL DETERMINATION TO USE THIS INDIVIDUAL AS A GOVERNMENT WITNESS."[11]

The December 20 wire followed by one day a ninety-minute meeting in a crowded car parked on a secluded Manhattan street, during which Matusow was interviewed by four prosecutors in the Smith Act case, all from the U.S. attorney's office in New York City. He had come to New York in response to a hurried summons from the FBI instructing him to catch the first flight from Dayton. An FBI agent drove him to the meeting. Although no longer a confidential informant, Matusow was introduced to the prosecutors only by the cover name "John Alden." "It was a strange type of conference," he recalled, with six men "sitting in a small sedan with the motor running and the heater on, all uncomfortable."[12]

A fast-talking and aggressive young prosecutor, Roy M. Cohn, only twenty-four (four months younger than Matusow) but already possessing a substantial reputation in the prosecution of "Communist" cases, asked most of the questions. Cohn had proceeded directly from Columbia Law School, where he graduated at age twenty, to the U.S. attorney's office, joining the Julius and Ethel Rosenberg prosecution team. He also participated in the high-profile perjury trial of William W. Remington, the young government economist accused by Elizabeth Bentley. When Remington's conviction was reversed on appeal, Cohn engineered a second indictment, charging him with perjury at his trial on the first indictment.[13]

Cohn directed his questions largely to whether Matusow could tie any of the Smith Act defendants to statements advocating forceful overthrow of the government. The names of the defendants were read, one by one; if Matusow knew the individual (as he did most of them), he was asked whether he had ever heard him or her (three of the defendants were women) say anything supporting forceful overthrow. Cohn asked particularly whether Matusow recalled any of the defendants referring to Andrei Vishinsky's *The Law of the Soviet State,* which had a passage urging violent overthrow of capitalist governments that the prosecution had tried unsuccessfully to place in evidence at the 1949 Foley Square Smith Act trial. Cohn was delighted, Matusow said, when he answered that he did recall one of the defendants mentioning the book.[14]

As the meeting ended, Matusow inquired whether he would be used as a government witness, and Cohn answered with a compliment, "I think you'll make as good a witness as Budenz." Budenz, Matusow knew, had the reputation of "a witness's witness."[15]

The next day, the U.S. attorney's office sought from the FBI, and immediately obtained, Matusow's true name and background. The prosecutors, impressed by Matusow at his interview, did not hesitate in deciding to use him, notwithstanding the bureau's reserve. The benefits to the prosecutors of winning a high-profile "Communist" case were evident. John F. X. McGohey, the U.S. attorney who prosecuted the 1949 Foley Square Smith Act case, was nominated for a federal judgeship the day after the jury verdict; his successor, Irving Saypol, who led the Rosenberg and Remington prosecutions, only recently had resigned to obtain election as a New York state judge. Roy Cohn, barely a year later, would parlay his successes in "Communist" cases into a powerful position as Joe McCarthy's chief counsel.[16]

Concerned that Matusow's forthcoming public appearance before HUAC might interfere with his subsequent use as a trial witness, the prosecutors worked out an arrangement with HUAC to avoid specified subjects at its hearing.[17]

* * *

Back in Dayton, Matusow, unemployed, spent much of his time with the Edmistons. When he returned from New York, arriving after midnight, they drove from their home in Waynesville to meet him. "Sat up with ed and martha till 4 A.M. talking about the good possibilities on the new commie hunt . . . all very happy about it," he noted in his diary.[18]

Matusow had resumed keeping a modest diary, albeit for only four more months. His entries reflect the repeated domestic crises created by Ed's excessive drinking and the Edmistons' tight financial situation—a condition Matusow fully shared. His diary is filled with references to borrowing small amounts of money and attempting to obtain credit. On December 27, for example, he applied to open a department store charge account. "If not," he wrote, "they are stuck with two suits and a coat which I bought." He borrowed $1,400 from his parents, for which he was repaying them $46.80 per month. "I will need to hit the jackpot in washington in order to pay off the world and get back on my feet," he lamented.[19]

Starting in early December 1951, in anticipation of his discharge from the air force, Matusow sought employment with *Counterattack*, a weekly newsletter designed to promote and enforce the political blacklist in the entertainment industry. American Business Consultants, formed by three ex-FBI agents and initially financed by Alfred Kohlberg, began *Counterattack* in 1947; three years later, it published (as a "Special Report" for subscribers) *Red Channels*, a listing of alleged Communists and Communist sympathizers in radio and television that served as a foundation for the blacklist. Persons named in *Red Channels* generally could not work unless they were able to make arrangements to be "cleared."[20]

Matusow approached Ted Kirkpatrick, one of *Counterattack*'s founders, at the company's New York office to seek backing for a proposed lecture tour, or at least to sell a story about his Communist Party activities. When the date for his air force discharge became firm, he followed up with a phone call from Dayton, citing as a further credential his upcoming public appearance before HUAC. He saw Kirkpatrick when he was in New York for his parked-car meeting. Kirkpatrick asked the FBI whether it had any objection to his employing a former FBI informant; the bureau answered "no comment." Kirkpatrick advised Matusow, however, that a lecture tour was out of the question and that *Counterattack* didn't buy stories. Matusow ended up selling twenty-four-dollar subscriptions to *Counterattack* in Ohio (his commission amounted to nine dollars). He would later assume a more important role with the publication.[21]

While selling *Counterattack* subscriptions, Matusow learned from a *Cincinnati Enquirer* reporter, Jim Ratliff, of the recent formation by the legislature of an Ohio Un-American Activities Commission, located at the state capitol in Columbus. Ratliff suggested that Matusow apply for a job and contacted the commission on his behalf. Following an interview with Matusow in Columbus, the commission hired him in January 1952 at a salary of $300 per month plus expenses. While he lacked an investigator's background, Matusow wrote, "[m]y familiarity with Communist literature, party doctrine and language was considered by the commission my most valuable asset."[22]

A modest operation, the commission had only a three-person staff, headed by its chief counsel, Sidney Isaacs, an ex-FBI agent and lawyer. The other employees were a former American Legion "anti-subversive" official and an ex-lieutenant in the local sheriff's office. For Matusow, hired as a "research assistant," the job had more prestige than peddling *Counterattack* subscriptions, and he concluded, "my plans for the future would be better served by the commission."[23]

His first assignment was to obtain the names of all Communists in Dayton. The city had been a stronghold of the United Electrical Workers, a large union expelled by the CIO (like the Mine-Mill union) as Communist-dominated. The commission planned to expose Communists and link them to the UE in each of several Ohio industrial cities.[24]

Compiling the Dayton list proved to be surprisingly easy: Matusow received ready access to the files of the Dayton police department; he obtained a twelve-year-old HUAC list of Communist Party petition signers; and the International Union of Electrical Workers-CIO, the UE's anti-Communist rival, heartily cooperated. At the commission's hearings on "Communism in Dayton," several UE officials were subpoenaed as witnesses—in the midst of the UE's contract negotiations with perhaps its largest shop in Dayton. Matusow (who had by then left his job with the commission) broadcast the hearings on a Dayton radio station.[25]

The commission also assigned Matusow, its expert on youth, to investigate Antioch College in Yellow Springs, Ohio, long known as a liberal institution, and the Labor Youth League in Ohio. But before he could complete these assignments, his HUAC appearance intervened.[26]

* * *

Matusow's public testimony before HUAC, on February 6 and 7, 1952, served as the centerpiece of hearings titled *Communist Activities among Youth Groups (Based on Testimony of Harvey M. Matusow)*. Prior to Matusow's appearance, he and the Edmistons sought to generate maximum publicity for the event and to sell an exclusive story to the newspapers, rather than simply giving his story away when he testified at the hearing. Before he left for Washington, the Edmistons distributed biographical material to the *Cincinnati Enquirer* and to the two Dayton newspapers and arranged for photographs.[27]

When Matusow and Ed Edmiston arrived in the capital, several days before his appearance, they booked a hotel suite, and grabbing a phone directory, began to call right-wing newspapers to sell the story. The *Chicago Tribune* and the Scripps-Howard chain declined. But Jack Clements, public relations director for Hearst publications, and David Sentner, the Washington bureau chief, came promptly to the hotel and bought the story for Hearst's *New York Journal-American*. Matusow and the Edmistons split the

$750 fee. "[B]eing able to sell a story," Matusow later wrote, gave him "a badge of importance" and made him "an authority," like Budenz and other informers whose writings had been published successfully.[28]

Matusow then headed for Hearst's New York headquarters to help write the story. There, J. B. Matthews, Hearst's resident expert on Communists, closely questioned him. A tall, gray-haired, distinguished-looking man, "Doc" Matthews, after decades spent in radical left-wing politics and then (having switched sides in the late 1930s) with the Dies committee, had an encyclopedic knowledge of the American left. An indefatigable collector of written materials (letterheads, circulars, posters, dinner programs), he kept extensive files on left-wing individuals and groups, expanded during his Dies committee years, that served in the 1950s as a source of personal political power and financial gain. The Hearst organization kept him on retainer, both as a resource for its Red-hunting columnists (notably George Sokolsky and Westbrook Pegler) and to insure that no left-wingers would write for, or receive favorable publicity in, Hearst publications. Matusow quickly passed Matthews's inspection.[29]

Howard Rushmore, an ex-Communist who had become a top reporter for the Hearst press, wrote the articles in four installments, on an "as told to" basis. He worked from the "autobiographical" document Matusow and the Edmistons had prepared in October. Rushmore, a towering man, turned right-wing after leaving his job as the *Daily Worker*'s movie reviewer in 1939 in a dispute over the party's insistence that he give a wholly negative review to *Gone with the Wind*. He now specialized in sensational stories; in the mid-1950s he would leave the Hearst organization to become editor of the scandalmongering *Confidential* magazine.[30]

In light of the articles' emphasis on his personal experiences, Matusow, with Rushmore and a *Journal-American* photographer, made a hurried trip to the Bronx to be photographed with his parents, who posed obligingly. "As I left my parents' home," Matusow recalled, "I could see the look of bewilderment on their faces. They didn't know what was going on."[31]

On Tuesday morning, February 5, the day before his HUAC appearance, the first of the articles appeared on the *Journal-American*'s front page, accompanied by Matusow's photograph, under the screaming headline: "Secret FBI Man Reveals: 3,500 Students Recruited Here for Red Fifth-Column." The "3,500" figure had been pulled from thin air.[32]

When the newspaper hit the streets, a New York FBI agent phoned Washington, and Hoover was advised by memorandum that the articles "will apparently reveal [Matusow's] connections as an informant of the FBI." Scribbling in the margin, the director grumbled, "Since the former informant is now writing articles I don't see how [HUAC] can be expected not to call him."[33]

* * *

Matusow's HUAC testimony, consuming more than a full day of hearings, amply indulged the committee's desire for public disclosure of the names of Communist Party members. He first listed individuals according to the places where he had met them—AYD, Camp Unity, LYL, People's Songs. Given the Weavers' celebrity, he wasted no time in supplying their names. Then, at HUAC's request, he gave a plenary list in alphabetical order. The J's included "Clint Jenks"; flatly contradicting his written statement to the FBI five weeks earlier, Matusow volunteered that Jencks, "in private discussion" with him, "admitted membership in the Communist Party." The committee treated Matusow with deference, at one point asking whether he had "any suggestion for the benefit of this committee in our obligation to report to Congress any remedial legislation."[34]

Well coached by the Edmistons, Matusow fashioned his testimony to achieve the broadest possible media coverage. The Communist Party, he said, lured American youth by preying on their areas of "weakness." "In their recruiting attempts," he explained, "the Communists will pick out your weakness, be it sex, then sex will be used to recruit you. . . . If it is intellectual discussion, then that will be used." "[S]exual immorality" was common among young Communists, he revealed, both in Greenwich Village and at Camp Unity. Elaborating, he named "Lenin's Rock," in the wilderness near Camp Unity, as "one of the places where these acts of sexual immorality at times took place."[35]

Communist indoctrination of the young, he continued, started between the ages of four and six, with the teaching of politicized Mother Goose rhymes. For example: "Jack Sprat could eat no fat, his wife could eat no lean, / Because the Congress done them in and picked their pockets clean."[36]

The press loved it all. The tabloid *New York Daily Mirror* headlined: "FBI Aide Says Reds Employ Sex as Snare." Back in Ohio, the *Columbus Citizen*'s headline blared, "Says Reds Used Sex to Lure Members." The United Press wire carried the text of his nursery rhyme.[37]

Matusow, however, still found fault with the press coverage. The newspaper headline he saw during the lunch break on his first day of testimony read, "King George VI Dead." "[W]hat a hell of a break for the king to die and just on my day of triumph," he wrote peevishly in his diary. "[P]ushed me right off the front page." Certainly, Matusow had no misgivings about testifying. "I believed that what I was doing was completely right," he wrote.[38]

FBI director Hoover viewed Matusow's press coverage from his own perspective. Writing in the margin of an internal report on the *Journal-American* articles, he complained, "We apparently have no control over informants."[39]

* * *

Observing Matusow's success before HUAC, Pat McCarran's Senate Internal Security Subcommittee promptly booked him for its own hearings. SISS wanted Matusow not only for its separate investigation of Communist youth activities but, more importantly, for its continuing hearings on Owen Lattimore and the State Department's China policy.

Matusow's testimony in the Lattimore hearings—testimony he would later recant—was first given in executive session on February 13, only a week after he completed his HUAC appearance. His public testimony came in March. In the interim, Lattimore suffered twelve days of hostile and detailed questioning by the subcommittee, which was attempting to create the basis for a perjury charge against him. Fred J. Cook termed it "the longest and most brutal interrogation of one man in all Congressional history up to that time."[40]

Months earlier, the subcommittee had received the testimony of Louis Budenz, who accused Lattimore of having secretly been a Communist Party member, part of a conspiracy to influence State Department policy in favor of the Chinese Communists. But Budenz's hearsay accusations had been rejected in 1950 by the Tydings committee, impeached by a variety of witnesses, and flatly denied by Lattimore. When Matusow appeared on the scene, the subcommittee was seeking to corroborate Budenz's charge by proving that Lattimore's writings followed the Communist Party "line" on China.[41]

Matusow's February testimony focused on his employment at the Jefferson School book shop. Lattimore's book *Solution in Asia,* published in 1945, he said, "was one of the books used in the book shop and suggested reading for a background on the party line, the Communist Party line in Asia." The party's State Education Committee, Matusow explained, "came out with a decision that Solution in Asia was one of those books which could give a Communist Party member a correct line, a Communist line, on the Asiatic situation in China and China specifically." By the time of his public testimony a month later, the Lattimore book had advanced from "suggested reading" to "required or recommended reading" at the Jefferson School. Matusow added that he himself had recommended Lattimore's book on numerous occasions, because "in my position in the bookshop, I knew by sight probably 10,000 Party members in New York," and when one of them asked for a book on China, he had been "told to recommend" the Lattimore book.[42]

The subcommittee used Matusow's executive-session testimony—which it characterized as the testimony "of an FBI agent here before this committee"—in its marathon interrogation of Lattimore two weeks later. "Well, Mr. Lattimore," Senator Homer Ferguson, Republican of Michigan, queried, "do you not think then that people may be justified in criticizing your book as following the Communist line when testimony before this committee from an employee, an FBI agent, has characterized it as having been adopted as carrying out the party line?" Lattimore protested that "many people of other points of view also used and commented favorably on Solution in Asia." "But," Senator Ferguson responded, "you would not criticize people now for following what this witness has said under oath; would you?"[43]

The Justice Department later indicted Lattimore for perjury, one of the charges being that he falsely denied to the subcommittee that he was a "follower of the Communist line."[44]

* * *

Matusow's appearance in SISS's hearings, which were given the title *Communist Tactics in Controlling Youth Organizations*, like his HUAC appearance, was at times comical. The core of his testimony, given in closed session on March 5 but not released until August (in the midst of the 1952 election campaign), was a description of Communist efforts first to undermine and later to infiltrate the Boy Scouts of America. "I had a chance to get 'documents' relating to the subject," Matusow later wrote (he had been given them by a SISS staff member), "and I made a fairly impressive showing."[45]

Matusow began by introducing a number of pre–Russian Revolution pamphlets by Lenin that were directed to the importance of youth in the Communist movement and by reading aloud selected passages. In 1905, he said, Lenin wrote: "The youth will decide the issue of the whole struggle, the student youth and still more the working-class youth. Get rid of all the old habits of immobility, respect for religion, and so on." He selected another Lenin instruction: "All that is needed is more widely and boldly; more boldly and widely, again more widely and again more boldly to recruit young people, and not to be afraid of them."[46]

Matusow then discussed the Communist Party's formation, in the 1920s and early 1930s, of a rival group to the Boy Scouts called the "Young Pioneers," producing for the subcommittee a dated party pamphlet that exhorted readers to "Smash the Boy Scouts! Join the Young Pioneers!" In the unmistakable rhetoric of the 1920s and 1930s, the pamphlet charged, "THE BOY SCOUTS IS AN INSTRUMENT OF THE BOSSES FOR MILITARIZING THE CHILDREN!" He read aloud the pamphlet's chilling chapter headings, including "Boy Scouts take part in murder of striking workers." But "the Young Pioneers," Matusow explained, "were never able to compete with the Boy Scouts," and the party's "line has changed drastically." Now, he said, the party, utilizing once more a policy articulated by Lenin, sought to infiltrate the Boy Scouts—he cited as evidence testimony by the Edmistons before the Ohio Un-American Activities Commission.[47]

Before he finished, Matusow's testimony took on a more familiar cast. He leafed through an AYD publication entitled *Youth*, finding on page after page the names of individuals he identified as party members. Turning to the Labor Youth League, he added, almost without pausing for breath, twenty-seven names of LYL leaders "[w]hom I know to be Communist Party members."[48]

Matusow's warning that the Communist Party sought to infiltrate the Boy Scouts led to a panicky nationwide alert from the chief executive of the organization, Arthur A. Schuck, to other Boy Scout officials. "Here is further evidence," Schuck wrote, "of how careful we must be to scan every adult applicant for membership in the Boy Scouts of America. In other words, we must be eternally vigilant."[49]

The following week, Matusow returned to SISS's witness stand to address in closed session his alleged friendship, first disclosed when he contacted the FBI in 1950, with two members of the Czech United Nations delegation. He told the subcommittee that the Czech government tried in 1951 to steal atomic secrets from Los Alamos. Matusow would repudiate this testimony when he recanted, stating that it was he who "approached" the Czechs, in order to "have something to report to the FBI." "It was," he told SISS in 1955, "a social relation."[50]

Before leaving Washington, Matusow stopped by to see two HUAC members, who spoke of the committee's successes against the Michigan Communist Party. Similar action was needed in New York, Matusow wrote in his diary: "half of the party members in the us are in nyc . . . Matusow you've got a job on your hands . . . the only way your going to do it, is by taking the mc carthy approach . . . 'keep punching' . . . give im hell."[51]

* * *

Matusow's appearances before the committees led immediately to additional employment. On February 8, two days after his HUAC appearance, William Jansen, New York City's superintendent of schools, wrote Matusow asking his assistance in the city's purge of Communist teachers. Following meetings with Jansen and Saul Moskoff, an assistant corporation counsel, during which Matusow named several teachers, the Board of Education hired him as a consultant for a ten-day period in March at twenty-five dollars per day. Later, after his recantation, Matusow testified that his knowledge of the subject was "so limited" that he had to cadge information from an investigator for the corporation counsel's office in order to justify his fee.[52]

Simultaneously with his HUAC appearance, a New York City booking agent, Clark H. Getts, Inc., recruited him for the lecture circuit. The promotional circular it prepared listed such lecture topics as "What Communist Youth Camps Mean" and "The Red Snare for Young People" and described Matusow's "exposures of Red perfidy," which had "been of immeasurable value in turning the tide of Communist influence here."[53]

In March, the Justice Department used Matusow as a witness before the Subversive Activities Control Board in the department's effort to compel registration of the Communist Party as a "Communist-action" organization—a statutory term defined as an organization dominated by a foreign government that (among other things) seeks to conceal the identity of its members. By way of proof, Matusow testified that in October 1948, at a meeting of a Communist youth club, the group was instructed it should "not support the United States in an imperialist war against the Soviet Union." And when he worked at party headquarters in 1949, he said, "[a] tin can was kept on all desks and any message with names, addresses and telephone numbers was burned as soon as it was read."[54]

By virtue of his passing reference before HUAC to Communist participation in a 1949 student strike at City College of New York, Matusow was retained by Lord, Day & Lord, a prestigious New York City law firm, one of whose partners was Herbert Brownell (soon to become attorney general of the United States). The firm's client, the *New York Times,* had been sued for $250,000 by the student council at CCNY for reporting that the strike was Communist inspired. Matusow gave a statement affirming that it was and earned $300, including traveling expenses from Dayton.[55]

In Dayton, Matusow continued his labors for the Ohio commission. He worked on hearings, commencing on February 11, in which informer Matt Cvetic had star billing. Matusow also assisted the commission's continuing campaign against the UE, an effort aided greatly by the employers at UE-organized plants in Ohio.[56]

His investigation of "subversive" influences at Antioch College, however, ran into problems. Not only did Matusow's methods ruffle community feathers, but the best he could come up with was a campus chapter of Young Progressives of America, an organization formed in 1948 to back Henry Wallace's presidential campaign. Not every YPA member was a Communist, Matusow conceded in testimony to the commission on February 25; but YPA membership, he said, served as "an easy stepping stone" to Communist Party membership.[57]

Matusow also told the commission that the Communist Party frequently used folk-singing and square-dancing events to attract young people. As in his HUAC testimony, he mentioned the Weavers, naming three of the group as party members and the fourth as a former party member. For the Weavers, however, the damage had been done the first time. Matusow's HUAC testimony, the Associated Press reported on February 7, resulted in cancellation of the Weavers' one-week booking (for $1,750) at the Yankee Inn in Akron, Ohio. The group had already performed part of the booking, the inn's owner said, but the "pressure of publicity" compelled him to cancel the remainder.[58]

* * *

Matusow's activities also affected other entertainers. One of the Matusow and Howard Rushmore *Journal-American* articles named Sam Levenson, a well-known TV humorist, as an entertainer whose bookings were made by the Communist Party–controlled People's Artists agency. Levenson, who indeed had been listed with People's Artists in the late 1940s, along with a number of other agencies, before he achieved success in television, suddenly found his career in jeopardy. He contacted Rushmore, who led him to Matusow. Matusow wrote a letter addressed to the Ohio commission absolving the entertainer of Communist ties; he signed the letter at the office of Jack Wren of the Batten, Barton, Durstine & Osborn ad agency, who often served as a "clearer" of blacklisted talent. With Matusow's letter in hand, Levenson made a voluntary appearance before SISS on March 20, where he read the letter aloud.[59]

He also had other letters proving his loyalty, Levenson anxiously told the subcommittee: "This is a letter from the mayor [of New York City] for participation in I Am an American Day ceremonies. I get invited annually. I have a letter from the Society of Former Special Agents of the Federal Bureau of Investigation, signed by Robert W. Dick, the president. I performed for them." Levenson, formerly a Brooklyn high school teacher, read from a laudatory letter written by "Dr. Lefkowitz, my principal from 1939 to 1946." "That is just one paragraph," Levenson said. "You can read the rest for yourself. He says I am a 100 percent risk, a most loyal American, and he would vouch for me. He himself is quite a well-known anti-Communist."[60]

Matusow later denied in courtroom testimony that he was paid for his letter absolving Levenson. But in a 1995 oral history, he said (in the context of his renewed association with *Counterattack* in the spring of 1952), "I was also on the take. . . . Sam Levinson's [*sic*] agent gave me an envelope with two hundred dollars in it, 'Go buy yourself a dinner.'" Levenson, Matusow added, "was just a liberal Jew."[61]

On the day following Levenson's appearance before SISS, Matusow wrote a letter for the Ohio commission to a Twentieth Century-Fox Film Corporation official, naming as Communist Party members writers, actors, and others associated with the 1950 production of *Longitude '49* by the Freedom Theater (a Camp Unity offshoot). The play was written, he said, by Herb Tank, a contributing editor to the *Daily Worker,* and one of the cast members was Sidney Poitier, "who played the role of a seaman." Three years later, Tank would become an actor in Matusow's recantation drama.[62]

* * *

For the moment, Matusow's myriad activities as an informer seemed to impress even the FBI. A bureau official commented in late April that Matusow "has proven to be a prolific fountain of Communist Party information within the past year."[63]

But although his rise to celebrity as an informer-witness could hardly have been more rapid, Matusow's career was still not in the top rank. Herbert Philbrick, for example, in addition to publication of his book, *I Led Three Lives,* began in May 1952 to publish a regular column, "The Red Underground," in the respected *New York Herald Tribune.* Matt Cvetic's story, *I Was a Communist for the FBI,* became not only a 1951 film but also, beginning in 1952, a syndicated radio show, with movie actor Dana Andrews in the lead role.[64]

Whittaker Chambers's *Witness* appeared in ten *Saturday Evening Post* installments starting in February 1952; Random House scheduled a spring release for the book; and the Book-of-the-Month Club made it a main selection. By June, *Witness* reached the top of the *New York Times* best-seller nonfiction list.[65]

Louis Budenz's third book, *The Cry Is Peace,* appeared in 1952, and when in April he was in the headlines again, testifying for fourteen days as the government's leadoff witness in the Smith Act trial of "second-string" Communists in New York City, he complained about it. "Constant testifying," Budenz wrote to Hoover and the Justice Department, had injured him "physically and financially," and it interfered "seriously" with his "plans for lecturing and writing and also with my teaching." He asked that he be given "a complete respite" for at least two years "from all testimony against the Communist conspiracy." Hoover was unimpressed, his reaction summed up in a handwritten note to his aides: "[Budenz] puts too many qualifying conditions upon his cooperation for one who for many years was engaged in traitorous activities against his country."[66]

Matusow, however, still a supporting player, welcomed the opportunity to testify at a major Smith Act trial, although he would have to wait until July for his turn. And still other opportunities would be provided by the 1952 election campaign now just underway, in which Communist "subversion," and the Truman administration's response, was certain to become a major issue.

But Matusow could not expect professional advancement living in Dayton. "Ohio was too small," he later wrote, "and didn't offer me the scope of anti-Communist identity that Washington and New York did." He had other reasons to leave. His job with the Ohio commission ended in early April. Matusow, his diary entries indicate, had repeatedly irritated his boss, Sid Isaacs. Five days before the end, he wrote of "a balling [sic] out" from Isaacs, adding, "matusow you have a big mouth, sometimes its to[o] damm big." His friendship with the Edmistons had also cooled. He wrote that Ed "is to[o] dam lazy . . . from now on I will have to work it alone . . . I'll do better that way."[67]

In May 1952, he returned to New York City.[68]

4 Blacklists and Election Campaigns

Counterattack held great appeal for Matusow, combining publishing, the entertainment industry, and informing. It also provided entreé to the profitable businesses on the underbelly of the radio-TV blacklist: "clearing" blacklisted individuals and assisting broadcast sponsors and their ad agencies in identifying and avoiding politically tainted talent who might pose a commercial risk.

While still living in Dayton, Matusow actively sought a job with *Counterattack* in New York City. On several occasions during February and March 1952, he arranged in the course of an East Coast trip to see Ted Kirkpatrick, the managing editor. In April, Matusow suggested that *Counterattack* employ him to compile an index, a suggestion politely declined. The newsletter did, however, publish his charges concerning the Weavers.[1]

When Kirkpatrick asked him as a favor to assist the Westchester County district attorney's office, still dealing with the aftermath of the 1949 Peekskill riots, in securing evidence that Communist concertgoers were the aggressors and the failure of local police to protect them was justified, Matusow jumped at the chance. He promptly gave a written statement that "[c]alls" to attend the concert "were sent out to Communist Party members from the whole New England, New York, New Jersey, and Penna, area." The Camp Unity group alone, he wrote, consisted of a convoy of forty cars, each carrying six people and "equiped [*sic*] with baseball bats, and some had lead pipes wraped [*sic*] in newspapers. One car carried a 22 hunting rifle. . . . Four Cars in the convoy were called trouble shooters. They carried six men in them, all of whom were ready for trouble and looking for it." He omitted any mention of the rock-throwing mob or having to hide Paul Robeson Jr. in the back seat of his car.[2]

In June, Matusow, now living in New York City, picked up $300 for an article in *American Legion Magazine,* although the "as told to" credit given Howard Rushmore, who also made $300, indicates he was the author. The piece, titled "Reds in Khaki," described itself as a "first-hand account by a GI who was recruited into the communist party by reds in Army uniform."[3]

The same month, Matusow finally succeeded in getting hired by *Counterattack,* as assistant to the editor, at a salary of $70 a week. He now had the chance, he wrote, "to get into the glamorous limelight of show business." He learned that the $24–a-year newsletter he had peddled in Ohio was used by its owners, American Business Consultants, to develop a business selling "protection services" (i.e., protection against hiring or keeping "subversive" employees) to large corporations, such as General Electric, at annual fees of $5,000 and up. But the role assigned Matusow, who was employed, he said, because of his "inside knowledge of Communism," consisted of writing articles and enforcing the entertainment industry blacklist.[4]

In view of the profit potential for its owners and allies when it named a radio or television talent—selling "protection" to the program sponsor or ad agency, or collecting fees for "clearing" the individual—*Counterattack* had an economic, not merely ideological, incentive to cast its net widely. It caught not only Communist Party members but also past and present members of fronts and civil-rights groups, petition signers, meeting-goers, and some who simply let their names get on the wrong letterheads. A few months after the attorney general's list of "subversive" organizations appeared in 1947, *Counterattack* published its own list of 192 fronts, adding 119 to those on the attorney general's list.[5]

Counterattack was formidable. It maintained comprehensive files on left-wing organizations and individuals. It had volunteer "informants" throughout the United States. "*Counterattack*'s standards of what constituted 'infiltration,' 'communistic associations,' and grounds for suspicion," John Cogley said in his 1956 study of entertainment-industry blacklisting (written for the Fund for the Republic, a Ford Foundation unit), "were almost universally adopted up and down Madison Avenue."[6]

An important consequence of the blacklist in the radio-TV industry, where careers were often lucrative but short, was to spawn a class of "clearers" who enabled a number of blacklisted actors, directors, and writers—each willing to make an abject confession and apology to HUAC or a patriotic group (e.g., the American Legion) and publicly to name names—to be "cleared" and to return to work. The "clearance" process, complicated and with its own etiquette, was operated by a class of paid "consultants," including Vincent

Hartnett, the reputed author of *Red Channels,* who was both a blacklister and a "clearer." Red-hunting journalists such as George Sokolsky and Howard Rushmore, of the Hearst press, and Victor Riesel, a *New York Daily Mirror* columnist, often assisted in the process, also earning significant income. "All those reactionary columnists were on the take," Matusow later remarked.[7]

Matusow named for *Counterattack* "many" young actors he had known in his Communist days. When he learned that comedian Jack Gilford, allegedly a member of Communist-front organizations, was to appear on television's *Colgate Comedy Hour* along with catcher Yogi Berra of the New York Yankees, he bombarded the Yankee office with phone calls, using a variety of voices, demanding that Berra be withdrawn from the program—although in the end it was Gilford who did not appear.[8]

* * *

While at *Counterattack,* Matusow became a protégé of Laurence A. Johnson, the elderly owner of four Syracuse self-service grocery stores, who intimidated broadcast networks, high-powered ad agencies, and corporate sponsors that failed to comply with the blacklist. "Johnson . . . took a liking to me," Matusow said. "He would take me on his visits to the agencies." The Syracuse grocer, whom Matusow described as "very jovial, full of life, but intense," worked hard to get results, constantly visiting, phoning, telegraphing, and writing letters to network and ad agency executives and sponsors.[9]

Johnson did not threaten to remove from his stores the products marketed by sponsors of noncomplying programs but rather something worse. Johnson's stores, Matusow wrote, would display the offending sponsor's goods with a sign reading, "Our boys are dying in Korea; the manufacturer of this product employs Communist-fronters"; alongside, the store would display a competing product with a sign saying, "They do not employ Communist-fronters." When needed, Johnson could obtain support from supermarket owners in other cities, including the large Safeway chain.[10]

Johnson's threats got results. He was treated, Matusow said, "with the same kind of fear they would treat anybody who could cut their legs off." For example, after another complaint involving Jack Gilford (for his August 29, 1951, appearance on CBS's *Arthur Godfrey and His Friends*), J. L. Van Volkenburg, president of CBS Television, apologetically wrote Johnson, "We want to thank you for being instrumental in having this matter brought to our attention and fully understand the reasons for your deep feeling about it." He assured Johnson that the show's sponsor, Liggett & Myers Tobacco Company, had "no responsibility for the selection of the guests who appear on this show." Gilford's appearance, he explained, "took place during the absence on vacation of the regular director-producer," and the comedian had been "engaged through a reputable talent agency for a one-time appearance."[11]

Johnson also looked out for his friends. On one occasion, a major ad agency, Lennen & Mitchell, caught in a breach of the blacklist involving talent on the television show *Schlitz Playhouse of Stars,* heeded his demand that Matusow be hired as a "consultant." Under Matusow's guidance, the agency purchased what it termed "Actor Clearance Lists" from *Counterattack* for $150. It got rid of the individuals named, including director Phil Brown, who, Matusow reported, "has still not shown himself to have taken any concrete action against Communism and the Communist fronts which his name has been tied to." Matusow's report to the agency concluded with good news: "I spoke to Mr. Johnson . . . and told him of the concrete action taken by the agency and assured him that from what I was able to gather, a situation such as this would never occur again at Lennen & Mitchell or with any of the accounts of Lennen & Mitchell."[12]

Matusow's accusations at times missed their target. During 1952, he informed Johnson, on the basis of a magazine photograph, that Sidney Lumet, director of the CBS television program *Danger,* had been a fellow member of his Communist Party cell. Johnson complained to the program's sponsor, Block Drug Company. But inquiry showed Lumet to have been in Korea at the time in question. Arnold Forster, general counsel of the Anti-Defamation League, with the help of "clearer" Victor Riesel, arranged a face-to-face meeting between Matusow and Lumet, at which Matusow acknowledged he "was thinking of somebody else" and had been "wrong and mistaken." The next day, he went to Forster's office, signed a written retraction, and collected fifty dollars—an amount, he later said, "accepted reluctantly."[13]

Johnson was among the many "countersubversives" embarrassed by Matusow's 1955 recantation. Still, his influence continued, as reflected in John Cogley's cautious treatment of the event a year later: "The grocer had no reason to believe that the young man [Matusow] was anything other than what he said he was, a sincere, knowledgeable, anti-Communist. . . . [T]he agencies which accepted Matusow as an 'expert' did so mainly to please the grocer and convince him that they were sincerely cooperating with his crusade."[14]

Johnson's activities came to an end in 1961, in the wake of litigation brought by John Henry Faulk, a blacklisted CBS radio personality, who was represented (without fee) by attorney Louis Nizer. Before the trial, Matusow (who had long since recanted) called Nizer to suggest that he use Frank Barton, a Lennen & Mitchell executive, as a witness to describe Johnson's methods. Barton, persuaded by Nizer to appear, testified to a 1952 meeting with

Johnson and Matusow in a Manhattan hotel dining room at which Johnson "got fairly angry with me and started to pound the table and raise his voice sufficiently to attract attention around the dining room." The dispute ended, Barton said, only after he agreed that his agency would hire Matusow. The jury returned a large damage award against Johnson and blacklister Vincent Hartnett. While the jury deliberated, Johnson died in a Bronx hotel.[15]

* * *

Throughout the spring of 1952, Matusow worked with federal prosecutors preparing for his appearance in the "second-string" Smith Act trial then in progress. On July 21, he took the witness stand for the first of six days of well-publicized testimony.[16]

The "most difficult task" facing the prosecution, Edward J. Dimock, the trial judge, later explained, was to prove that each individual defendant had the intent to bring about the overthrow of the government by force and violence. While "Communist classics" advocated the necessity of forcible overthrow, the judge stated, the Communist Party of the United States and the defendants in the case contended that this "tenet" had been "abandoned." "From the standpoint of the Government, therefore, proof of individual advocacy of the use of force and violence was necessary." Matusow skillfully shaped his testimony to this task.[17]

He had learned as early as his December parked-car interview, for example, that the prosecutors hoped to introduce into evidence against defendant Alexander Trachtenberg the passage endorsing forcible overthrow contained in Andrei Vishinsky's *The Law of the Soviet State.* But until shortly before his appearance at the trial, Matusow could only connect Trachtenberg to the book by ambiguous statements of third persons—a link so remote that the prosecutors decided not to use the book against him. Then, a few days before he testified, Matusow recalled that during the time he worked at the Jefferson School Book Shop, Trachtenberg, who managed publishing for the party, directly instructed him to promote the Vishinsky book because it was the latest description of Soviet law, and American party members should become familiar with it.[18]

At the trial, despite this testimony, Judge Dimock initially refused to admit the proffered passage from the book into evidence because Trachtenberg's instruction to Matusow "did not constitute an endorsement of the part about the necessity of violence." But Matusow then conveniently remembered another statement by Trachtenberg—that the book showed "how the diametrically opposed classes could be eliminated"—tying him more closely to the book and its advocacy of violence. Dimock ultimately admitted the extract as evidence of Trachtenberg's intent. "Matusow," the judge later wrote, "had saved the day."[19]

The Vishinsky passage, read to the jury to prove Trachtenberg's intent, stated that "violent seizure of authority by the proletariat, the demolition of the exploiting society's machinery of state, and the organization (in lieu of the old state machinery, now reduced to fragments) of a new state is the most important thesis of the Marxist-Leninist doctrine of proletarian revolution."[20]

In similar fashion, Matusow initially recorded (in his October 1951 "autobiographical" report) an instruction by defendant George Blake Charney, another Communist Party official, prior to Matusow's Puerto Rico trip, that he arrange for the sending of a Puerto Rican delegate to a Communist youth festival in Budapest. Thereafter, Matusow remembered a series of progressively more damaging statements by Charney. By the time of trial, he recalled Charney's statement "that Puerto Rico was being used as a military base by the United States, and an independent Puerto Rico would help to destroy those bases and [crip]ple the Caribbean defense." Charney "pointed out," Matusow continued, "that the only time Puerto Rico would get its independence was when we had conducted an effective struggle for socialism and had overthrown the bourgeoisie."[21]

Again, Matusow remembered during an early interview with prosecutors that Pettis Perry, an African American defendant, had urged in a speech that a separate "Negro nation" be established in the "black belt" in the South. In a subsequent interview, he recalled Perry saying that establishment of the "Negro nation" would require overthrow of the capitalist system and its replacement by Communist-run socialism. By the time of the trial, he added Perry's statement that "the bourgeoisie would not sit back and let it [socialism] come to power peacefully, and therefore the working class led by the Communist Party would have to forcibly overthrow this bourgeoisie to set up the Negro nation while establishing socialism."[22]

"Matusow's stories developed gradually," Judge Dimock wrote after Matusow's recantation, "and his successive statements [to the FBI or prosecutors] and 'trial briefs' [by the prosecutors] enable us to watch their unfolding." "In every case," Dimock found, "the effective thrust was finally given in connection with something about which Matusow had first given his interrogators a comparatively innocent statement."[23]

But Judge Dimock's revelation came later, not at the time of the trial. Then, although he acquitted two defendants, finding the evidence against them insufficient to submit to the jury, thirteen other defendants, including Trachtenberg, Charney, and Perry, were convicted. The incendiary Vishinsky passage, Dimock later found, "was the strongest single item of evidence against

Trachtenberg and the conversation about Puerto Rico was almost the only persuasive evidence of Charney's personal intent."[24]

The lengthy trial ended in mid-January 1953, with sentencing of the thirteen convicted defendants early the following month. In an unusual action, Judge Dimock gave each defendant the choice between a prison sentence or exile to the Soviet Union. None chose exile. Defendant Elizabeth Gurley Flynn, a feisty sixty-two-year-old member of the Communist Party's national committee, said, "We feel we belong here and have a political responsibility here." Claudia Jones, a native of Trinidad whom the government was seeking to deport, found the judge's inquiry "a strange request." "I am fighting deportation to earn my citizenship," she told him. Alexander Bittelman, an elderly party theoretician, who was born in Russia, stated, "I adopted this land of my own volition and I intend to stay here the rest of my life."[25]

The next day, Judge Dimock imposed prison sentences on each of the defendants, ranging from a year and a day to three years. Given the opportunity to make a statement, defendant Flynn condemned the prosecution's "motley array of bought and paid-for informers, stoolpigeons and renegades." The *New York Times* gave the story front-page coverage: "13 Secondary Reds Get Their Wish: Jail Sentences Instead of Russia."[26]

* * *

While still in Dayton, Matusow had worked briefly in Senator Robert A. Taft's unsuccessful effort to win the 1952 Republican presidential nomination. After completing his appearance in the Smith Act trial in July, he again took note of the national election campaign and the opportunities it afforded.[27]

Never lacking in cheek, Matusow walked into Joe McCarthy's Senate office in Washington, announced that he had just testified against the Communists, and volunteered to campaign for McCarthy, who was running for reelection and facing opposition in the Wisconsin primary. To McCarthy and his staff, Matusow's FBI connection, his HUAC and SISS appearances, and his recent courtroom testimony against Communist Party officials were all attractive credentials. After preliminary scrutiny of his speaking skills, they accepted his offer. Jean Kerr, the senator's assistant, phoned the FBI to ask how Matusow's past relationship with the bureau should be characterized; "he was in fact an FBI informer," she was told.[28]

McCarthy did need help in his primary campaign. The principal problem was not his opponent, Len Schmitt, an attorney who had lost a gubernatorial primary two years earlier, but McCarthy's health. After a sinus operation in June, the senator in July underwent major surgery for the repair of a herniated diaphragm. The operation necessitated a twenty-four-inch incision and removal of a rib. His constant drinking complicated the problem. Mc-Carthy made only a single campaign speech, carried on a statewide radio hookup, prior to the September 9 primary.[29]

In August, Matusow, as a McCarthy surrogate, flew to Wisconsin, where he delivered speeches in Green Bay, Madison, and Ashland, under the auspices of the McCarthy Club. His Green Bay address, "The Inside of the Communist Plot against McCarthy," was broadcast, and in Madison he appeared at a statewide rally with the Republican governor, Walter J. Kohler. Matusow asserted that Communists on the staffs of New York City newspapers had launched a "smear campaign" against McCarthy but that the senator "makes no accusations or says anything about anybody unless there is documentation to back it up." When his appearances proved successful, the McCarthy organization extended Matusow's tour to Wausau and Kohler.[30]

In the course of the campaign, Matusow forged a friendship with McCarthy, characterized by much kidding back and forth. It began when Matusow phoned the Milwaukee hotel room of Urban Van Susteren, McCarthy's close friend, and, recognizing the senator's voice at the other end of the line, identified himself as Harvey Matusow, the man who was giving speeches for "that fascist son of a bitch" McCarthy—eliciting loud guffaws. On a later occasion, he substantially convinced McCarthy that a tiny statue of Tom Paine stood atop the Washington Monument, before the senator realized that Matusow was putting him on. The two men, fellow pranksters, seemed to share an enjoyment of the rough-and-tumble as well as the theatrical side of politics.[31]

McCarthy won his primary election handily and invited Matusow to the boozy victory party. Matusow had (as he later wrote) "hit the jackpot."[32]

His accomplishments during the primary campaign were remarkable. With only minimal experience in election politics (the 1948 Wallace campaign in New York City), Matusow stepped into a high-profile, pressure-filled statewide election, in a locale foreign to him, and made five successful speeches before large audiences. If McCarthy had a weak opponent, and Matusow's message was shrill and undifferentiated, he had nonetheless delivered the goods for a candidate in distress. Not least, he had made Joe McCarthy, an enormously powerful politician, his friend.

McCarthy, recognizing election talent, invited Matusow to campaign in the general election for Republican senatorial candidates favored by him in several western states.[33]

Nationwide, the Republican strategy was to make full use of the "Communist" issue against the Democrats. With Richard Nixon, who built his career on the Hiss case, as Dwight D. Eisenhower's running mate, and with McCarthy a readily available weapon, the GOP was well-positioned to do so.

* * *

In early October 1952, before he began campaigning in the West, Matusow testified in Salt Lake City at SISS hearings directed at the Mine, Mill, and Smelter Workers union. That these hearings were scheduled for Salt Lake City only a month before election day was not a coincidence: Senator Arthur Watkins of Utah, a conservative Republican and a SISS member, was running for re-election, and chairman Pat McCarran (although a Democrat himself) did not wish to see Watkins replaced by a liberal Democrat. The hearings, with Watkins prominently displayed, were supported by the CIO, which had expelled the Mine-Mill union. Matusow was joined by J. B. Matthews, soon to become his friend and frequent host, who appeared as an "expert" witness.[34]

The thrust of Matusow's testimony, delivered in a hearing room jammed with union members, was that the Mine-Mill union sought to cut off copper production needed in the Korean War when it struck Kennecott Copper. Matusow again accused Clinton Jencks. Jencks told him at the San Cristobal Valley Ranch, Matusow stated, that "the Communists within the union" were seeking to bring about a strike in the copper industry "under the guise of wage increases, etc., and better working conditions," in order "to cut down the production of copper for the Korean war effort." (He would later recant this testimony.)[35]

Asked whether Jencks had "identif[ied] himself to you as a member of the Communist Party," Matusow, once more contradicting his December 29 written statement to the FBI, answered flatly, "Yes." "The substance of the conversation," he reiterated, "was that Mr. Jencks was a Communist Party member."[36]

Matusow managed to drag into his testimony accusations against the New York City media he had previously discussed with McCarthy. He volunteered that having attended Communist Party caucuses for the American Newspaper Guild, he knew that the *New York Times* employed "well over 100 dues-paying members" of the Communist Party, and *Time* magazine, 76. These allegations, like his testimony about Jencks, would be recanted.[37]

Senators McCarran and Watkins, observing the crowd of union members in the hearing room and realizing that a large number of mine employees would vote in their home states, took pains to emphasize their solidarity with rank-and-file workers. The portly McCarran, an unwavering friend of large corporations, announced that he "came from the loins of labor" and was "reared in a labor home." Watkins claimed to be "the son of a hardrock miner myself," who "had to work with my hands for much of my life."[38]

Afterward, McCarran invited Matusow to meet privately with him at his hotel suite. He wanted to discuss Hank Greenspun, the outspoken editor and publisher of the *Las Vegas Sun* and his political opponent. The senator told Matusow that he believed Greenspun to be a Communist or Communist-fronter and asked him to try to develop some evidence to this effect. Matusow requested a list of the names of employees of Greenspun's newspaper, which McCarran's office provided a week later.[39]

* * *

Matusow spent most of October 1952 campaigning for Republicans and being well paid in the process. On October 5, he delivered a speech in Libertyville, Illinois (the hometown of Adlai Stevenson, the Democratic presidential nominee), for which he received $300. By election day, he had campaigned in Idaho, Montana (he made $1,000 there), Utah, and Washington (where he was paid $500). While he received speech material from his sponsors, he spoke without notes.[40]

In Idaho, where his engagements included an address to the student body at the local high school in Pocatello, Matusow's scheduled thirty-minute talk was so well received—the local press said he held the audience "spellbound"—that he ended up speaking for two hours. The explanation for his success, Matusow said, was that he "brought Communism down to the teenage level by talking their language, and it had the desired effect."[41]

But charges made in his Pocatello speeches—that all churches except the Mormon church had been infiltrated by Communists and that the head of the Methodist church was a Communist—engendered heated complaints. (The charge of Communist infiltration of the Protestant clergy was hardly new; J. B. Matthews, a one-time Methodist minister, regularly voiced it.) Because Matusow flaunted his FBI connection, the Butte FBI office quickly received word. The director sent instructions to Butte to limit comment; an editorial note typed by one of his aides stated, "Matusow is rapidly becoming another Andrew [*sic*] Cvetic." The bureau had dispensed with Cvetic's services as an informant in 1950 and viewed his subsequent career, premised on his FBI connection, with a jaundiced eye.[42]

Matusow flew on to Montana in an airplane chartered by the Republican Party. Appearing on behalf of "Montana Citizens for Americanism," his objective was to defeat Mike Mansfield, a Democratic congressman running for the Senate, whom McCarthy disliked. Matusow began with a full day in Great Falls, where he made daytime appearances at two high schools and at the local air force base, followed by a brief personal appearance (for a fifty-dollar fee) at a drive-in theater. He then addressed a packed house at the city auditorium, where he suggested to his small-town audience that while Communists could be found everywhere, they gathered in big cities—for example, 500 Communist teachers in New York City and 126 Communists working for the Sunday *New York Times*. (The Sunday *Times* had fewer than 100 employees in total.) Matusow repeatedly implied in his Montana appearances that the Communist Party supported Mansfield.[43]

As in Idaho, his added implication of a close relationship with the FBI led a number of Mansfield supporters to direct inquiries to the bureau. Lou Boedecker, a Montana prison warden in good standing with Hoover, wired him on October 23, "IS OR WAS HARVEY MATUSOW WITH THE FBI AND [I]F SO IN WHAT CAPACITY." The director's response gave him little solace. While "Matusow has never been an employee of the FBI," Hoover wrote, "[h]e has . . . furnished this Bureau with information pertaining to the national security." Methodist Bishop G. Bromley Oxnam (who would later play a role in Matusow's recantation) also complained to Hoover, citing Matusow's charge in a Great Falls speech that the Methodist church was infiltrated by Communists and naming Oxnam. Hoover replied that Matusow "does not speak in any sense directly or indirectly" for the FBI. Mansfield, despite the charges, went on to win the election.[44]

Matusow next visited Utah where, at McCarthy's request, he assisted Senator Arthur Watkins in his successful reelection campaign. (Less than two years later, Watkins would be chairman of the committee that recommended McCarthy's censure.) In Washington state, he campaigned for Senator Harry Cain, a conservative Republican engaged in a losing reelection effort against a youthful Democratic congressman, Henry M. ("Scoop") Jackson.[45]

The FBI, after the complaints it received from Montana and Idaho, made sure that local FBI agents attended Matusow's Seattle speech. They reported that he returned to the themes of Communist infiltration of the Protestant clergy (naming not only Bishop Oxnam but also Presbyterian and Episcopalian clergymen) and the New York City public schools and newspapers. Matusow also attacked a special McCarthy enemy, columnist Drew Pearson—with whom the senator in 1950 had come to blows in a Washington, D.C., coat-check room—charging, the agents reported, that "next to DEAN ACHESON, DREW PEARSON was the most evil person in the United States."[46]

Matusow concluded his tour in Las Vegas, where Pat McCarran was working successfully to defeat Thomas B. Mechling, a moderate Democrat, who had beaten McCarran's handpicked Senate candidate in the primary and was running against a conservative Republican incumbent. In a less than three-month period, Matusow had made about seventy-five speeches in six states.[47]

On October 27, as a fillip to Matusow's very successful election season, he was introduced from the audience in the course of McCarthy's nationally televised "Alger—I mean Adlai" speech in Chicago. The speech, with the senator waiving papers in the air, was vintage McCarthy. Stevenson had once given a character affidavit for Hiss, with whom he worked in 1945 in the formation of the United Nations, and during the election campaign, he tried to pass off his endorsement as merely lukewarm. McCarthy seized on this comment: "A man is either loyal or he's disloyal. There is no such thing—[t]here is no such thing as being a little bit disloyal or being partly a traitor." Although the pro-Eisenhower *New York Times* said afterward in an editorial that the speech "was not an official expression of the G.O.P. as such," the Republican Party's practice of using McCarthy to brand Democrats "soft" on Communism was manifest.[48]

A tired Matusow, at J. B. Matthews's invitation, welcomed the Republican landslide at a posh election-night party in Washington, D.C. Among other reasons to celebrate, McCarthy, easily reelected, would now have his own investigating subcommittee in the Republican-controlled Senate. The senator had also assisted in the defeat of a bitter Senate foe, William Benton of Connecticut, the author of a troublesome anti-McCarthy resolution.[49]

The party, attended by two hundred guests, was held at the plush Foxhall Road home of a major McCarthy contributor, Arvilla Bentley, the wealthy ex-wife of Alvin Bentley, a Republican congressman. Matusow found Mrs. Bentley, who was blond and blue-eyed and the mother of three young children, to be a gracious hostess and most attractive.[50]

The only negative consequence from Matusow's campaigning was the FBI's reaction. On election day, Louis Nichols, a top Hoover aide, dispatched a memorandum to Clyde Tolson (Hoover's deputy and closest friend) stating, "Now that the elections are over, I think we should tackle Harvey Matusow and in no uncertain terms let him know that we do not appreciate the extravagant stories he has told, which he has not been able to support with fact." When the bureau found that Matusow's charges of large-scale Communist infiltration of the *New York Times* and other publications did not appear anywhere in his FBI file, the New York office was instructed to call him in for an interview.[51]

The weeks following the election proved eventful for Matusow. On Thanksgiving Day, responding to an urgent summons from J. B. Matthews and his wife, Ruth, Matusow spirited Arvilla Bentley to Nassau, Bahamas, to avoid Senate investigators probing McCarthy's financial affairs. She had contributed $7,000 to McCarthy, which he had reportedly used to speculate in commodities, and a Senate subcommittee headed by Thomas C. Hennings Jr., Democrat of Missouri, had begun an inquiry. Arvilla also feared that, if served with a subpoena, she would be questioned about a reported $75,000 contribution during the 1950 election campaign, used by McCarthy to defeat his Senate enemies—Millard Tydings in 1950 and Benton in the election just completed. The subpoena threat, only temporary, would evaporate during the first week of January 1953, when the Republicans assumed control of the Senate.[52]

The Bahamas trip had a cloak-and-dagger character. Arvilla first traveled by train, in a locked compartment, from Washington to New York City, where Matusow met her. The two then left Pennsylvania Station via a little-used exit and drove to Idlewild (now JFK) Airport; there, they boarded a late-night flight (Arvilla using her maiden name) to Miami and from there flew to Nassau. Two days later, Matusow returned alone to New York City to respond to a subpoena from the defense in the closing days of the Smith Act trial. But the subpoena was withdrawn, and after submitting to the FBI interview concerning his election-campaign speeches, he rejoined Arvilla in the Bahamas. Before leaving, he stopped in Washington to report to McCarthy and bask in his gratitude.[53]

While traveling, Matusow sent playful picture postcards to J. B. and Ruth Matthews in New York City. "On my way—still single," he wrote from Miami on December 5; "FROM A SHORT FAT MAN," he added from Nassau the next day. Matusow spent a pleasant week with Arvilla in Nassau, during which a romance began. Arvilla's nickname was "Billie"; Matusow called her "Duchess."[54]

The couple returned to Washington in mid-December—via a chartered plane to West Palm Beach (after making and canceling airline reservations to confuse would-be pursuers) and then by train—and Arvilla waited out the last days of Democratic rule hidden in her home.[55]

* * *

For Matusow, 1952 had been a year of astonishing success. Only a year before, he was an unknown young man living in Dayton, just released from the air force, with few friends and with his first public appearance as an informer-witness still ahead. Now an established informer, indeed a public figure, he had important friends among the "countersubversive" elite—J. B. Matthews, Ted Kirkpatrick, Laurence Johnson, even Joe McCarthy himself. The powerful Pat McCarran had welcomed his assistance.

Matusow's relationship with the FBI, to be sure, had become strained—but nothing more. In his interview on December 1, about his statements during the election campaign, Matusow seemingly assuaged the bureau's concerns. As to his claim that all Protestant churches except the Mormon church had been infiltrated by Communists, the interviewing agent reported, "he stated he was misquoted." His assertion that 126 Communists worked for the *New York Times* "was merely a figure given to him" by a party member who was a member of the American Newspaper Guild. His charge that there were 76 party members at *Time* magazine was simply based on information from 5 or 6 party members who worked there. He assured the bureau, moreover, that excepting only testimony for government entities, "he does not intend to make any political speeches as in the past, but rather intends to make a living in the radio-television industry doing work that has nothing to do with Communism or his past activities in the Party."[56]

On Christmas day, Matusow attended a party at the home of George Sokolsky—who, he said, "was short and fat" and "reminded me of all my uncles." Roy Cohn was also a guest.[57]

5 Fruits of Triumph

For "countersubversives" the Republican sweep in the 1952 elections marked a sweet and long overdue victory. After two decades spent chafing under the dominance of New and Fair Dealers, whom they viewed as Communist dupes or sympathizers (or worse), their warnings had at long last been heeded by the American electorate. In late December, J. B. Matthews, George Sokolsky, Alfred Kohlberg, and their wives made a brief and enjoyable visit to Washington, D.C., the conquered land.[1]

Matthews, whose labors in the wilderness dated back to the Dies committee in the late 1930s, and whose files containing tens of thousands of names provided an invaluable resource for friends and associates, was the group's unofficial dean. Ruth Inglis Matthews, his third wife, well educated and with a similar political outlook, had become, after their marriage in 1949, a partner in his work. They lived in a spacious Manhattan penthouse apartment and gave frequent dinner parties attended by a right-wing elite. Ruth later called it "a modest salon." Author Ayn Rand and Hearst columnist Westbrook Pegler were among the most frequent guests, along with the Sokolskys, the Kohlbergs, Joe McCarthy, Roy Cohn, authors Max Eastman and Ralph de-Toledano, Hearst president Richard Berlin, and informers Louis Budenz and Harvey Matusow.[2]

Following his October 1952 appearance with J. B. at SISS's Mine-Mill union hearings, Matusow became a favorite. The Matthewses invited him to dinner on November 16, with the Sokolskys, film director Leo McCarey, and Elizabeth Bentley. He was also their Thanksgiving dinner guest, came by for cocktails on December 17, and attended a small dinner on January 11 and a larger one on February 9, along with Ayn Rand and writer-editor Suzanne

LaFollette (who, two years later, would join young William F. Buckley Jr. in founding the *National Review*). On December 4, Matusow lunched at the Abbey Hotel with Ruth Matthews and Elizabeth Bentley.[3]

Matusow had become friendly with Elizabeth Bentley, who at the time drank heavily and was financially strapped. On October 3, 1952 (his twenty-sixth birthday), they shared dinner at a Greenwich Village restaurant, and Bentley poured out her troubles to him. She couldn't find work as a language teacher, he recalled her saying; she had spent the money from her book, and the government kept pressuring her to name new names. When Matusow recanted in 1955, this dinner would become a subject of controversy at SISS's hearings and give rise to an FBI investigation.[4]

* * *

On February 13, 1953, Matusow attended a black-tie testimonial dinner for J. B. Matthews at the Waldorf-Astoria. Organized by George Sokolsky, the dinner honored "Doc" Matthews (the nickname had been conferred by Martin Dies) for his past efforts in the cause and also reflected current (and well-founded) reports that he was in line for a senior staff position with Joe McCarthy's investigating subcommittee. With McCarthy as the principal dinner speaker and Sokolsky as master of ceremonies, the dinner was a "must" event for "countersubversives," three hundred of whom turned out.[5]

The "regulars" were there—Kohlberg, Rabbi Benjamin Schultz of the American Jewish League against Communism (which served the important function of shielding the "countersubversive" community against charges of anti-Semitism), Roy Cohn (whose party included Jean Kerr, the future Mrs. Joe McCarthy), Matt Cvetic, Herbert Philbrick, and Elizabeth Bentley. The right-wing writing world was well represented. In addition to Rand, Eastman, and deToledano, the names of William F. Buckley Jr. and L. Brent Bozell (the soon-to-be authors of *McCarthy and His Enemies,* a vigorous defense of McCarthy), and Victor Lasky (the coauthor with deToledano of *Seeds of Treason,* a 1950 book on the Hiss case) appeared on the guest list. Television broadcaster Lawrence Spivak also attended.[6]

Vice President Nixon sent regrets, enclosing a small check to be used toward a gift for Matthews and asking Sokolsky to "extend to Doc my commendation and appreciation for his many years of outstanding service in the anti-Communist field." Sokolsky read Nixon's message to the appreciative dinner guests.[7]

The guests responded enthusiastically to McCarthy's dinner address. They laughed at his double entendre, delivered to an audience familiar with the Right Reverend Hewlett Johnson, the so-called Red Dean of Canterbury: McCarthy referred to "the great Red Dean, Acheson."[8]

* * *

Arvilla Bentley accompanied Matusow when he dined with Ruth Matthews at the Westbury Hotel on March 2. He had been visiting her regularly in Washington since their return from the Bahamas. Compassionate and a lively companion, Arvilla, following her divorce, was starved for attention and welcomed Matusow's visits. The couple eloped and were married on March 6 at a local court in the Virgin Islands, the bride wearing a mink stole. They spent their honeymoon in the Caribbean. When Joseph Stalin died on the day of their wedding, Matusow excitedly wrote J. B. and Ruth from St. Thomas, "I wonder if the shock of our marriage killed Comrade Joe S. It was a very nice wedding present."[9]

Upon their return, Matusow moved into Arvilla's impressive Washington mansion, with its staff of servants and spacious grounds. He reveled in the thirty-plus rooms and elegant library. For once, he impressed his parents. Matusow's next-door neighbor, George Humphrey, was Eisenhower's secretary of the treasury. He and Arvilla entertained State Department diplomats and members of Congress, including, on frequent occasions, Joe McCarthy. "I was living high on the hog," Matusow recalled, "and I looked like one."[10]

Arvilla's wealth constituted only one of their differences. Young, stocky, and rumpled in appearance, aggressive and forward in manner, Matusow came from a Jewish immigrant home via a Bronx street corner. Arvilla was more than a decade older, a mother, refined in appearance and manner, and, while by no means a snob, accustomed to wealth and upper-crust society. From the outset, she loathed Matusow's career as an informer-witness and repeatedly implored him to abandon it. He had no such intention.[11]

* * *

In early February 1953, Matusow, having been recommended by Matthews, had testified for the Texas and Pacific Railway at an employee-discharge hearing, picking up an easy $500. The railroad had charged the employee, a hapless clerk named William McAnear, with attempting to buy radio time for the National Committee to Secure Justice in the Rosenberg Case, and Matusow supplied testimony purporting to link the organization to the Communist Party. The hearing didn't amount to much—the employee (who had been suspended) did not appear, and his union representative sought principally to convince Matusow of his own militant anti-Communism—and the employee was fired.[12]

In January, columnists Joseph and Stewart Alsop had suggested that the Justice Department investigate the use of professional informers, citing Matusow, Budenz, and Paul Crouch, but Matusow saw no need to respond. He ignored Alfred Kohlberg's letter offering financial assistance if Matusow were to bring a libel action—"If you are inclined to do anything may I suggest you give me a ring." Matusow accurately gauged the situation: no threat existed.[13]

Rather than investigate Matusow, the Justice Department, in April 1953, asked him to testify before a federal grand jury in El Paso, Texas, considering prosecution of Clinton Jencks for filing a false non-Communist affidavit under the Taft-Hartley Act. Matusow welcomed the opportunity to testify before a federal grand jury. It was, he later wrote, "the highest honor in witnessdom," one that put him "on a par with Paul Crouch, Louis Budenz, Matt Cvetic and the other stellar performers of the witness world."[14]

Before the grand jury, Matusow testified to statements Jencks allegedly made at the San Cristobal Valley Ranch in July and August 1950. He said that when he asked Jencks what he, as a Communist, was doing about the Korean War, Jencks answered, "we are going to try and cut down production by means of strikes." Matusow had "[n]o doubt whatsoever," he told the grand jury, that Jencks was a Communist Party member at that time—only three months after submitting his non-Communist affidavit. The grand jury indicted Jencks within hours of Matusow's appearance.[15]

In May, Matusow was a witness in the Goldie Davidoff deportation proceeding. Davidoff, a Canadian, worked for the *Daily Worker,* and Matusow testified that the newspaper only employed party members. A deportation order followed.[16]

* * *

Contemporaneously with the Justice Department's use of Matusow as a grand jury and deportation-case witness, his already difficult relationship with the FBI worsened. Following his postelection interview in December, the bureau's New York office had informed headquarters that "[i]t was forcefully impressed upon MATUSOW that he had given a false impression concerning his statements" during the election campaign, particularly the implication that his information "was available to the Bureau." In April 1953, a further report to the director's office stated that Matusow "has been considered as unstable and unreliable in the past and has made irresponsible statements for which he has been reprimanded."[17]

Much of Matusow's FBI problem stemmed from his inability to give the bureau the names of the hundreds of Communists who he charged had infiltrated the New York City press. On April 1, he did come up with thirty-three names; but almost all worked for Communist-line newspapers (including seven for the *Daily Worker,* six for the *National Guardian,* and four for the *Morning Freiheit*), not the *Times* or other mainstream publications. After that he simply stalled—he had to check his records in New York, he was going on vacation, and so on. One agent commented that he "DID NOT APPEAR TO HAVE THE SLIGHTEST IDEA WHO WAS TO BE INCLUDED ON THE LIST."[18]

In May, George Sokolsky advised Louis Nichols that Matusow and his wife were drinking heavily and quarreling. Sokolsky said he tried to phone Arvilla on May 6; but he called during a party, and "apparently there was quite a brawl." He "hung up when he found that they couldn't make sense." (The event was a giant birthday party for Arvilla.) Sokolsky expressed concern at Matusow's "gross exaggerations." Nichols told him that "we [the FBI] had washed our hands of Matusow" and "he was a free agent as far as we were concerned."[19]

The disconnect between the FBI's assessment of Matusow as "unstable," "unreliable," and "irresponsible" and the decision by Justice Department lawyers to continue using him as a government witness in criminal and deportation cases was complete. The bureau, however, which had not the slightest sympathy for defendants in "Communist" cases, saw no need to force its assessment upon the prosecutors. The prosecutors, anxious to win "Communist" cases, were interested only in the usefulness of Matusow's testimony and his effectiveness as a witness.

* * *

On May 5, 1953, Joe McCarthy invited Matusow to join the staff of his investigating subcommittee—still another feather in Matusow's informer's cap. He received the offer over lunch at a Capitol Hill restaurant with McCarthy, committee counsel Roy Cohn, and G. David Schine, a wealthy young man serving as a "consultant" to the subcommittee (who, a year later, would become a focal point of the Army-McCarthy hearings). Like Schine, Matusow was hired as a one-dollar-a-year "consultant," a consequence of having a wealthy wife. McCarthy was then at the apex of his power—in command of a well-publicized and much-feared investigating subcommittee, with a staff of investigators that included several experienced ex-FBI agents.[20]

McCarthy wasted no time in giving Matusow a major assignment. The senator was then engaged in a battle with critical elements of the New York City press. The liberal *New York Post,* in particular, had sharply criticized him in a seventeen-part series. On May 6, Matusow received instructions from McCarthy at a televised hearing, while seated in the subcommittee's witness chair: "The CHAIRMAN. I would like to have you, if you will, supply us in executive session with the names of all the Communists, those known to you as Communists, who have infiltrated the various news media [in New York City], whether it is radio, newspapers, television. I know that will be quite a monumental task, so we will not set any definite date, but you can get that for us at your convenience."[21]

"The assignment was given to Mr. Matusow," the *New York Times* reported, "a day after McCarthy's second clash with James A. Wechsler, editor of The New York Post, over the editor's membership, between 1934 and 1937, in the Young Communist League." Matusow's assignment constituted an implicit but unmistakable threat that McCarthy would pursue and embarrass news media hostile to him.[22]

* * *

Unknown to McCarthy, Matusow's assignment posed a separate problem for him, because it called for the creation of a list of names substantially the same as the one he had been stalling the FBI about for weeks—the names of Communists employed by mainstream New York City media. This fact was not easily lost upon the bureau. On May 8, the FBI's New York office wired Washington, "NYO FEELS THIS [list] SHOULD BE IN THE POSSESSION OF BUREAU BEFORE IT IS MADE A MATTER OF RECORD OR PUBLISHED BY THE COMMITTEE." In Washington, a top bureau official concluded that "[i]nasmuch as Matusow has promised to furnish the FBI a list of Communists in the newspaper field and inasmuch as Senator McCarthy has requested him to furnish such a list . . . the Bureau should maintain contact with Matusow only for the purpose of obtaining this list."[23]

But Matusow continued to stall. Contacted by the FBI on May 29, he "ADVISED HE DOES NOT CONTEMPLATE WORKING ON THE LIST AS LONG AS WIFE IS IN HOSPITAL, PROBABLY SIX WEEKS." On June 9, the Washington field office was directed immediately to reinterview him, which it did on June 15. Matusow, however, was "unable" to add to the thirty-three names he had earlier given the bureau. He "admitted," the report of the interview stated, "that he cannot compile any additional names from records in his possession and that to obtain additional names he must do considerable research work in New York City"; but he "does not anticipate a trip to New York City" before the end of July. Several days after the interview, Matusow phoned the bureau to advise that he himself would be confined in a Washington hospital for at least one month. VA hospital records show that he was admitted for observation and treatment of chronic back pain on June 17, and after a weekend pass on June 26 he simply failed to return.[24]

* * *

On May 6, the day he received his assignment from McCarthy, Matusow appeared as a witness before the senator's subcommittee in its ongoing investigation of State Department overseas libraries—in particular, the libraries' inclusion of books by alleged Communist authors.[25]

The subcommittee's investigation featured a well-publicized, whirlwind tour of the overseas libraries in Europe by Roy Cohn and G. David Schine. The young men (both twenty-six) visited libraries in twelve cities in six countries in seventeen days—forty hours in Paris, sixteen in Bonn, twenty-three in Belgrade, six in London—behaving rudely and sowing confusion. In Vienna, they visited the State Department's library and the Soviet Union's House of Culture, finding several books selected by both sides, including works by Mark Twain. "The two brash young men," an observer wrote, "left Americans abroad alternately laughing and grinding their teeth."[26]

Matusow was preceded to the subcommittee's witness stand by Louis Budenz, who again received star billing. While Budenz's testimony was predictable—the display of books of Communist authors in the overseas libraries, he said, evidenced hidden Communists at work inside the government—his treatment by the Democrats on the subcommittee was noteworthy. In 1950, at the Tydings committee hearings, the Democrats had sharply cross-examined Budenz; now they fawned over him. Stuart Symington of Missouri asked: "Because of your experience in the field—and if it is out of order, please do not answer it—but I was just wondering what you thought the result to the Soviet system would be from the death of Stalin and the rise of Malenkov?" "[T]here will be no change, whatsoever," Budenz announced, "because of the fact that communism is bigger than a man." John McClellan of Arkansas wondered whether the fact that authors publish books "derogatory to the American system and favorable to the system that prevails in Russia" was not itself "a very reliable test of whether they are really Communists or Communist sympathizers." "Most decidedly," Budenz responded.[27]

By comparison, Matusow's subsequent appearance was ordinary. He identified as Communists two authors, Herbert Aptheker and Philip Foner, who had taught at the Jefferson School, and an artist, William Gropper, cartoonist for the *Daily Worker*. Roy Cohn, who led the questioning, commented that on his (and Schine's) trip he had seen one of Aptheker's books in the information library in London. "Are these books on the open shelf?" Senator Charles Potter, a Republican, asked anxiously.[28]

Brought before the subcommittee, Aptheker, a Marxist historian sharply critical of American society, invoked the Fifth Amendment in response to questions concerning Communist affiliations. But he willingly engaged the subcommittee members in a discussion of informers—"a political term," he suggested. As to Matusow, however, he saw little room for discussion: "I think that his whole career and performance and function and appearance are dastardly."[29]

The investigation had a severe impact on the International Information Agency, the State Department unit in charge of the overseas libraries, whose top officials resigned. The State Department directed that "no material by any controversial persons, Communists, fellow travelers, etc., will be used by IIA." In the panic that followed, IIA employees removed scores of books from overseas library shelves, and some were actually burned.[30]

The latter event prompted President Eisenhower, in a commencement address at Dartmouth College on June 14, to urge the graduates, "Don't join the book-burners. . . . Don't be afraid to go in your library and read every book." But when asked about McCarthy at a press conference three days afterward, Eisenhower backed off. He never indulged in personalities, the president said, and had not intended his Dartmouth speech as an attack or reflection on anyone.[31]

* * *

Matusow continued his labors for McCarthy during July, although much of the time he was in Nevada, where Arvilla had established residence preparatory to obtaining a divorce. A host of factors had doomed their marriage: differences in age and background, Matusow's highly public and controversial career as an informer-witness, his nearly total economic dependence, his instability, and Arvilla's overriding need to maintain custody of her children against an ex-husband who strongly disapproved of Matusow.[32]

Arriving in Las Vegas on July 20, Matusow contacted a local FBI agent to advise that *he* was establishing residence there to obtain a divorce from Arvilla. He added, the agent reported, that he wanted "to be of assistance to the FBI in furnishing information regarding the Communist Party and criminal activities in Las Vegas and vicinity." A week later, Matusow told the bureau that he had taken a job with a magazine in Las Vegas.[33]

While in Las Vegas, Matusow pursued a covert task for McCarthy, attempting to insinuate himself into the good graces of Hank Greenspun, the publisher of the *Las Vegas Sun* and a political enemy of both Pat McCarran and McCarthy. In a written report, delivered to McCarthy aide Richard O'Melia, Matusow described a July 25 lunch with Greenspun (referred to only as "H.G.") and his wife at their Las Vegas home. Upon arriving, Matusow had checked out the Greenspuns' library: "The books in the library are no[t] of a political nature." During lunch he told the Greenspuns, "I don't like McCarran and McCarthy, for they are not helping in the fight against Communism," and "I only worked for McCarthy and the Committees so I could fight them, just as I had done when I was in the Communist party working for the FBI." Matusow concluded in his report that "[i]t is going to take a few weeks before I get any real information from [Greenspun], but I'll watch out, and work at it."[34]

On July 30, he volunteered to the FBI that he had been "very closely associated" with Walter Lowenfels, a writer/editor for the *Daily Worker* recently arrested and later tried in Philadelphia on Smith Act charges, and was available to testify against him—information that the bureau passed on to the Justice Department.[35]

During his stay in Nevada, Matusow attempted, ultimately in vain, to save his marriage. His actions, and Arvilla's as well, reflected intense emotion. When Matusow learned that, despite his pleas, Arvilla had obtained a divorce decree in Reno on August 25, he "hit her with a full fist across the face" in a public garage and knocked her down (his own description). Still, he managed to persuade her to join him in Santa Fe, New Mexico, where he had been offered a job at a radio station and hoped to live with her. The couple remarried in Santa Fe on September 4. Matusow had given the FBI word of the impending marriage the day before.[36]

The second marriage had a very short duration. After only two weeks, Matusow filed for a New Mexico divorce, asking in his suit, the *Albuquerque Journal* reported, "a $20,000 judgment to restore his pre-marriage standard of living." He later told SISS that he was merely seeking cancellation of a $20,000 promissory note that evidenced a loan from Arvilla during their marriage. On September 28, Arvilla obtained a second Nevada divorce. Matusow, who had signed a prenuptial agreement, departed the marriage with only their new Buick station wagon.[37]

* * *

The breakup of Matusow's marriage left him bereft. Despite his behavior, he had affection for his wife, who also provided financial support he sorely needed. He found himself largely friendless, no longer a sought-after guest in the homes of Matthews and Sokolsky. His relationship with Arvilla had been a significant factor in his acceptance by them; but even before the divorce, his lack of discipline and loose tongue had diminished his standing.[38]

On August 24, the day before Arvilla obtained her first Nevada divorce, Matusow, in a Reno hotel, addressed an emotional and remorseful letter to Joe McCarthy, taking stock of his life, even suggesting he contemplated suicide. Written only an hour after Arvilla had rejected his plea for reconciliation, Matusow's letter began: "Next month I will be twenty-eight—twenty-eight years of being a coward and being dishonest. Or should I say most of the time. I have gone through life hurting the things I love and believe in . . . being dishonest with them for I was afraid that if I were honest I would be

hurt by them—I was wrong." He agreed with a defense lawyer in the Smith
Act case who said Matusow would "do anything for a buck," disclosing that
he had sold to Drew Pearson for $250 the story of his trip with Arvilla to the
Bahamas to evade the Senate's investigation of McCarthy.[39]

Matusow had decided, he told McCarthy, to abandon his present career:
"If I go on—I don't want to go near politics ever again, and I never want to
be part of the Communist question—pro or con. It might be that you look
at this as the cowards [sic] way out . . . but if I am to go on as an honest—
honest with myself—human being I have to use saltpeter in my living. . . . I
have to tone down the temptations that made me dishonest." But this decision, he made clear, reflected no change in his political outlook: "I did one
honest thing, and that was when I went to the FBI in relation to my activities in the Communist Party, and also when I testified before the Committees in Washington." His closing comment to McCarthy: "Goodby [sic], and
God speed in your crusade . . . I know now that I am with you."[40]

McCarthy didn't bother to respond.

6 Mixed Messages

Following his divorce and the letter to McCarthy, which ended his tenure with the subcommittee, the focus of Matusow's life changed. He continued to testify, but a little less frequently, and mostly for the Justice Department, not the congressional committees. Nor did he (with one exception in early 1954) seek out witness assignments, testifying only when requested. Matusow also began a process of "apologizing" to persons he had accused—not the hundreds of individuals he had named as Communist Party members but influential people, politicians and journalists. Faced with the need to earn a living, he thought increasingly of writing a book, cashing in on his remarkable experiences of the preceding few years.

While he spent much of August 1953 in Nevada, Matusow began writing a book that same month, working at Drew Pearson's Washington, D.C., office. He later told his book publishers that he trusted Pearson and Jack Anderson, Pearson's assistant, "implicitly." "When I was working with McCarthy," he said, "I gave them a lot of stuff on Joe. They were the first ones I told when I got the idea of doing this book. I started typing it in their office." To his vast amusement, Matusow typed on stationery headed "Organizing Committee for the J. Edgar Hoover Foundation," which Pearson and Anderson kept around the office as scrap paper. In Nevada, he boasted to a coworker at the Las Vegas magazine where he was employed that he planned to go to Mexico "to write a book about his former activities as an 'FBI Undercover Agent.'"[1]

In September, Matusow contacted the *New York Post* about doing a series of articles on the "inside" workings of the McCarthy subcommittee, and James Wechsler arranged to have him flown in from New Mexico to discuss the matter. Wechsler assigned his friend William Dufty, a writer whose background was in public relations work for the United Auto Workers (UAW), whom Wechsler had hired for the *Post*, to talk to Matusow. Dufty met Matusow at his parents' apartment in the Bronx and became the audience for Matusow's description of Keystone-cops antics by McCarthy and his staff— a comic account in accord with Dufty's own view of McCarthy as less a grim ideologue than a mischievous American Legion conventioneer. While he recommended that the *Post* not publish the articles Matusow proposed, Dufty told Matusow that he had the makings of a book—one with a light and mocking tone, not a serious expose.[2]

Matusow soon returned with a book chapter, which Dufty found amusing and publishable. Dufty had connections in the book business, and since he liked Matusow, he undertook to find a publisher for the book. But to his surprise, he got nowhere; friends didn't return his phone calls. Anybody who would talk to him said that no publisher wanted to be in the position of making fun of Joe McCarthy.[3]

Matusow's series of "apologies" were related to his need to support himself while writing his book. He apologized to a sizable number of persons, as he explained to SISS in 1955:

> Mr. SOURWINE [SISS counsel]: Have you testified you called upon or called on the telephone and apologized to the following persons for wrongful attacks you had made upon them: Drew Pearson, Marquis Childs, Elmer Davis, James Wechsler [all prominent journalists], Senator [Henry] Jackson, Senator [Mike] Mansfield, Senator [James] Murray, Senator [Hubert] Humphrey, and Senator [Herbert] Lehman.
>
> Mr. MATUSOW: Senator Lehman's administrative assistant, I believe, not Senator Lehman himself.
>
> Mr. SOURWINE: And the other names are correct?
>
> Mr. MATUSOW: I spoke to Senator Murray; Senator Mansfield's administrative assistant, not Senator Mansfield. I spoke to Senator Jackson, Senator Humphrey, Drew Pearson, Marquis Childs, James Wechsler, they are accurate, either on the phone or being—
>
> Mr. SOURWINE: Why did you pick those nine persons to apologize to?
>
> Mr. MATUSOW: Those are the only ones I could recall apologizing to; the list is much longer.

Asked whether he hadn't sought money from each of the persons named, Matusow admitted requesting a loan from Pearson and offering to sell a story to Wechsler. The others, he said, he simply asked for help in finding a book publisher. "You were trying to get money?" Sourwine persisted. "I was trying to get a subsidy to write a book," Matusow responded.[4]

While the senators (all Democrats) and journalists to whom Matusow apologized were liberals or moderates, his actions reflected not so much a shift in political allegiance as an attempt to find favor—somewhere. Late in the summer of 1953, Matusow drove to Ohio to visit, unannounced, his one-time friends, the Edmistons, with whom he had had a falling out more than a year earlier. Unable to enter their property, he parked his car on a country road in front of Martha's mother's home and waited. When Martha drove up in her car, Matusow told her, according to her later affidavit, that he wanted to "right" himself with her and Ed and be forgiven for his behavior. He said, she recounted, that he was "through with being a witness" and had "made a mess in Washington." Martha brushed him off and drove away.[5]

* * *

In late September 1953, Matusow, on his own initiative, gave the *New York Times* a written affidavit repudiating his repeated allegation during the 1952 election campaign and in his October testimony before SISS in Salt Lake City that he knew of more than one hundred Communists employed by the *Times*.

The puzzling sequence of events began on Friday, September 25, with Matusow in Reno. (Arvilla received her second Nevada divorce the following Monday.) Phoning the *Times* in New York City, he said he was "bothered by his conscience" and wanted to give the *Times* a story "you will find very interesting." After he refused to elaborate over the phone, and the *Times* declined to send a representative to Reno to see him, Matusow agreed to give his story to the newspaper's West Coast correspondent, Gladwyn Hill, based in Los Angeles. The *Times* wired him $300 for expenses, and Matusow flew to Los Angeles, checking in at the Hollywood-Roosevelt Hotel. There, he dictated an affidavit to Hill and, on Saturday, signed it before a notary.[6]

Matusow's affidavit was hardly a conscience-clearing apology. After explaining that, in his SISS testimony and in numerous campaign speeches, he had charged the *Times* with having employed 120 Communist Party members, the affidavit recited: "While these statements were intended to serve a constructive purpose in the cause of anti-communism, extended reflection has convinced me that their generalized nature was such as to cause incorrect inferences and reflect unfairly on the Times, and thereby defeat their purpose." Matusow's statements, it continued, were "susceptible to the inference" that he "personally knew of 120 or more specific" Communists at the *Times*, but "[t]his is not correct." Rather, he had made only "an unverified estimate" and was "able at this time to name no more than six employees" as party members, "[a]t least one" of whom had since left the *Times*. The affidavit named no names; but Matusow, it said, was "willing to give the

Times the names of these individuals." Soon afterward, he did so, providing to Hill the names of five of the six individuals.[7]

Matusow described his financial arrangement with the *Times* at SISS's 1955 hearings. He firmly rejected any suggestion that he had provided the affidavit in exchange for $300. The *Times,* he said, had advanced him this amount because its correspondent "could not come to Reno where I was," with the understanding that he would return any unspent portion. But while Matusow's expenses were less than $200, no funds were returned, he said, because $1,100 of his money (in cash and hidden in the pages of a book) "was stolen when I arrived at the hotel" in Los Angeles. The *Times* "accepted the fact that the money was stolen, and therefore didn't press the issue." Most of the $1,100, Matusow explained, had been won "in a dice game" in Reno.[8]

While the receipt of Matusow's affidavit surely was news fit to print (an important government witness retracting a sensational and well-publicized allegation under unusual circumstances), the *Times* did not publish the story, choosing instead to take the affidavit to the FBI. Julius Ochs Adler, general manager of the *Times,* met with a Louis Nichols aide on October 2 and delivered to him a letter to Hoover, communicating the text of the affidavit and describing how the *Times* obtained it. Adler pointed out that Matusow had made his charge against the *Times* (now repudiated in the affidavit) not only in election speeches but also in sworn testimony before SISS. Hoover, never a Matusow fan, wrote in the margin of Nichols's report: "Yes. There may be perjury here." Adler also passed on to the FBI the names of the five *Times* employees that Matusow gave to Hill, asking the bureau whether the individuals were ever Communists. "See what we have," Hoover instructed his staff, "but we will give Adler *nothing*" (emphasis in original).[9]

On October 8, Alan H. Belmont, a top FBI official, wrote a memorandum comparing Matusow's affidavit and his earlier SISS testimony. Belmont concluded, "there is no question that Matusow cannot support his testimony that 'The New York Times' has well over 100 dues-paying Communists." "However," the memorandum continued, "[t]he possibility exists if Matusow is charged with perjury that this may be used as the basis for a new trial in the cases in which he has appeared as a witness." Belmont recommended that "the possibility of perjury on the part of Matusow be brought to the attention of the Department for its consideration."[10]

The next day, Hoover forwarded Matusow's affidavit to Warren Olney III, head of the Justice Department's Criminal Division. Noting that Matusow had testified for the government in the 1952 Smith Act trial and was being considered as a possible witness in a pending Subversive Activities Control

Board proceeding, the director told Olney that the affidavit "is being brought to your attention for your consideration in view of the possibility that Matusow may have committed perjury."[11]

* * *

By the time the FBI passed to the Justice Department the issue of his perjury, Matusow had left Santa Fe, where he had hoped to live with Arvilla, and was headed back to New York City and his parents' apartment. Stopping in Washington, he visited the bureau's local field office and told the interviewing agent that he had not "completed any work" since his June 15 interview "toward the compiling of the list of Communists who allegedly have infiltrated the newspaper field." "MATUSOW added," the agent's report continued, "that he does not intend to work on that list in the near future, as he will be tied up with his work with the Justice Department."[12]

The Justice Department, ignoring the FBI's warning that Matusow may have committed perjury, elected again to use him as a witness, this time in an SACB case aimed at forcing the Labor Youth League to register as a Communist front. Matusow testified at the SACB's hearing in Washington on December 9 and 10.[13]

The hearing was presided over by former Senator Harry Cain, Republican of Washington, for whom Matusow had campaigned in the 1952 election and who, following his election defeat, had been appointed an SACB member. Cain treated him, Matusow recalled, with a "friendly and sympathetic" attitude. On his first day, in testimony aimed at showing Communist Party domination of LYL, Matusow told of obtaining funds at party headquarters to purchase literature for LYL. The following day, he testified that in 1949 he accompanied Joe Bucholz, a Communist Party youth leader (and Matusow's friend), to party headquarters, where Bucholz received funds to buy train tickets for a group attending LYL's organizing convention in Chicago.[14]

On December 11, before leaving Washington for the Bronx, Matusow again checked in with the local FBI office, and for the first time he disclosed to the bureau his plans to write a book. The agent's report stated: "With reference to a book he anticipates writing, he stated that his book will deal exclusively with politics such as interpretation of politics with a philosophical vein. He further stated that there will be no mention of Communism as such, the FBI, or the Department of Justice. He pointed out that there would be no discussion about his past activities in the Communist Party for the FBI." Matusow "has only a tentative outline for the book at this time" and "volunteered to make a copy available to" the bureau prior to its publication.[15]

* * *

Judged only by his activities in the December 1953–January 1954 period, Matusow's bustling career as an informer-witness had hardly changed.

In the week preceding his December appearance before SACB, he had testified in Austin at the invitation of the Texas Industrial Commission in its investigation of three unions expelled from the CIO as Communist dominated. The commission's goal was now to expel them from Texas. "The hearings are being held," the Texas Department of Public Safety advised the FBI, "as a predication for court action to bar from the State of Texas any organization found to have Communist officials." The bureau instructed its San Antonio office "to discreetly follow the hearings."[16]

The five-member commission had assembled a cast of star witnesses, including, in addition to Matusow, Matt Cvetic and John Lautner. At Matusow's December 4 appearance, where he was given free rein by commission counsel, he again traced his history as an American Youth for Democracy and Communist Party member and volunteered names. Discussing once more the party's indoctrination of tots, he added new political nursery rhymes to those he had given HUAC two years earlier.[17]

As to the three unions under investigation, Matusow testified first about a strike by the Distributive, Processing, and Office Workers of America at a Hecht's department store in New York City. A Communist Party organizer employed by the union, he said, recruited AYD members to "disrupt the sales personnel who were not on strike by going in and trying on sweaters and clothing and not purchasing, breaking toys, just in general keeping them too busy to wait on legitimate customers."[18]

Matusow next testified that he "did some work" with the International Fur and Leather Workers Union, the second union under inquiry, and identified several of its officers as Communist Party members. The union "contributed heavily," he said, to "communist functions" such as "the communist lobby to defeat the McCarran Internal Security Act of 1950."[19]

The third union was the Mine, Mill, and Smelter Workers, and Matusow's testimony turned predictably to Clinton Jencks, under indictment in El Paso and soon to be tried, and their conversations at the San Cristobal Valley Ranch. "Did he [Jencks] identify himself personally to you as a member of the Communist Party?" he was asked. "He did." Another series of questions elicited that Jencks had invoked the Fifth Amendment at SISS's October hearings rather than answer Matusow's charges.[20]

While in Texas, Matusow, lacking steady employment, discussed with a representative of the Texas Department of Public Safety doing undercover work for the department, even trying to rejoin the Communist Party—discussions that were fruitless.[21]

* * *

In January 1954, Clinton Jencks went on trial in El Paso, charged with filing a false non-Communist affidavit. Before leaving for El Paso, Matusow recalled, he spent "many days" with Justice Department prosecutors in Washington "going over" his testimony, and in El Paso he "rehearsed some more." While there, he bragged later, he would sneak across the border at night and work as a stand-up comic in a Juarez night club. "El Paso was very profitable for me," he wrote, "I was paid $9 a day, normal witness per diem, plus $25 a day expert witness fee, plus my income as a comic in Juarez."[22]

The prosecution had witnesses other than Matusow to testify that Jencks had been a Communist Party member in the period prior to April 1950, when he filed his non-Communist affidavit with the National Labor Relations Board. Only Matusow, however, provided testimony that Jencks was a party member subsequently, in July and August 1950 at the San Cristobal Ranch, negating any possible claim that Jencks had resigned from the party before he signed the affidavit.[23]

Matusow did not testify that Jencks specifically admitted party membership to him—as he had told SISS, HUAC, and the Texas commission and had once informed the FBI (in his October 1951 report, contradicted in his signed statement two months later). When the prosecutor, Holvey Williams, an assistant U.S. attorney in El Paso, asked, "did Mr. Jencks, in those conversations identify himself as a Communist Party member?" defense counsel objected, and Williams withdrew the question.[24]

Instead, Matusow described several conversations with Jencks about party activities, where the context indicated that both were party members. Matusow stated, for example, that after telling Jencks of his intention to move to New Mexico or California, Jencks commented, "we can use more active Communists out here." Matusow testified that after describing to Jencks his party unit's weekly "do-days" (no meetings, all work), Jencks said he would "bring that idea back to some of his fellow Party members in Silver City." When the conversation turned to the "Communist-sponsored Stockholm Peace Appeal," Matusow testified, Jencks described his discussions with "Communist union organizers" in the Mexican miners union aimed at achieving common contract-expiration dates, "so that they would be able to end all mining and smelting . . . in an attempt to cut off production or slow it down for the Korean War effort." And when Matusow stated he had joined ANMA (a militant, left-wing Mexican American organization), Jencks replied, according to Matusow, that "this was proper Communist Party concentration work."[25]

Defense counsel John McTernan, a West Coast union lawyer whom Matusow had run into in earlier proceedings, cross-examined him at length. McTernan questioned Matusow closely as to whether he had included in his reports to the FBI each of the conversations with Jencks to which he testified on direct examination. Matusow repeatedly gave an evasive answer—"I don't recall if that was a written report or an oral report." But the defense's motion seeking production of the text of the reports was denied by the trial judge. Adhering to the Catch-22 procedure then in effect, the judge, Robert E. Thomason, ruled that the defense could obtain the reports only by showing first that they would contradict Matusow's testimony.[26]

The trial was one-sided. Jencks did not testify, and the defense called no witnesses. Its affirmative case consisted essentially of introducing Jencks's military record—he won the Distinguished Flying Cross for service in the Pacific during World War II. A jury verdict for the prosecution swiftly followed (the jury deliberated less than half an hour), with Jencks receiving a five-year prison sentence.[27]

* * *

After the Jencks trial, Matusow resumed his schizophrenic behavior of the preceding months. In early March 1954, he wired HUAC: "[I] have further detailed important documentation between Communist Party and Nationalist Party Puerto Rico. Please contact." He directed the same communication to Francis Carr, a top McCarthy staffer. His action had been triggered, Matusow later testified, by the attempted assassination of members of Congress by Puerto Rican nationalists. But his communications, he conceded, were an "offer to testify" before the committees. Neither committee was interested.[28]

Only three weeks later, Matusow gave *Time* two affidavits repudiating his allegation, made in October 1952 during SISS testimony and in election speeches, that the magazine employed 76 Communist Party members. The first affidavit stated that he did not know the names of any present or former party member "who is now or ever was" employed by Time, Inc. "Any prior statements" to the contrary, he said, "were based on conjecture and surmise on my part for my own personal motivations, and have no basis in law or in fact." In a "supplemental" affidavit dated the same day, he added that his reasons for making the accusation were first to show "the American public the serious threat of Communism and secondly to further my own political ambitions in becoming one of the fair-haired boys of the extremes in the anti-Communist movement." He had been "encouraged," he said, by Senator McCarthy.[29]

Two months after the *Time* affidavits, Matusow sent a lengthy and bizarre letter to the Soviet ambassador in Washington, seeking a visa to visit the U.S.S.R. Matusow informed the ambassador that he was an American-born veteran of World War II and the Korean War, adding, "I state all this sir, for you see, I am also a Russian. Both my Mother and Father were born in your country." Acknowledging that he was once a CPUSA member, who "sniffed the confused air of Marxism-Leninism" but found that "it soon became a stagnant stillness that lacked honest humor," Matusow finally got to the point, his "challange" [*sic*] to the Soviets: "My challange says—Grant me, Harvey Marshall Matusow, a visa—A visa to travel in the Soviet Union. I would like to visit the birthplace of both my Mother and my Father."[30]

Matusow next wrote to Secretary of State Dulles, applying for a passport and enclosing a copy of his letter to the Soviets. He advised the secretary, "[w]ith all the depth that my love for the United States can muster, I mean every word I say in my letter to the Soviet Ambassador."[31]

When he stopped at the FBI's Washington field office ten days later, Matusow also told the bureau about his letter. While he said he was not optimistic he would receive a visa, he would, if he did receive it, "tour all of Russia; return to the United States and write and lecture on his experiences." He intended to contribute the "funds derived from this lecture tour" to a scholarship for Russian schoolchildren to come to the United States "'to experience an education in a democracy.'"[32]

* * *

Throughout the spring of 1954, an entire nation camped in front of television sets tuned to the Army-McCarthy hearings, which began on April 22 and continued until June 17. The precise goal of the disorderly hearings, held before McCarthy's own subcommittee (with Karl Mundt of South Dakota, the second-ranking Republican, as temporary chairman), eluded many viewers. For the most part, the hearings seemed to be about the army's induction of G. David Schine, its refusal to grant him a commission for which he didn't qualify, and its unwillingness, despite pressure from McCarthy and Roy Cohn, to assign Schine to the subcommittee to continue his work as a "consultant." McCarthy, in turn, charged the army with failing to root out Communists in its ranks. But the television audience had the opportunity to observe the senator in action, day after day, over an extended period.[33]

The climax came with McCarthy's attack on a young colleague of Joseph N. Welch, the army's attorney, a partner in an old-line Boston firm. When McCarthy gratuitously charged that the young lawyer had been "a member of an organization [the National Lawyers Guild]" that had been named as "'the legal bulwark of the Communist Party,'" Welch gave his famously devastating response: "Little did I dream you could be so reckless and cruel as to do an injury to that lad. . . . Have you no sense of decency, sir, at long last? Have you left no sense of decency?"[34]

The hearings altered the public's opinion of McCarthy. During a six-month period in 1954 that encompassed the Army-McCarthy hearings, Gallup polls showed an increase in the senator's "unfavorable" rating from 29 percent to 45 percent and a decline in his "favorable" rating from 50 percent to 34 percent.[35]

* * *

Matusow devoted much of the spring of 1954 to trying to find a publisher for his book and, more important, funds to support himself while he wrote it. He contacted, unsuccessfully, Doubleday, Simon & Schuster, Harper Brothers, and Parker Publishers. He was essentially broke.[36]

When *The Nation* devoted most of its April 10 issue to a lengthy Frank Donner article on political informers, Matusow made a beeline for the magazine's offices. He knew of Carey McWilliams, *The Nation*'s editorial director, because he had accused him in 1952 election speeches of membership in dozens of Communist-front organizations. Matusow told McWilliams that "[i]nformers, like I have been, are a lot more bastardly than this article has them set out to be," and he "was trying to undo some of the harm I had done in unjustly attacking people" by writing a book. "I saw Mr. McWilliams a dozen times during that period," Matusow later testified, "in relation to getting somebody to publish the book."[37]

He also contacted R. Lawrence Siegel, a New York attorney who was general counsel to *The Nation*, and, commencing in April, held a series of meetings with him about funding for the book. One of the meetings included a visit to the New York apartment of actress Gloria Swanson, a Siegel client deemed a potential investor. The discussions, however, which extended over six months, were not successful—and later would prove disastrous for Siegel.[38]

When Matusow advised McWilliams he "probably could help" in the case of Edward Lamb, then in the midst of his prolonged battle to retain FCC broadcast licenses in the face of charges of Communist affiliations, McWilliams referred him to Lamb's law firm. On April 30, Matusow met in Washington with Russell Morton Brown, a partner in the law firm. Matusow said he had "definite specific documentary information" concerning Lamb, Brown wrote in a memorandum of the meeting, and brought "voluminous files" with him from New York. But upon examination, Brown found that "Edward Lamb's name was nowhere listed." Matusow, moreover, told Brown (perhaps intending to be humorous) that "I am not to be trusted under any circumstances. . . . If I give you some information which is helpful, you check it 100% because I don't even trust myself."[39]

Matusow showed Brown a rough outline for his proposed book and requested a $1,500 loan to enable him to complete it—Brown refused. Matusow then asked for $200 to help him obtain an apartment in New York and again was refused. Brown did end up paying Matusow's fare from New York and his expenses in Washington, including a three-day hotel bill. Brown formed the "distinct impression" that Matusow had arranged the meeting with him "solely for the purpose of getting his expenses paid for a trip to Washington where he could visit with his old friends."[40]

* * *

On April 27, three days before his meeting with Brown, Matusow sought out G. Bromley Oxnam, the Methodist bishop of Washington, who was participating in a radio broadcast, the "Tex and Jinx" talk show, at a New York City hotel. Not only had Matusow named Oxnam in his 1952 election speeches but also the Bishop had been a HUAC target, having been grilled at a marathon session in July 1953. Oxnam wrote a book about his HUAC experience and was promoting it on the "Tex and Jinx" show.[41]

Matusow approached Oxnam, identified himself as having worked for McCarthy and HUAC, and asked to meet with him after the broadcast. When Oxnam inquired, "why do you want to see me?" Matusow replied, according to Oxnam's memorandum of the incident, "that he had had a religious experience of considerable significance and was a completely changed man. He said, 'I have lied again and again in my statements to these committees and in my reports, and I want to go to each individual about whom I have falsified to ask his forgiveness.'" After the broadcast, Matusow told the bishop that he planned to write a book titled "World of McCarthy." Asked why he had lied, Matusow said that "one fabrication led to another and there was a thrill in being involved in such revelations." He added, Oxnam wrote, "that his relationship to God was the occasion for seeking me out."[42]

Matusow obtained a second and longer (almost an hour and a half) meeting on May 31 at Oxnam's Washington office. There, as recorded in the bishop's diary, Matusow gave a performance. He acted out "skits" with pipe cleaners—one of them, a story about a "very lonely little poodle dog," which he told while "his nimble fingers" twisted a pipe cleaner into the shape of a poodle, Oxnam found "screamingly funny." Matusow confided his plans to publish a volume of his poetry (in addition to the McCarthy book) and gave the bishop some of his poems to read, including (Matusow recalled) one about the atom bomb, "For Whom the Boom Dooms." The first poem shown him, Oxnam wrote, "was a striking creation of mood and, I think, of considerable value." The bishop noted in his diary, "He may be a genius; he may be a charlatan. . . . He may be a poet of unusual ability; he may be a panhandler." His conclusion: "I really can't fathom the fellow."[43]

Oxnam's credulity did have limits. Matusow, he wrote, "talks about Christian charity and all, but down underneath I think he is more interested now in getting his poems published than in anything else. He is writing a book which he thinks he needs $1,500 for." "His primary interest, I think," Oxnam said, "was finding $1,500 for his book of poems." Still, the bishop "didn't want to send the man away hungry. I asked if he had had dinner. . . . I gave him $5 and told him I thought that might help to get supper somewhere." Matusow took the $5.[44]

* * *

The next day, June 1, Matusow appeared at the FBI's Washington field office and mentioned again he was writing a book, now tentatively titled "McCarthy's World—As I Have Lived It." He explained, the interviewing agent reported, that "there was very little in the book concerning MCCARTHY and McCarthyism as such but that the name of MCCARTHY in the title might assure sensational sales." The book would be "highly critical" of profit-making entities such as *Counterattack*, the report continued, because "[h]e does not feel that a person can be serious about combating Communism if his livelihood depends upon his revelations." Matusow assured the bureau that "the book will not reveal his past activities with the FBI" but instead "will follow a philosophical vein." He also advised, the agent added, that he is performing a comedy monologue, "two shows nightly," under the name "Harvey Marshall," at a Washington nightclub.[45]

Matusow's night-club act included a spoof of the Army-McCarthy hearings, featuring his Joe McCarthy imitation. But after a local newspaper called attention to Matusow's identity, the nightclub owner, fearful of McCarthy, let him go. In New York City, Matusow picked up a couple of short-lived nightclub jobs; he had also worked as a children's entertainer, calling himself "The Traveler." "I was a clown on the nightclub floor in the evening," he wrote later, "and a government witness during the day."[46]

In the days following his FBI visit, Matusow testified for the Justice Department in SACB proceedings against the National Council for American-Soviet Friendship and the Veterans of the Abraham Lincoln Brigade. Later, he said he had tried unsuccessfully to dissuade the department from using him. He testified that he told Justice Department attorneys that "my testimony in the past was not right, in some cases, I didn't say I had lied; I just said I felt I was too unstable a witness and that I didn't belong in a witness chair, and would they please get someone else." But on June 3, in the NCASF proceeding, he testified and named as a Communist Party member Albert Kahn, who, only months later, would be the copublisher of his book. His testimony in the VALB case, on June 7 and 8, marked his final appearance as a government witness.[47]

* * *

On June 7, Matusow's confessions of having lied caught up with him. The *Washington Evening Star* reported that Bishop Oxnam told a Methodist conference in Westminster, Maryland, that Matusow twice sought him out "to say that he had had a religious experience and wished someone to undo 'all the lies I have told about many people.'" Hoover passed this information to Assistant Attorney General Olney, pointedly reminding Olney of Hoover's earlier letter posing the issue of Matusow's perjury at the time of his affidavit to the *New York Times.*[48]

Soon after the *Evening Star* article appeared, Matusow received a phone call from Donald Appell, advising that a HUAC subpoena awaited him and asking that he testify before the committee on July 12. When Matusow took the stand, HUAC's counsel, Frank S. Tavenner Jr., promptly inquired whether his February 1952 testimony (which named over 180 individuals) "is in error, or any statement in it which is false." For a moment, Matusow fenced with the committee. He had "told the truth," he said, but he didn't "appreciate or realize the full scope of what the testimony would mean. . . . My name was in the headlines and I did not appreciate all that was going on around me. It was happening too quick. In the past few months I have had time to reflect." Then he backed off: "There are no lies." He reviewed the various committees before which he had testified, the SACB cases, and the dates. "Sir," he stated, "I do not believe I told any untruths at any time under oath."[49]

Anticipating he would be questioned about Oxnam, Matusow volunteered that "I have told somebody I found a stronger faith and belief in God . . . and that I have had a very warm and, shall we say, friendly, honest religious experience not in relation to any specific church." When Tavenner read to him the *Evening Star* report of Oxnam's speech, Matusow responded that press reports often include "much fiction and coloring," but "I did not say and I do not say now that I ever lied under oath." Representative Gordon H. Scherer, an Ohio Republican, was not satisfied: "If the bishop was correctly reported by the newspapers, did he tell the truth?" "If he was correctly reported by the newspapers," Matusow answered, "the bishop is a dishonest man." The committee chairman thanked him for his testimony.[50]

*　*　*

Only two weeks before his HUAC appearance, Matusow had moved from New York City to Dallas. He arrived in Washington to testify, he told HUAC, after an all-night flight from Texas "having worked all day and half the night before." Seven months later, when he recanted, he would say that with a good night's sleep prior to his HUAC appearance, "I might have come out and said I lied. [But] I was too tired to fight with anyone that day."[51]

"This Could Spoil The Whole Racket, Men"

▲ "This Could Spoil The Whole Racket, Men." From *Herblock's Here and Now* (New York: Simon & Schuster, 1955). Reprinted by permission of The Herb Block Foundation.

◀

Matusow posing for the camera in anticipation of his maiden appearance in closed session before HUAC. Fall 1951. Courtesy of the Harvey Matusow Papers, University of Sussex.

▲ Matusow working with Hearst reporter Howard Rushmore (himself an ex-Communist) on *Journal-American* articles that accompanied his first public HUAC appearance on February 6, 1952. Courtesy of the Harvey Matusow Papers, University of Sussex.

▶

Matusow testifying before before HUAC, February 1952. Courtesy of the Harvey Matusow Papers, University of Sussex.

▲ Martha and John J. ("Ed") Edmiston, Matusow's mentors in the political informer trade, had themselves been HUAC witnesses. © Bettmann/CORBIS.

◀

Matusow broadcasting in Green Bay, Wisconsin, in support of Joe McCarthy's reelection, Republican primary, August 1952. Courtesy of the Harvey Matusow Papers, University of Sussex.

▲ Matusow celebrating with friends at the Thunderbird Hotel, Las Vegas, November 1, 1952. Courtesy of the Harvey Matusow Papers, University of Sussex.

▲ A Methodist minister and left-wing radical turned top staffer for the Dies committee, J. B. Matthews compiled voluminous files on left-wingers that earned him political power and commercial reward in the McCarthy era. Courtesy of the Rare Book, Manuscript, and Special Collections Library, Duke University.

▲ George Sokolsky, a Hearst syndicated columnist, played a major role in administering the motion picture industry blacklist. Courtesy of the Hoover Institution, Stanford University.

▲ Senator Pat McCarran (D-Nev.), the powerful chairman of the Judiciary Committee, led SISS's lengthy investigation intended to prove Communists in the U.S. State Department were responsible for the "loss" of China, January 1954. © Bettmann/CORBIS.

▲ Senator Joe McCarthy (R-Wis.) and Roy Cohn, chief counsel to the investigations subcommittee, having a whispered conversation during the McCarthy-Army hearings, 1954. © Getty Images.

▲ Mine-Mill union official Clinton Jencks and his wife, Virginia, on the set of *Salt of the Earth,* a film made by blacklisted Hollywood talent, in which both appeared, 1953. Courtesy of the Wisconsin Center for Film and Theater Research.

▲ Matusow with Charles Herring (right), the U.S. attorney in El Paso, and Holvey Williams (left), the prosecutor at the trial of Clinton Jencks, January 1954. Courtesy of the Harvey Matusow Papers, University of Sussex.

▲ Senator William Jenner (left, R-Ind.), SISS's chairman in 1953–54, with Attorney General Herbert Brownell and FBI Director J. Edgar Hoover (right) at subcommittee hearings attacking former President Truman's handling of the Harry Dexter White case, November 17, 1953. © Bettmann/CORBIS.

▲ Publishers Angus Cameron (left) and Albert Kahn, prime targets of SISS's investigation of Matusow's recantation, at a press conference, February 17, 1955. © Bettmann/CORBIS.

▶

Matusow's explosive book was published in March 1955 by Cameron & Kahn.

▶

Matusow in El Paso for the hearing on Clinton Jencks's motion for a new trial, March 7, 1955. Courtesy of the Harvey Matusow Papers, University of Sussex.

◀

Senator James Eastland (D-Miss.), an avowed segregationist, was SISS's chairman when it investigated Matusow's recantation. © Bettmann/CORBIS.

▲ An elderly "Job" Matusow, photographed by one of the authors, in Salt Lake City, December 1996.

7 Matusow's Odyssey

Matusow later wrote that he came to Dallas, at the end of June 1954, "on the run while attempting to hide from myself." But he also came because he had found a job there, selling souvenir programs at the Melba Theater, which exhibited "3-D" films made by the Cinerama Corporation. He obtained the position, which paid him a monthly income of $467, through a family friend who worked for the Program Vendors Union.[1]

Matusow had other Dallas jobs in mind as well. When he checked in with the FBI's local office, he said he "WAS MAKING ARRANGEMENTS TO PARTICIPATE AS [AN] ENTERTAINER IN TELEVISION SHOWS AND NIGHT CLUBS IN THIS AREA." He looked up William McDowell, an attorney with the Texas & Pacific railroad (with whom he had worked on the 1953 employee-discharge case), and asked his help in obtaining backing for a children's TV show, one with a patriotic slant. He corresponded with a right-wing Idaho publishing firm about selling its books in the Dallas area. He worked briefly as an all-night disk jockey at a radio station and in theater production at the state fair.[2]

For almost all of his three-and-one-half-month stay in Dallas, Matusow lived in a two-room suite at the White Plaza Hotel, for which he paid $5.50 per day. In his final two weeks, he moved to a furnished apartment. "In Dallas," he recalled, "I unwound, turned off, and relaxed for the first time in I couldn't remember how long." He became friendly with a young woman who worked at the Melba Theater. And he pursued a developing interest in the Mormon faith. He testified later to "[r]egular attendance at church, and not only on Sunday." In a letter to J. B. and Ruth Matthews, written about two weeks after arriving in Dallas, Matusow spoke of "this new found faith, that I now try to live."[3]

Matusow's rambling, not always coherent letter to the Matthewses voiced his desire for a more ordered, less frenetic life: "This letter is being written by one who now works—Every day (6 days a week),—I arrive at a given time, and leave at a given time—I draw a pay check, and I enjoy it. . . . Disipline [sic] is a wonderful thing for people like I use to was—as I've been, and has-been. . . . Credit for my relaxed feeling toward life, I beleive [sic] is in the fact that I have finally learned how to listen." He mentioned that he had lost eighty pounds of "lard."[4]

Matusow's interest in the Mormon faith was ignited, he said, by colum-nist Jack Anderson and Senator Arthur Watkins, a Mormon elder. "I go to church with [Anderson] regularly," he testified in 1955. Matusow did not regard himself a "convert," because he had not abandoned the Jewish reli-gion, only "expanded" on it. The Mormon faith attracted him, he said, be-cause it was the only Christian denomination that never practiced anti-Semit-ism. While in Dallas, Matusow testified, he discussed with "leaders of the Dallas Stake" having lied in his testimony. On October 1, 1954, he was bap-tized in the Mormon faith.[5]

* * *

The Mine-Mill union had followed closely the press reports of Bishop Ox-nam's statement that Matusow admitted lying repeatedly. On August 4, Rod Holmgren, a union employee at its Denver headquarters, wrote to Oxnam asking for details: "It happens that the same Matusow has, on two occasions, testified against our Union—a subject on which he knows nothing. We are convinced that on both occasions he perjured himself. . . . Would it be pos-sible for you to send us the full text of whatever you said or wrote in which Mr. Matusow was quoted?" Within a few days, the FBI obtained the text of Holmgren's letter, either from an informant or via a surreptitious break-in. The bureau passed it on to the chief of the Justice Department's new Inter-nal Security Division, William F. Tompkins, reminding him that Matusow had been a government witness in the Jencks trial.[6]

Jencks's lawyers, including Nathan Witt, a New York lawyer who represent-ed both Jencks and the Mine-Mill union, scrutinized the statements by Ox-nam and by Edward Lamb's attorney, Russell Morton Brown, from the stand-point of whether Jencks might be able to obtain a new trial based on newly discovered evidence. The Harvard-educated Witt, a National Labor Relations Board official during the New Deal, was a veteran advocate for left-wing unions and Communist causes—he had been named by Whittaker Cham-bers as a member of the Ware group of Communists in federal agencies in the 1930s. Witt drafted a motion for new trial for Jencks, based on the Oxnam-Brown revelations, and circulated the draft to his co-counsel in the case, John McTernan, an old friend with whom he had worked at the NLRB, and El Paso attorney Edmund B. Elfers. "McTernan particularly felt that a motion based that way would be insufficient," Witt later testified, "and therefore I sat on it hoping for something to happen, hoping—perhaps hoping that Matusow would suddenly turn up on my door step or somebody would deliver him to me or something."[7]

Although Witt "was convinced from the beginning of the Jencks trial that Matusow hadn't told the truth about my client," the lawyers could not consider contacting him about the case for fear of being charged with tampering with a government witness. McTernan, when he met with Witt in New York City in mid-September, came up with a different approach, one that took account of the reports they had received of Matusow's efforts to find a book publisher. As Witt explained it: "[McTernan] said to me, he was in my office . . . 'Why don't we see if we can't get a publisher to help [Matusow]? He is trying to write a book, obviously he is trying to tell the truth.' And the idea never struck me before. I said, we'd think about it and see what we can do." In late September, at a meeting with top Mine-Mill union officials in Butte, Witt received authorization "to do all in my power to keep tracking this down" and "to make expenditures on behalf of the union up to a thousand dollars, in connection with this Matusow matter, with reference to the Jencks case"—that is, a thousand dollars to pursue McTernan's idea.[8]

About two weeks after his return from Butte, Witt met with Jencks, free on an appeal bond and in New York City to raise funds to cover his legal costs. At Witt's suggestion, Jencks and his wife discussed the Matusow situation with Albert Kahn, whom they had met at the San Cristobal Valley Ranch. Kahn's background as an investigative writer and, more recently, a publisher made him a logical choice. Their discussion with Kahn at his suburban home led to a meeting the next day at Witt's office, attended by Witt, the Jenckses, and Kahn.[9]

Then in his forties, a Dartmouth graduate, and an author specializing in political exposés, Albert Kahn, like Witt, had a political history. Elizabeth Bentley had named him in her lengthy November 1945 statement to the FBI, immediately after her defection. Bentley told the bureau that Jacob Golos, her spy handler-lover, introduced her to Kahn in 1942 and that she knew him briefly as a "dues paying Communist Party member" who supplied Golos with information concerning the Ukrainian Nationalist Movement and "miscellaneous information taken by him from the files of the Anti-Defamation League." Kahn, she said, "acted very mysteriously on the occasions I met him."[10]

In 1952, his writing career on hold in the prevailing political climate, Kahn joined with Angus Cameron, formerly editor-in-chief of Little, Brown & Company, in a small book-publishing venture. Cameron had been forced to resign his job in 1951; *Counterattack* had denounced him, and in August of that year, Louis Budenz named him before SISS as a Communist Party member. Cameron & Kahn sought to provide, Cameron wrote, "a publishing outlet for blacklisted writers and progressive books." Richard Rovere described it in 1955 as "a house that up to now has specialized in Communist literature."[11]

Kahn told Witt, when they met at Witt's office, that "his publishing firm was breaking up, that they were in a bad way for money." He said, Witt testified, that "if he was to engage in this [Matusow book] project he would like to know that they could get some money from us [the Mine-Mill union] for an advance on the order of the book." Witt replied that the union "was prepared to buy a thousand dollars worth of books." For that sum, Kahn told him, the union would get two thousand paperbound books. Witt agreed to advance $250 to Kahn "to start with, win, lose, or draw"; but, he testified, he did not pay any more of the $1,000 until after Kahn had obtained a signed book contract from Matusow.[12]

Witt emphasized to Kahn that, to avoid any tampering or bribery charge by the Justice Department, Matusow should not be informed of the Mine-Mill union's order "until after we had secured our affidavit [from Matusow repudiating his testimony at the Jencks trial] if we did." As Witt's comment suggested, Matusow's book meant little to the union if his disclosures failed to support a motion for a new trial for Jencks.[13]

* * *

Matusow did not testify again as a government witness after his June 1954 appearances before the SACB. He has variously described the moments in time and the circumstances in which he made the decision to relinquish his hard-earned role as an informer-witness.

In his book, he told of entertaining small children on the flight back to Dallas after his July HUAC testimony. The children impressed him, he wrote, with "[t]he simplicity of their attitude, their inquisitiveness about things, places and people," and "[i]t was then that I knew that I would no longer testify." In courtroom testimony, he said that his decision was made while he "performed puppet and magic shows" in a children's polio ward in Dallas. Years later, he told interviewers that he decided to recant after reading an inscription on the wall of the Jewish Theological Seminary in New York City (which he remembered as "Do justice, love mercy, and walk humbly with thy

God"), a decision that led to the affidavits he gave the *New York Times* and *Time* magazine. The inscription, Matusow said, "became a mantra for me. That became my breakthrough."[14]

In the first week of October 1954, Matusow sealed his decision in a letter to Attorney General Herbert Brownell, which, although apparently never received by the Justice Department, he took care to communicate to the *Dallas Times Herald*. His letter protested the court-martial sentence of life imprisonment given Corporal Claude Batchelor, a Korean War POW who, upon his return, had been charged with cooperating with his captors. Batchelor's sentence, Matusow believed, was unduly harsh. In a phone call to the *Times Herald*, he told "[t]he man at the copy desk" that he would not appear at any of the six hearings at which he was scheduled to testify, because "my conscience will not let me be a party to any future Claude Batchelor cases."[15]

Of course, given his damaging admissions to Oxnam, now public information, it is doubtful that the Justice Department, in early October, intended to make continued use of Matusow as a witness. And any doubt evaporated with the appearances of Oxnam and Russell Morton Brown at SACB hearings later that month, as witnesses called by the Veterans of the Abraham Lincoln Brigade and the National Council for American-Soviet Friendship to testify to Matusow's admissions.

Oxnam appeared in the VALB case on October 18 and used the occasion to condemn the Justice Department for relying on "the testimony of a person like Harvey Matusow in any legal proceeding." The next day, the bishop wrote to Attorney General Brownell, describing his interviews with Matusow and concluding that while "we must rely upon the testimony of some former conspirators . . . we need to be sure that we are not using men who have no regard for the truth."[16]

On October 25, Troy Conner, the Justice Department attorney handling the NCASF case, informed the FBI that Brown, a former Justice Department lawyer, would testify later in the week and that "the purpose of Brown's testimony will be to discredit Harvey Matusow, a former Bureau informant who was utilized as a Government witness" against NCASF. Conner expected Brown to testify that Matusow, at their April meeting, made statements to the effect that "he was an unreliable individual and a person who could not be trusted." "Conner advised," the FBI's report added, "that he would make every effort to block the testimony of Brown before the Board."[17]

* * *

By then, Matusow had left Dallas and embarked on an unusual journey, by foot, bicycle, and hitchhiker's thumb, headed, he said, for Utah. He gave differing rationales for his trip. In February 1955, he testified that he planned to work in radio or television with friends in Salt Lake City. The following month, he testified that he intended to meet a friend, Richard Cardell, and two men employed at the Melba Theater, with the "plan" that one of the group would work in Salt Lake City to support a uranium-prospecting effort by the others. Years later, he told a radio interviewer that he left Dallas to find a Mormon bride in Utah.[18]

But Matusow has also indicated that he left because he feared physical violence stemming from the government's knowledge of his admissions to Oxnam and his intention to write a book. He decided on the flight back to Dallas following his July HUAC testimony, he wrote later, "that I would have to be out of Dallas by the beginning of October—no later, and that would be cutting it extremely close." His friend William Dufty, experienced in the violent labor-management wars in the automobile industry, had warned him that if his book confessed to perjury as a government witness, his life would be at risk. Matusow believed it, and he stated repeatedly afterward that Hoover and the FBI tried to track him down after he left Dallas and wanted to take his life. His departure took place within hours after he received a lengthy wire from the Justice Department. He also had just learned that Angus Cameron, whom the government surely regarded as a Communist, was trying to contact him, having left word with Matusow's mother.[19]

Fear of government-instigated violence may likewise explain Matusow's decision to depart Dallas on foot, avoiding airports and railroad or bus stations. He later said he had trained for the journey throughout the summer, taking early morning hikes under a heavy load. On the other hand, his mode of travel may have been attributable to a lack of funds; he was apparently broke, owing the Melba Theater sixty-two dollars and his landlord a week's rent when he left without notice. He departed on a Saturday evening, October 16.[20]

* * *

During Matusow's Dallas stay, in Washington the once-omnipotent Joe McCarthy faced censure charges at the hands of the Republican-controlled Senate, and both Republicans and Democrats positioned themselves for the 1954 election campaign.

The censure resolution, introduced in July by Ralph Flanders, a Vermont Republican, was referred to a six-member bipartisan committee chaired by the upright Arthur Watkins. The committee's report, issued on September 27, found against McCarthy on two of the counts. The Senate Republicans did not condemn McCarthy for making false or reckless accusations of treason and Communist ties but rather, as David Oshinsky put it, "for transgressing the rules and the spirit of the club to which he belonged." Support for the resolution did not pose undue political risk, for McCarthy had become vulnerable by virtue of the shift in public opinion against him following the Army-McCarthy hearings.[21]

The Republicans' 1954 election campaign likewise distanced itself from McCarthy but not from his message. The GOP adopted a strategy, in Richard Nixon's words, of "ignoring McCarthy, emphasizing vigorously the Administration's anti-Communist record, and attacking the other side for its past and present softness on the issue."[22]

Senate Democrats, led by Hubert Humphrey, responded to the "soft on Communism" charge by introducing on the Senate floor, on August 12, the Communist Control Act of 1954, a mischievous piece of legislation to outlaw the Communist Party and, as enacted, to strip it of its "rights, privileges, and immunities" under federal and state law. In an election year, not a single senator voted against the bill when it emerged from a House-Senate conference less than two weeks later.[23]

* * *

Matusow's journey from Dallas, which began on October 16, never reached Utah, ending instead, as did his 1950 trip, in Taos, New Mexico. He had in mind stopping off in Taos, he later testified, the "main reason" being "to visit the Mormon Church" but also "to visit old friends." The details of his trip became the subject of intense scrutiny in two federal courts and before SISS.[24]

Matusow left Dallas on foot, he testified, walking, at times hitchhiking, and carrying "a knapsack and a musette bag full of puppets, canteen, trench knife, boots, some extra clothes, a recorder, that is, like a flute, a musical instrument, two harmonicas and a jew's-harp," along with a Hermes typewriter. His load, mounted on an aluminum frame, weighed one hundred pounds. The puppets, he said years later, represented Old Testament characters, and he used them to entertain children in hospitals on his route and also at a revival meeting and a ranch, in return for overnight shelter, food, and a shower. He had a partial beard, often wore a beret, and carried perhaps fifty dollars with him.[25]

According to Matusow's testimony, after mostly walking his first night, he acquired a secondhand bicycle in the morning, at a store about thirty miles outside of Dallas, near Denton. He traveled the following night "on the back of an oil rig truck taking some pipe up to Wichita Falls." There, he earned a meal washing dishes at a truck stop and then caught another ride that "took me down north of Lubbock." Outside of Lubbock, two Border Patrol officers stopped him along the highway, thinking he "looked a little weird" with his beret and beard, but they left after he showed identification. He spent most of that day picking cotton on a farm between Lubbock and Amarillo, after which, hitching a ride with "an Air Force man," who tied Matusow's bicycle to the trunk of the car, he reached Amarillo, late Tuesday afternoon, October 19.[26] Matusow had an eventful, if brief, stay in Amarillo. He testified that his bicycle broke down; he left it with some kids; and he purchased another bicycle for three dollars. He attended a Mormon chapel, met a local couple there, and spent the night at their home.[27]

In addition—of this there is independent evidence—local police officers checking on a prostitute stopped, frisked, questioned, and nearly arrested him in the lobby of a sleazy, dollar-a-night hotel. Matusow testified that he checked into the hotel to bathe, to take a nap "for maybe an hour," and to leave his baggage while he shopped for a bicycle. He talked his way out of an arrest by telling the police officers that he was an undercover operative for the FBI and had sent a top Communist to jail in San Antonio, displaying as proof a copy of his 1952 article and photograph in *American Legion Magazine*. A report of the incident quickly found its way to the FBI.[28]

Leaving Amarillo by bicycle and also hitchhiking, Matusow headed north and west, through Dumas and Dalhart, toward New Mexico. Near Dalhart, he testified, he "worked on the combine harvesting maize." He reached Raton, New Mexico, on a produce truck. At Eagle Nest, east of Taos, his second bicycle broke down; but a farmer with an old truck gave him a lift to Taos, loading the bicycle on the back of the truck. He arrived late in the day on Thursday, October 21.[29]

When he reached Taos, Matusow traded his bicycle for lodging at the Taos Inn, where he had worked in 1950 and knew the owner, and borrowed ten dollars from his friend Doughbelly Price. On Friday morning, he phoned Angus Cameron in New York City (responding to the call he had learned about before leaving Dallas) but failed to reach him. A short time later, he received a return call from Albert Kahn.[30]

Their conversation was brief and to the point. Kahn expressed interest in seeing Matusow's manuscript; Matusow said he was headed for Salt Lake City and had left the manuscript in New York. When Kahn asked him to come to New York, Matusow replied that he would come if Kahn had a serious interest in publishing his book but that he needed a round-trip airline ticket in the event "it doesn't work out." Matusow in testimony first said that Kahn would agree to send only a one-way ticket; later, he testified that Kahn acquiesced to his request. Kahn, in fact, purchased a one-way TWA ticket to be picked up in Albuquerque.[31]

During his stay in Taos, Matusow visited the office of Ruth Fish, the local Associated Press representative, and had an extended phone conversation with the AP correspondent in Albuquerque, who wanted his reaction to Bishop Oxnam's testimony before the SACB. Matusow recalled he became angry during the conversation, and "in a fit of temper I believe I might have said I never lied under oath." Oxnam gave the press "half-truths," Matusow told the AP.[32]

Afterward, he boasted to Fish that Cameron & Kahn, a New York publisher, intended to publish his book and wanted him to come to New York for discussions. Fish passed this information to another local resident, Craig Vincent, proprietor of the San Cristobal Valley Ranch, who was dumbstruck. He couldn't believe it, Vincent said, because Kahn had spent considerable time at the ranch.[33]

On Saturday night, Matusow took a bus from Taos to Albuquerque, where he boarded an early Sunday morning flight to New York City, carrying with him one hundred pounds of baggage. Before boarding, he shaved off his growth of beard. The TWA ticket agent, David Atchison, later told the FBI that, in the course of a rambling conversation, Matusow had commented that "some people" were sending him to New York to write a book, and "[i]f they are crazy enough to pay me, I will write anything." Matusow denied making the statement.[34]

* * *

Years later Matusow remained convinced that the FBI was on his heels during his Dallas-to-Taos journey. He told an interviewer, "I believe the FBI wanted to kill me. Hoover wanted me dead. They would've killed me if they'd found me walking down the road. . . . You ask me what proof I have; I don't have proof." He wasn't found, he told a second interviewer, because the FBI never figured that he would be walking across the state of Texas with a knapsack full of Old Testament puppets. Albert Kahn wrote that the FBI arrived in Taos looking for Matusow twenty-four hours after his phone conversation with Kahn.[35]

Matusow's FBI file (as released by the bureau), however, gives no indication of an FBI search—and not because the bureau had no hint of trouble. On October 9, a week before Matusow left Dallas, the FBI's Los Angeles office sent a teletype message to the director and five field offices, reporting information apparently obtained (given the phonetic rendering of Matusow's name) from a wiretap or microphone at the Mine-Mill union:

QUOTE MONTEUSE [*sic*] UNQUOTE, PHONETIC, DESCRIBED AS A GOVT WITNESS IN RECENT TRIAL OF CLINTON JENKS [*sic*], HAS PHOTOS AND AFFIDAVIT WHICH WILL PROVE THAT FALSE EVIDENCE WAS PRESENTED BY THE GOVT IN ABOVE TRIAL. QUOTE MONTEUSE UNQUOTE IS WILLING TO TESTIFY HE LIED AT THE

TRIAL AND WILL INTRODUCE ABOVE MENTIONED EVIDENCE. QUOTE MONTEUSE
UNQUOTE HAS TRIED TO SELL ABOVE INFO TO VARIOUS PUBLISHERS, INCLUD-
ING THE PUBLICATION QUOTE NATION UNQUOTE. . . . INFO AVAILABLE THIS
OFFICE REFLECTS POSSIBILITY THIS WAS HARVEY MATUSOW, WHO TESTIFIED IN
THE JENKS TRIAL.

The director's memorandum, three days later, to Assistant Attorney General Tompkins, largely redacted by the bureau's Freedom of Information Act
(FOIA) censors but described in part in later FBI documents, contained even
more explosive information: "that Matusow was to receive $4,000 from the
Union" in return for an affidavit retracting his testimony.[36]

But the FBI neither interviewed Matusow before he left Dallas nor (so far
as his file shows) did it monitor his movements after he left. The report concerning his near arrest by local police in Amarillo on October 19 appears to
have reached the bureau's Dallas office the same day. But that office did not
communicate the report to headquarters until November 15, three weeks after
Matusow had flown back to New York.[37]

Rather than aggressively pursuing the potentially important lead it had
received, the FBI evidently decided to pass the matter to attorneys in the
Justice Department—choosing, in other words, to distance itself from an
impending embarrassment, not to risk compounding the problem by arranging physical injury to Matusow, as he feared.

* * *

On October 25, the day following his return to New York, Matusow met Kahn
and Cameron for lunch at the Delmonico Hotel on Park Avenue, a venue
selected by Kahn. The headwaiter in the "quiet, luxurious dining room,"
Kahn recalled, "warily eye[d]" Matusow, who was dressed in a "black tur-
tleneck sweater, jeans and cream-colored buckskin moccasins" and carrying
"a bulky briefcase."[38]

When Cameron was delayed in arriving, Matusow showed Kahn some of
his poetry. Kahn, like Bishop Oxnam, perceived merit in his poems: "To my
surprise, though somewhat trite and sentimental in content they showed an
inventive use of language and an unusual sense of imagery." Matusow also
displayed to Kahn a notebook he termed his "prospectus" as a nightclub
entertainer. But the publisher found the notebook, "bordered with hand-
drawn figures of rabbits, dogs, monkeys and other animals," to be "pathet-
ically pretentious and tawdry." Undeterred, Matusow next fashioned a collection of animals from pipe cleaners, beginning with his poodle routine that
had so amused Oxnam. He continued with a creditable Winston Churchill
imitation, "relish[ing]" Kahn's laughter.[39]

After Cameron arrived, Matusow showed the two publishers an outline for a book entitled "Blacklisting Was My Business," two sample chapters written in August 1953 and reflecting his situation at that time, and a preface, which referred to his "past of hate" and his belief "in one absolute, God and faith in all he created." These materials can only have distressed the publishers. His "one hate," Matusow had written, was a "hate for communism and all it stands for," and he had praise for the FBI, which "had accomplished a very important thing . . . Safeguarding the security of the United States." His only reference to Jencks was a negative one; Jencks, he had written, "helped reaffirm my faith in why I had gone to the F.B.I." Nothing in Matusow's outline referred to his testimony in the Jencks case. Nor did his sample chapters mention any lies he told from the witness stand.[40]

When Kahn alluded to the risk of a perjury charge if Matusow wrote the book, Matusow stated flatly, "I never committed perjury." He wanted to write the book, he said, because "I want to live with myself." Matusow estimated that the book would take two or three months to complete and asked for a $1,500 advance. The publishers replied, with misgivings, that they would draft a preliminary contract.[41]

The following day, after a pleasant, family dinner at Kahn's Croton-on-Hudson home, Matusow signed a two-page, typed letter agreement with Cameron & Kahn to publish his book. It called for a $900 advance against royalties, $250 of which he would receive immediately and the remainder in $50 weekly installments. After publication of the book, he would receive an author's royalty based on a percentage of sales. While the publishers, of course, could not provide in the agreement that the author would admit to having lied at the Jencks trial, they did state: "One of the fundamental purposes of this book—as you have put it—is to 'undo some of the harm done' to other individuals by your activity and testimony, much of which, as you have pointed out, was not a true and complete reflection of the actual facts." Matusow voiced no objection.[42]

While his agreement with Cameron & Kahn fell short of a confession of perjury, it marked the completion of a 180–degree shift in Matusow's position. Less than eighteen months earlier, he had been an enthusiastic informer-witness for the congressional committees and the Justice Department, a colleague of Joe McCarthy, and a darling of the "countersubversive" elite. Now, he not only had become unusable as a government witness and unwelcome among the "countersubversives" but also had allied himself with pro-Communist publishers in the writing of a book in which, to a greater or lesser extent, he would admit to perjury as a government witness. Several possible explanations exist for Matusow's dramatic switch.

An ideological motive can be ruled out. Pragmatic, not ideological, Matusow turned against the Communist Party when he saw his personal ambitions floundering. He actively pursued a career as an informer-witness until his prospects again diminished; only then did he decide to write a book critical of the committees and the Justice Department. He didn't choose a left-wing publisher for his book; only Cameron & Kahn would consider publishing it. A "religious experience," Matusow's initial explanation, may likewise be discounted. He later termed it "a cover for the real story"—the prevailing view among observers at the time. In the late 1970s, Matusow did become a serious and observant Mormon, but at the time of his recantation he separated himself from the Mormon church. His contemporaneous 1955 book asserted more an awakening of "conscience" than religious belief.[43]

Nor, as the government would conclude, did Matusow, made vulnerable by financial circumstances, become a pawn in a Communist plot. Able to exist on little money and possessing well-developed survival instincts, Matusow would not subject himself to a likely perjury prosecution solely to earn the modest advance and uncertain future royalties his publishers promised. The rumor of a $4,000 payment by the Mine-Mill union had no substance. The perceived "plot," moreover, consisted of little more than an effort by Jencks's lawyers (and, subsequently, lawyers for the Smith Act defendants) to do what defense lawyers, whatever their politics, might be expected to do upon learning that an essential witness against their client might repudiate his trial testimony—attempt to obtain the witness's changed testimony and to exonerate their client.

A more credible explanation for Matusow's very public recantation lies in his unbounded need to be the center of attention. "Hell for him is the condition of going unnoticed," Murray Kempton observed. Matusow himself had referred (in his sample chapters) to publicity as a "narcotic" and his need for it as an "addiction." Judge Dimock, after listening to seven days of Matusow's testimony at the new-trial hearing in the Smith Act case, concluded that his recantation "was not induced by friends of these [Smith Act] defendants, nor I must admit, by any preference that Matusow had for truth as against falsity. It was induced by Matusow's yearning for a place of importance. He had squeezed dry the orange of informing and was prepared to begin on the orange of recanting." Matusow, Dimock said, had "a passion for the limelight." To be sure, given the peril of Matusow's undertaking, considerations of conscience—doing right, making amends—must have played a role in his thinking. But his recantation was triggered primarily by the realization that he would create a *sensation*.[44]

Kempton accurately described Matusow's situation when Kahn phoned him in Taos: "The committees had used him up; the private entrepreneurs of the search for treason had cast him forth; he had not . . . a friend in the world." Another individual in his situation might have elected to write off the political scene and to look for a nine-to-five job; Matusow elected to write his book and to face the consequences.[45]

8 Writing and Recanting

Justice Department attorneys had no trouble locating Matusow upon his return to New York City: they phoned him at his parents' apartment. On the day he lunched with Kahn and Cameron, Monday, October 25, Matusow also had a phone conversation with an attorney named Daly. "My recollection of the conversation," he testified, "is that I told Mr. Daly if Bishop Oxnam told him I lied Bishop Oxnam was wrong." Daly wanted Matusow to come to Washington, and they made an appointment for Wednesday. But Matusow called back and cancelled it, because he had "done something to [his] back" during his trip and his "left leg was partially paralyzed." "I was very evasive with Mr. Daly," he acknowledged.[1]

On Friday, two Justice Department attorneys, Troy Conner, whom Matusow knew from the NCASF case, and Harold Koffsky, came to his parents' apartment to interview him. (Albert Kahn had advised Matusow not to see Justice Department attorneys without his own lawyer present, but he told Kahn, "it is none of your business who I see.") Apprehensive that Conner brought a "witness" with him, Matusow again was "evasive." "I just didn't intend to tell them much," he testified, "because I felt they were up there to gather information for use . . . against me." He did tell the two attorneys, however, that he had never lied on the witness stand.[2]

Conner, who was dissatisfied with the interview, sought assistance from the FBI, asking that the bureau "attempt to determine Matusow's current activities and associations through every available means, including a mail cover and a surveillance." But the bureau received his request coolly.[3]

In a November 10 memorandum to the director, Leland Boardman, a top aide, explained Conner's concern that Matusow might be in the hands of "leftwingers." Matusow, at his interview with Conner, "advised that he plays chess with Carey McWilliams, an editorial director of 'The Nation' and often associated with other individuals he termed 'leftwingers,' whom he did not identify." Boardman reminded the director that on October 12 "the Department was advised an informant had overheard a conversation which indicated that an individual believed to be Matusow may have suggested that, in consideration of $4,000, he could testify he had lied as a Government witness in the Jencks case. Matusow reportedly was willing to introduce photographs and an affidavit which would prove that false evidence was presented by the Government in this case."[4]

Yet Boardman recommended that the FBI decline Conner's request for surveillance. The Justice Department, he wrote, "does not indicate exactly what it intends to do with this information. If the Department is aware of what it intends to do, they should tell the Bureau specifically so that proper consideration can be given to the advisability of further investigation." "[I]nvestigation at this time," Boardman believed, "would merely verify information concerning [Matusow's] unreliability and association with certain 'leftwingers,' which information is already known."[5]

Hoover agreed. The requested surveillance, he advised Assistant Attorney General Tompkins, "would require a great deal of manpower" and "is not deemed advisable in the absence of some indication as to what action is to be taken with the information obtained concerning Matusow."[6]

* * *

About November 1, Matusow moved into a small, two-room apartment on Bleeker Street in Greenwich Village, a neighborhood in which he was very much at home. Kahn "couldn't have imagined a less suitable place." "It was a drably furnished, cold-water flat in a dilapidated section," he wrote, and "[t]o reach it you had to climb three creaking flights of stairs." If the FBI wished harm to Matusow, Kahn believed, the apartment left him isolated and vulnerable. But Matusow loved the place. "He found enchantment," Kahn marveled, "in its every dingy corner."[7]

Matusow's files, which arrived at the apartment shortly, included correspondence, scores of press clippings, transcripts of committee hearings, reports he gave the FBI, and almost anything else that had mentioned his name. He spent nearly three days taking Kahn through the material. Kahn's attention was drawn to a February 1954 letter from Charles F. Herring, the U.S. attorney who prosecuted Jencks, thanking Matusow for his "fine cooperation" and his testimony, which was "absolutely essential to a successful prosecution."[8]

On November 7, a television interview by Drew Pearson briefly interrupted the writing effort. In the interview, which dealt with his association with Mc-Carthy, Matusow described his "break" with the senator: "One day I came to realize that Senator McCarthy was using the tactics of the Communist Party and these were in direct opposite [sic] to my beliefs that the Christian—I've since joined the Church of Latter Day Saints and try to be a good, Mormon."[9] At his apartment, Matusow seemed to suffer from writer's block. He "wasn't putting anything on paper," Kahn recalled, and "[a]s the days went by, he found one reason after another for not writing." About mid-November, Kahn suggested an alternative procedure: that he himself "go through the stuff" in Matusow's files, "organize it into various categories," ask Matusow "questions about it," and tape-record and then transcribe both the questions and Matusow's answers. Matusow, sensitive to any claim that Kahn ghostwrote his book, remembered that it was he who invited Kahn as his "editor" to "sit in on sessions where I dictated and where I was a little ambiguous, or not clear, . . . ask pointed questions, which would maybe more fully develop the story which I was writing."[10]

The tape-recorded question-and-answer process continued for about four weeks. Kahn maintained duplicate tapes, which he kept in a safe deposit box; he also sent a copy of each tape and transcript to Nathan Witt. "I wanted to be sure," Kahn said, "that no matter what happened, there would be a permanent record of our conversations." While he told Matusow of these arrangements, Kahn "deliberately refrained from mentioning the advance order Cameron & Kahn had received from the Mine-Mill union." During the October–December period, Kahn received from Witt $1,250 of the union's money, a $250 increase over the amount initially authorized. Witt also gave Kahn a copy of Matusow's testimony in the Jencks trial, "so he would know what it was all about."[11]

The taped discussions had a chess-game character. "Matusow clearly wanted to avoid incurring any legal risks by his disclosures," Kahn wrote, while "I wanted to steer clear of any questions that might make him think I was trying to inveigle him into incriminating admissions." Matusow readily admitted to Kahn that he viewed testifying as a performance, consciously selected themes he thought would attract media attention, and frequently employed half-truths, distortions, and innuendo. But, Kahn said, "he stubbornly avoided admitting he had ever perjured himself."[12]

Many of Matusow's comments were doubtless unwelcome to Kahn. He and Joe McCarthy were both "natural-born actors," Matusow said; they were "two people cut from the same mold," "as much alike as peas in a pod." He described the perjury-prone informer Paul Crouch as a tragic figure who "has much love" and blacklister Ted Kirkpatrick as a man "who had a heart," "was more anxious to clear people than he was to list them," and was consumed by guilt because he "hurt innocent people and he knew it." Matusow admitted that he himself helped write the *Counterattack* articles "that got [Angus] Cameron fired or forced to resign from Little, Brown."[13]

Matusow later testified that "I did not tell Mr. Kahn or anybody the real facts because I didn't trust any of them because Bishop Oxnam and Mr. Brown had betrayed my confidence." His distrust of Kahn, however, diminished as he developed a friendship with Kahn, his wife, Riette, and their young sons and visited their home "almost every weekend."[14]

On December 14, Matusow's and Kahn's taped discussion addressed the issue of Matusow's testimony in the Jencks case:

MATUSOW: I knew Jencks was a party member and I said so. I can't say here that Jencks wasn't a party member after he signed the [Taft-Hartley] affidavits because I know that he was. But I shouldn't have testified. That's the important thing.

KAHN: Why do you say you know he was?

MATUSOW: I say I know he was—I mean in this way. Men like Ben Gold who have been indicted on the same charge. He officially resigned from the Communist Party. Jencks also officially resigned from the party. Or he could have. Let's put it that way. But in—to my mind— then, in my thinking, it made him no less a Communist because he put a piece of paper down and said "I'm no longer a Communist Party member." As far as I was concerned, Jencks was still under Communist Party discipline. And there's a difference. He legally, according to the law, might not have been a member of the party. I didn't know that difference. Jencks didn't change his thinking because he issued that scrap of paper.[15]

The tape recording ended there. But Matusow told Kahn, off the tape recorder, according to his testimony, that he would give him "the whole story, how I feel about Jencks and the other things, after I see Mr. Witt and get his assurance that my confidence won't be violated." He wanted Witt to guarantee that "he will not use any of this material until I tell him he can." Matusow explained, Kahn wrote, that he was unwilling "to take the chance of screwing up the book"—that is, the chance that his confessions would be seized upon and made public by the lawyers and the book project compromised or even abandoned. Late in the afternoon of December 14, the two men went to see Witt at his office. The attorney assured Matusow that none of the taped materials would be used without his consent. "It's a hell of a weight off my mind," Matusow told Kahn when they left, "to know nothing will break until the book's done."[16]

"[I]t was after seeing Mr. Witt," Matusow testified, "that I told the truth even to Mr. Kahn about the whole story about Jencks." Moreover, he stated, "I specifically told Mr. Witt on the day I met him and told him I was prepared to file an affidavit or write and sign an affidavit in [the Jencks] case." Kahn recalled that Matusow said, "I'm going to give an affidavit saying I lied against [Jencks]. I plan to do it in the Flynn [Smith Act] case, too, or any other case where it's necessary."[17]

Thereafter, Matusow and Kahn discontinued the practice of tape-recording their discussions. They hired a stenographer, and Matusow began rapidly to dictate the manuscript of the book. He agreed to discard his tentative title, "Blacklisting Was My Business," in favor of Kahn's choice, "False Witness." The emerging manuscript, reflecting its new title, told a story of how a young man's excessive ambition led him to become an FBI informer and a less-than-truthful government witness, until for reasons of conscience he decided to make amends.[18]

* * *

In the November 1954 elections, the Democrats regained control of both houses of Congress. A number of liberal candidates for the Senate won in the face of red-baiting campaigns against them, including Paul Douglas of Illinois and Joseph C. O'Mahoney of Wyoming, who returned to the Senate despite having served as one of Owen Lattimore's attorneys. But liberals would not control the investigating committees in the incoming Congress. HUAC's new chairman would be Francis E. Walter of Pennsylvania, best known as the author of restrictive immigration legislation. SISS, which still bore the stamp of Pat McCarran (who had died a year earlier), would be headed by James O. Eastland of Mississippi, an arch-conservative and ardent segregationist. Joe McCarthy's replacement as chairman of the investigations subcommittee of the Government Operations Committee would be John McClellan of Arkansas.[19]

The outgoing, lame-duck Congress, however, debated and voted on McCarthy's censure. Commencing on November 8, Senate Republicans engaged in a harsh and divisive debate, while Democrats, under the discipline of their leader, Lyndon B. Johnson, remained largely silent. When Democrats did speak, they withheld any criticism of excesses on McCarthy's part and at times praised his "good work" in fighting Communism. "We have condemned the individual," Herbert Lehman observed, "but we have not yet repudiated the 'ism.'"[20]

The final vote, on December 2, was a lopsided 67–22, with Democrats voting unanimously for censure and Republicans evenly divided.[21]

* * *

With Matusow dictating and a stenographer typing his words, the book manuscript, Kahn wrote, "grew at a remarkable rate." The two publishers were pleased by the product: Matusow's account of SISS's Salt Lake City hearings, Kahn found, "brought the whole scene alive." "It's got pace, all right," the skeptical Cameron commented. Kahn noted, however, that while Matusow readily described "what he had done, he revealed a good deal less on why he had done it."[22]

A timing problem arose in late December 1954, when Kahn learned from Harry Sacher, the attorney for Elizabeth Gurley Flynn, the lead defendant in the Smith Act case, that the two-year period for filing a new-trial motion based on newly discovered evidence would expire on February 3, 1955. Although Matusow's book could not possibly be published by February 3, any affidavit recanting his trial testimony in the case would have to be filed in court by that date.[23]

Kahn discussed the problem with Matusow. While Kahn earlier had "assured him there's no need to write any affidavits before the book is published," Matusow decided to supply affidavits in both the Smith Act and Jencks cases before the February 3 deadline. He commented, according to Kahn, that "I obviously can't undo the harm in this [Smith Act] case unless I give an affidavit before the deadline. It's that simple, isn't it?" Jencks wrote Matusow a letter of gratitude, "welcoming [him] back to the human race."[24]

In early January, Witt traveled to Denver with Matusow's chapter on the Mine-Mill union and Jencks "to show Mr. Jencks and the leaders of the Union." By the middle of January, a first draft of the book had been completed, and Matusow and the lawyers were at work on the affidavits repudiating his testimony in the two cases.[25]

When Matusow and Witt met on January 17, Matusow asked the attorney whether the government would be likely to prosecute him for perjury if he executed the affidavits, and Witt (according to his testimony) "analyzed all the possibilities for him." Matusow denied in courtroom testimony that he got an answer to his question before he executed his affidavit in the Jencks case. But he acknowledged that Witt told him afterward that "it would be difficult for the Government to prosecute me because of the conflicting statements, that they would not want to prosecute me." And he stated in his SISS testimony:

Mr. SOURWINE: Were you told that you could not be convicted for perjury on the basis of your recanting of your previous testimony?
Mr. MATUSOW: I believe I was told the Government would have a
difficult time in proving it.
The CHAIRMAN: . . . that the Government would have a difficult time
in securing a conviction.
Mr. MATUSOW: That is right, sir.[26]

As a consequence of Matusow's decision to provide affidavits, Cameron
& Kahn had to advance the scheduled publication date of his book—to
March 1955—so it wouldn't be "old" news when it appeared. Also, the primary locale for work on the book, both writing and readying it for publication, was moved uptown from the Greenwich Village apartment to a two-
room suite at the Chelsea Hotel on 23rd Street. After Mine-Mill union officials
"expressed concern about some injury which might be done him," Kahn
hired a bodyguard for Matusow, a former merchant seaman, amateur boxer,
and playwright named Herb Tank—whom Matusow in 1952 had named as
a Communist Party member.[27]

In mid-January, Kahn traveled to Washington and delivered a copy of
Matusow's manuscript to columnist Stewart Alsop, who, with his brother
Joseph, had questioned the credibility of several McCarthy-era informers.
Alsop told Kahn, "I think I may do a column or two on it." Kahn left a second copy of the manuscript with Abe Fortas, Owen Lattimore's lead counsel, who had phoned Kahn to request it. Fortas learned that Matusow would
say in the book that his 1952 testimony before SISS, charging that Lattimore's
books were used as the "official" Communist Party "guides" on Asia, was "a
complete falsehood."[28]

* * *

Matusow signed his affidavit in the Jencks case on January 20, and Jencks's
attorneys filed it eight days later in federal court in El Paso, as part of Jencks's
motion for a new trial. In his affidavit, Matusow repudiated his trial testimony concerning his conversations with Jencks at the San Cristobal Valley
Ranch. "It is untrue," he stated, that Jencks said, "'we can use more active
Communists out here'"; Jencks "made no such statement." His testimony
reciting Jencks's comment about working with Mexican Communists to "be
able to . . . cut off production" for the Korean War effort "was untrue." His
testimony that Jencks told him joining ANMA was "proper Communist Party
concentration work" "was untrue." "There was no basis," Matusow said in

summary, "for my stating that Clinton E. Jencks was a member of the Communist Party at the time I so stated in court."[29]

On January 31, three days in advance of the deadline, defense counsel in the Smith Act case filed Matusow's affidavit in federal district court in Manhattan, as part of a motion for a new trial by the thirteen defendants. Matusow averred that he had given false testimony against four of the defendants—Alexander Trachtenberg, George Blake Charney, Pettis Perry, and Arnold Johnson. His testimony that Trachtenberg told him that the Vishinsky book showed "'how the diametrically opposed classes could be eliminated'" was "false," he said. His testimony that Charney stated that Puerto Rico "'would get its independence'" when it had "'overthrown the bourgeoisie there'" was "entirely false." And Matusow swore he "gave false testimony" when he testified that Perry said that establishing "'a Negro nation in the black belt'" required "'the working class to . . . forcibly overthrow this bourgeoisie.'" His false testimony, Matusow added, was given with the knowledge and assistance of prosecuting attorneys. Roy Cohn, he charged, helped concoct his testimony about Trachtenberg and the Vishinsky book: "We both knew that Trachtenberg had never made the statements which I attributed to him in my testimony."[30]

Following Matusow's execution of the affidavits, the financial arrangements for his book were modified modestly in his favor—an action upon which the government would soon place great emphasis. A substitute contract for publication of the book, signed on February 1, provided for a $1,500 (rather than $900) advance, the added amount having already been paid to Matusow in $50 weekly installments, and a reduction in the number of books required to be sold before he received an increased royalty percentage. Also, he learned after signing his Jencks affidavit that the Mine-Mill union would purchase 6,700 copies of his book (a sharp increase from the 2,000 Witt and Kahn initially discussed).[31]

On the day Jencks's motion was filed, the *New York Herald Tribune* and more than a hundred other newspapers published Stewart Alsop's initial column on the subject of Matusow's recantation, the start of an avalanche of press comment. Simultaneously with Alsop's column, Charles Allen, a savvy journalist associated with *The Nation*, whose assistance Kahn and Cameron obtained, supplied a three-article "exclusive" to a prestigious small-city newspaper, the *York (Pa.) Gazette and Daily,* which in turn shaped coverage of the story by the conservative wire services.[32]

The influential Alsop termed Matusow's forthcoming book "a remarkable political confession which may cause major explosions." "Legal lying by such professional ex-Communist informers as Matusow, which has been tolerated by all three branches of the American government," he wrote, "has done irreparable harm" both to "individual American citizens" and to "the whole American political process."[33]

* * *

The FBI learned of Matusow's affidavit in the Jencks case on January 25, three days in advance of its filing. The bureau's first concern was not taking responsive action but placing the blame elsewhere. As deeply rooted as Hoover's anti-Communist sentiments were, his overriding priority remained protection of his agency's (which meant his own) reputation.[34]

Alan Belmont's January 25 memorandum, which conveyed the news of Matusow's probable recantation to the FBI's top echelon, emphasized the Justice Department's failure to heed the bureau's repeated warnings about Matusow. As early as January 1952, Belmont wrote, "[t]he Department was furnished a copy of a report setting forth a signed statement from Matusow taken in connection with the Jencks investigation [presumably his December 29, 1951, statement] which indicated that Matusow did not have information concerning Communist Party affiliations of Jencks which would make his testimony valuable in this case." Yet, Belmont continued: "On its own initiative, the Department interviewed Matusow and based on the results of that interview, decided to use him as a witness in the Jencks case. Matusow had previously testified in the second Smith Act trial in New York City and statements made by him subsequent to that trial indicated the possibility that his testimony was not entirely accurate. The Department was aware of this situation."[35]

Belmont did not minimize the consequences of a Matusow recantation. "A retraction on the part of Matusow in connection with the Jencks case," he wrote, "would have a serious effect on the Government's security program in that it would undoubtedly shake public confidence. It also might have the effect of setting the stage for new trials or rehearings of cases in which he has testified." But Belmont made clear where responsibility would lie: "The Department has been fully advised of the Matusow situation . . . [and] went ahead and used Matusow as a witness in spite of information furnished by the Bureau indicating that he did not have knowledge of some of the facts to which he testified."[36]

The same day, the director wrote to Assistant Attorney General Tompkins, briefing him on the situation and adding: "No action will be taken at this time by the FBI in connection with this matter. In the event that Matusow does publicly retract his testimony in the Jencks' case, you are requested to advise whether you desire that a perjury investigation be initiated. Should you desire to contact Matusow the last address which we have for him is 1491 Macombs Road, Bronx, New York, telephone CYpress 9-7563."[37] The bureau was not entirely passive, however. On January 28, Hoover dispatched a wire to his New York and Albuquerque offices, promptly circulated to all FBI offices, directing that files containing reports from Matusow be labelled to indicate that his information is "of unknown reliability"—a designation quickly changed to "of known unreliability." The task proved herculean.[38]

* * *

Matusow's recantation, as might be expected, generated intense and varied comment in the media. The *New York Times* in an editorial condemned "[t]he shabby business of the paid professional informer, which has reached new dimensions under governmental encouragement during the past few years," stating that Matusow's action "affords a new warning against the unquestioning acceptance by political and judicial authorities alike of the accusatory statements of the professional informer." In an article the next day, however, a *Times* commentator (perhaps with an eye to the FBI's reaction) drew a distinction between "the army of turnabout [i.e., ex-Communist] informers for profit" and "loyal Americans" recruited "on patriotic grounds" by the FBI "in its difficult task of infiltrating the Communist party," a group that "has performed commendable and reliable service."[39]

The anti-McCarthy *Milwaukee Journal* wrote that the "fervor for witch-hunting has invited irresponsible, pathological or sinister individuals like Matusow to smear, falsify, and fictionalize." *The Worker* was jubilant, hailing "the most flatfooted and sweeping exposure of frameup methods in the long history of United States antilabor frameups." But informer Herbert Philbrick warned in his column in the *Herald Tribune* of "a long planned and well coordinated Communist campaign to destroy public confidence in government witnesses for investigation and prosecution of the Red conspiracy."[40]

The television networks and newsreels rushed to interview Matusow. In a CBS interview on February 2, he said he gave false testimony because he "was looking for what I call an identity, that is to be somebody, and I wanted the newspaper headlines in addition to seeing my name in print, and . . . I didn't care what happened to Owen Lattimore or to other people who I'd testified about." Asked by an ABC reporter about the consequences of recanting, he answered, "The thing is I can live with myself and nobody can take that away from me." "Even going to jail?" the reporter persisted. "How could that hurt?"

Matusow responded. Appearing before the cameras of UP Movietone News, he told his interviewer that "I was paid to lie, and that's what I did," but "I finally decided to quit the racket, and that's what I've done."[41] The media attention put Matusow, in Kahn's words, in "a high state of excitement." Accompanied by his bodyguard, he would leave his sanctuary in the Chelsea Hotel, return with his arms full of newspapers, and then sit on the floor with a pair of scissors, clipping all of the items that dealt with his recantation. He told Kahn that previously as an informer he "wanted headlines for their own sake" but "now I've got reason to be proud of these stories."[42]

At the same time, Cameron & Kahn moved to assure that Matusow's forthcoming book would not be forgotten in the excitement, scheduling a February 3 press conference to announce its publication. Held at the Biltmore Hotel in New York City, with fifty or more journalists in attendance, including many from right-wing publications (some of whom had worked with Matusow on "Communist menace" stories), the press conference proved a disorderly event. An FBI source called it an "ANTAGONISTIC PRESS CONFERENCE," and Kahn doubted "whether there was ever another press conference quite like [it]."[43]

Matusow, introduced by Angus Cameron, read a short statement and then responded to questions. As an informer, he said, he became addicted to the "type of glamor enjoyed by the professional ex-Communist." Now, he was telling the truth to "right some of the wrongs" he had committed. A *New York Times* reporter inquired about reports he had received psychiatric treatment; Matusow answered that he "had a nervous breakdown" while in the air force in 1951, spent eight days at the base hospital, and met with a psychologist on two occasions. Another reporter asked, "How do we know you're telling the truth now?" "There's no way you can be sure," Matusow admitted, "but I've documents proving much of what I'm saying." Many of the questions implied that he was under Communist sponsorship: "Are Cameron and Kahn members of the Communist party?" "How about the slave camps in Russia?" and "Are you being blackmailed, Mr. Matusow?"[44]

Matusow in later testimony described the scene: "There were two or three questions coming at me at a time, and there were people in the room who were doing a little shouting, a few—one newspaperman, I believe, Mr. [Victor] Riesel, was shouting and another man . . . was waving his finger at me; the INS man was getting a little violent . . . he was angry because I had worked on a story with him before."[45]

When Matusow's attempts to answer questions were drowned out by loud heckling and several Mine-Mill union members in the rear of the room came to his defense, I. F. Stone, a small, middle-aged, bespectacled man, respected by all sides, restored order, angrily shouting to his colleagues, "You call yourselves newspapermen! You make me sick!"[46]

Victor Riesel discussed the press conference in his syndicated column the next day, concluding that Matusow's recantation "may teach the anti-Communists the terrific price of carelessness and ineptitude in choosing some of their associates." When Hoover received the column, he circulated it to his top aides, noting in pen on the routing slip, "Very Good."[47]

* * *

In Washington, the signals were more ominous for Matusow. Senator Henry M. Jackson, a member of the investigations subcommittee previously chaired by McCarthy, urged that a "thorough examination" be conducted because the "Matusow incident may make it difficult for the Government to prosecute future cases effectively." HUAC chairman Francis E. Walter, charging that Matusow had been a Communist "plant" all along, urged the Justice Department to prosecute him. Vice President Nixon, who owed his high office in no small part to the Hiss-Chambers case, contacted the FBI's Louis Nichols to express his concern that "what the critics were trying to do was to discredit Chambers and all former Communists."[48]

Direct government action came quickly. On February 7, Attorney General Brownell announced a "vigorous" investigation of Matusow's recantation, to be headed jointly by Assistant Attorney General Tompkins and J. Edward Lombard, the U.S. attorney in Manhattan. SISS announced its own investigation. It "felt obligated" to pursue the matter, counsel J. G. Sourwine advised Nichols, because Matusow had given his "original" testimony about Jencks at SISS hearings. The subcommittee's investigation, Senator William Jenner (its former Republican chairman) told the United Press, would encompass the publishers of Matusow's book, as SISS's records showed that Angus Cameron had invoked the Fifth Amendment when asked if he was a secret Communist. However, SISS postponed its planned questioning of Matusow to allow him to be brought before a federal grand jury in New York City.[49]

In conjunction with Brownell's announcement, the FBI launched a comprehensive investigation of Matusow and "UNKNOWN SUBJECTS," directed to "SUBORNATION OF PERJURY; PERJURY; OBSTRUCTION OF JUSTICE."[50]

But initially the bureau had difficulty finding its man. Its Phoenix office had wired headquarters and nine field offices on January 25 "regarding the probability of Matusow's retraction." But for the next eight days, the bureau did not know his whereabouts and searched for him in vain. The task had some urgency because the Justice Department wanted to serve Matusow with a grand jury subpoena immediately. On February 1, Hoover demanded to know "why we had not located Matusow"; this led to instructions to the New York office that "there is nothing of more importance now than to locate Matusow, and that every resource should be devoted to it."[51]

The FBI kept Matusow's parents' Bronx apartment under twenty-four-hour surveillance; it made "pretext" phone calls to the apartment; it watched Cameron & Kahn's offices during business hours (the suggested use of a "technical installation" having been rejected); a report that Matusow was en route to New York by train resulted in "surveillance on trains arriving in New York." Ultimately, on February 2, the FBI found him and served him with a grand jury subpoena, when he showed up at the Hotel Dauphin in New York City for his ABC television interview. Hoover demanded an explanation from his subordinates, and when the report arrived, he scrawled in the margin, "It is obvious that here is another case of 'slow motion' action."[52]

From the outset, the FBI disclaimed any responsibility for Matusow's recantation. By February 2, Alan Belmont had prepared three detailed memoranda in response to "the Director's inquiry" whether the testimony "repudiated" by Matusow in the Smith Act case "was based on information which he had previously furnished to the FBI." Belmont reported that "[a] review of the Bureau files on [the four defendants] . . . failed to reflect any of the revolutionary statements attributed to them at the trial by Matusow"; "the revolutionary statements," he concluded, "were not given to the FBI but developed in the United States Attorney's Office." Leland Boardman performed a similar analysis of Matusow's testimony in the Jencks case, concluding that "[w]e did not furnish the Department with any of the [seven] items of information which Matusow has specifically retracted." Instead, Boardman's report emphasized, the bureau had advised the department "of Matusow's unreliability" and had repeatedly cited his December 29, 1951, statement that he had no direct evidence Jencks was a party member.[53]

The next day, the director advised Attorney General Brownell that the FBI had reviewed Matusow's affidavit in the Smith Act case, and "a check of our files fails to reflect that the specific testimony which Matusow now repudiates was based on information furnished to the Department by the FBI." Similarly, as to his affidavit in the Jencks case, the bureau had "determined that the specific items of testimony which Matusow has retracted were not items of information which were furnished to the Department by the FBI."[54]

Having excused itself of responsibility for the problem, however, the FBI conducted, on an expedited basis, an extensive and thorough field investigation. The bureau combed bank records of Matusow, Cameron & Kahn, and the Mine-Mill union for evidence that Matusow was bribed. Its agents compiled reports describing his activities and associates in cities in which he had resided even briefly—Taos, Dayton, and Dallas.[55]

The bureau also interviewed individuals who had known Matusow well, particularly those who knew him during his days as an informer-witness. Arvilla Bentley, remarried and living in Florida, was interviewed on February 3. She "knew of no circumstances in Matusow's life which might make him subject to blackmail by the Communist Party," the agent reported. "She could only attribute his retraction to his intense desire to see his name in the newspapers." J. B. Matthews, in his interview two days later, made a similar comment, reported in the agent's wire to the director: "HE THINKS THAT MATUSOW IS SO ERRATIC THAT HE WOULD WILLINGLY GO TO JAIL OR BE EXECUTED JUST FOR THE SAKE OF PUBLICITY."[56]

* * *

The mere filing of Matusow's affidavits in the Jencks and Smith Act cases did not mean, of course, that new trials would be granted. Rather, the trial judge in each case was required to conduct a hearing and determine whether Matusow had in fact, as he now claimed, perjured himself at the trial. In El Paso, Judge Thomason set a March 7 hearing date for Jencks's motion. In New York City, Judge Dimock held an extended hearing in the Smith Act case, beginning on February 10.

Dimock's hearing initially had been set for a date in early March; but the situation changed when the Justice Department served Matusow with a subpoena requiring that he testify first before a federal grand jury. The subpoena he received on February 2 (when he showed up for his ABC interview) required him to appear before the grand jury the following day. Fearful of the impact upon their motion for a new trial if Matusow were first delivered up to prosecutors to testify in secret before a grand jury, the defense attorneys moved to quash the subpoena. In response, Judge Dimock extended the subpoena's return date and, on February 8, barred any appearance by Matusow before the grand jury until after he had testified at the hearing on the new-trial motion. Dimock ruled, the *New York Times* reported, that a prior grand jury appearance "would interfere with the motion for new trial." But he also ordered that the new-trial hearing would begin only two days later.[57]

Despite the short notice, Judge Dimock compiled an exhaustive hearing record. Not only did he hear seven days of testimony by Matusow, including five days of cross-examination, but also he received voluminous documentary evidence—Matusow's reports to the FBI, his fragmentary diary entries, his testimony before HUAC and the SACB, Bishop Oxnam's notes of his conversations with Matusow, the transcripts of Matusow's taped discussions with Kahn, the manuscript of his book, and, importantly, a series of "trial briefs" prepared by prosecutors in the Smith Act trial, which traced the evolution of Matusow's testimony throughout the period of trial preparation.[58]

At the hearing, in response to attorney Harry Sacher's questions, Matusow confirmed the allegations in his affidavit. He described the meetings with prosecutors at which his trial testimony in the case was crafted and then traced the turnabout in his career, beginning with his "soul-cleansing" letter to McCarthy and his near admissions of perjury in affidavits to the *New York Times* and *Time* magazine and in conversations with Oxnam.[59]

The lengthy cross-examination by U.S. Attorney Lombard emphasized Matusow's destitute state at the time of his arrival in Taos and the financial rewards of recantation. Appearing "squat, sallow," the *Times* said, the witness acknowledged that his publishers gave him improved economic terms after he signed the affidavits and that the Mine-Mill union agreed to buy more copies of his book, including a five-thousand-copy order by the union's Canadian affiliate.[60]

In his written decision two months later, Judge Dimock carefully considered Matusow's motives and credibility, citing the "very extensive" opportunities afforded him as judge at the hearing and earlier at the trial "for getting an understanding of Matusow's character." "[T]he course of Matusow's life," Dimock found, "has been determined by his inability to reconcile himself to the position of a man of no importance. . . . Each of the two turnabouts that Matusow has taken since joining the Communist Party has been calculated to increase his importance." Matusow, he concluded, "is a completely irresponsible witness . . . a man without regard for the truth, with a passion for the limelight and with the need for a few dollars."[61]

But the essential question remained, "Which was the lie, the original story or the retraction?" Judge Dimock had little doubt: "The internal evidence all points to the original story as the lie. . . . Not a single one of the damaging statements made by Matusow on the stand was recounted by him in its damaging form the first time that he referred to it in the course of his preparation as a witness." Yet Dimock cleared Roy Cohn and the other prosecutors of complicity in Matusow's perjury. Refusing to "accept the word of a proved perjurer against theirs," he found that "all of Matusow's fabrications were his own suggestions."[62]

The judge's exoneration of the prosecutors was unquestionably a prudent course given the period, for even his grant of a new trial to defendants Trachtenberg and Charney (but none of the other defendants), based on his finding that Matusow testified falsely at the trial, drew a sour "no comment" from the prosecution side, which moved quickly to retry them. The two defendants were again convicted, although the convictions were later reversed on appeal.[63]

* * *

When Judge Dimock temporarily shielded Matusow from the grand jury's subpoena, the prosecutors turned their attention to his publishers. Albert Kahn and Angus Cameron received subpoenas on February 7 demanding their appearance before the grand jury the very next day, along with the production of documentary materials relating to Matusow's book, including all manuscripts, drafts, and galley proofs of the still-unpublished work. Kahn initially refused to turn over the requested documents, citing the First Amendment guarantee of freedom of the press. But he was immediately taken before a federal district judge, John W. Clancy, who directed him to produce the documents and, when he again refused, sentenced him to six months in jail for contempt. Kahn, however, succeeded in evading the contempt charge and jail sentence by releasing the next day to the press and public, as well as to the grand jury, all of the materials he had previously withheld. His further interrogation before the grand jury on the subject of Communist Party membership was routine stuff, to which he routinely invoked his Fifth Amendment privilege.[64]

The following week, SISS's inquiry began. Angus Cameron appeared before a closed session of the subcommittee on February 17 and, the *New York Times* reported, "turned over all pertinent data and documents relating to the disclosures in Matusow's book." The newspaper also reported Cameron's and Kahn's charge that the Justice Department was "putting pressure" on printers and binders to prevent publication of the book.[65]

A SISS source told the press that the subcommittee intended to question Matusow on "every word" of his prior testimony before it.[66]

9   At Center Stage

During the early months of 1955, Matusow's recantation occupied the spotlight, receiving close scrutiny in a variety of forums and constant attention in the media. The Justice Department's grand jury in Manhattan, augmented by federal grand juries in El Paso and Washington, D.C., considered issues of perjury, conspiracy, and obstruction of justice. FBI agents examined bank and telephone records and conducted interviews in a host of cities, searching for evidence Matusow was bribed or coerced. A federal court hearing in El Paso on Jencks's motion for a new trial placed Matusow on the witness stand for several more days, again to repudiate earlier testimony. But from the standpoint of publicity, SISS's hearings, held in a grand Senate hearing room before a packed house, with floodlights, movie cameras and radio equipment to record the event, and the Washington press corps in attendance, were unmatched—and Matusow responded with a bravura performance.[1]

SISS selected him as the leadoff witness at its first two days of public hearings, February 21 and 22. An Associated Press wirephoto of Matusow shows a neatly dressed young man, in a dark suit and striped tie, seated with hands clasped in front of him, waiting patiently for the proceedings to begin. The *New York Times*'s reporter, Russell Baker, recalled him years later as "a rather good looking young man with dark hair and cool demeanor." Matusow, the *Herald Tribune* reported, "kep[t] his voice and emotions under control as he stared unblinkingly into the spot lights and movie cameras beside the committee table." Stanley Faulkner, a left-wing attorney whom Nathan Witt had selected, accompanied him.[2]

Chairman James O. Eastland's opening statement touched upon the subcommittee's main themes. "As a result of testimony taken in this hearing," he said, "it may appear that Mr. Matusow told the truth in his original testimony before us and is now lying when he says that his original testimony was not the truth." "It may appear," Eastland continued, that "his motive for this shabby performance is merely low personal greed" or "that he has been the victim of pressure brought by Communists . . . and has finally broken under this pressure."[3]

Eastland spoke also in defense of ex-Communist informers, who had served the congressional committees and the Justice Department well, and whom he deemed threatened by Matusow's recantation. He extolled "the importance of the ex-Communist in this worldwide struggle to preserve human freedom" and deplored the "assault on the ex-Communist." Eastland referred in particular to "the vicious assault on Whittaker Chambers and Elizabeth Bentley after they came forward with their stories of Communist traitors." Chambers, he said, "proved his case" with the "pumpkin papers," and "hundreds upon hundreds of documents" showed that Bentley "had been flawlessly truthful."[4]

Subcommittee counsel J. G. Sourwine then commenced a wide-ranging examination of Matusow, which would consume all or part of six days of hearings. "[A] squat, soft-spoken 47-year-old former newspaper man from Reno" (the *New York Times*' description), a McCarran holdover, Sourwine sought confirmation of the subcommittee's view that Matusow's recantation was the product of a Communist plot, aimed at discrediting government witnesses. He began by focusing on Matusow's ethnicity, eliciting that the witness's parents were immigrants from Russia and that his mother's maiden name was "Stolpen." "Was that sometimes written as Stolpensky?" Sourwine asked. Lest anyone miss his point, he asked the witness, "Do you speak Hebrew or Yiddish?"[5]

In response to questions concerning the abrupt turns in his political life, Matusow stated that he became an informer in 1950 out of "fear" of prosecution as a Communist: "I felt if I would testify I would get off the hook, so to speak; and once I started, it just—I just got carried away with it, you might say." He lied at the Jencks trial in January 1954, he said, because "I didn't have the courage to admit I had lied before," to the grand jury, to HUAC, and to SISS at its October 1952 hearings.[6]

The plodding and often inept character of the subcommittee's questioning, however, seemed to embolden Matusow, whose responses increasingly had little, if any, connection with the questions and volunteered information the subcommittee had no wish to hear. He began to fence with the subcommittee, to bait and mock it—employing all of the witness skills he had gained in the preceding four years.

When asked by Sourwine about being "used as a tool of the Communists," Matusow gave a discursive answer that discussed Roy Cohn, criticized the government for not "us[ing] good judgment because they used me as a witness," and ended with the claim that "Miss Elizabeth Bentley, I believe, gave false testimony. . . . I am basing that on conversations with Miss Bentley, not on hearsay." When Senator Jenner asked why, if he had had "such a cleansing of [his] heart," he associated with individuals like Kahn, Cameron, Witt, and Herb Tank, Matusow answered, "I believe in God and Christian charity."[7]

The subcommittee seemed fascinated by Tank, Matusow's bodyguard, who it believed, and wanted Matusow to agree, had been assigned by the Communist Party to keep a round-the-clock watch on him. But Matusow disagreed, pointing out that Tank served three weeks of jury duty the preceding month "and wasn't with me quite a bit of time." Tank's "present duties," he said, consisted of "working on a play dealing with this subject, dealing with the book," and "[t]hat is the only reason he has been with me so constantly that I know of."[8]

The subcommittee persisted:

The CHAIRMAN: Do you think [Tank] is a Communist?
Mr. MATUSOW: I do not think he is a Communist.
The CHAIRMAN: Why did you accuse him then of being a Communist?
Mr. MATUSOW: Because I was a perpetual and habitual liar.
The CHAIRMAN: When you accuse somebody, you are not lying then, are you?
Mr. MATUSOW: When I accuse somebody I am not lying now.[9]

Sourwine tried another approach:

Mr. SOURWINE: Since you agreed to write this book have you been allowed to be alone with any non-Communist for any length of time at all?
Mr. MATUSOW: Yes, sir.
Mr. SOURWINE: When?
Mr. MATUSOW: During the complete writing of this book, in the early stages I shared an apartment with a member of the Young Republican Club in New York. . . .
Mr. SOURWINE: Are you a member of that club?
Mr. MATUSOW: I am.
Mr. SOURWINE: Who proposed you for that club?
Mr. MATUSOW: I don't recall who proposed me. It was 1 of 2 or 3 people.

Mr. SOURWINE: Wasn't it the man whose apartment or room you shared, as you have just testified?

Mr. MATUSOW: No; that is another Young Republican in another apartment.

Mr. SOURWINE: Who is the young man whose room you shared?

Mr. MATUSOW: This apartment? Which one are we talking about now?[10]

Nor would the subcommittee let lie Matusow's admission that he had been "a perpetual and habitual liar":

Senator MCCLELLAN: You kind of intrigued me by a description of the kind of liar you are. Could you possibly be a congenital liar?

Mr. MATUSOW: Well, sir, there are many adjectives to describe liars.

Senator MCCLELLAN: I know.

Mr. MATUSOW: And I think most of them would have fit my past.

Senator MCCLELLAN: What I wanted to determine is whether this is a capacity or faculty that you have developed or did it come natural with you; was it congenital from birth? . . . When did you develop the capacity to lie?

Mr. MATUSOW: I think you have got a point; I think all develop it at birth.[11]

At the close of the day's hearings, Eastland commented to reporters, "I think he is part of a shrewd plan to get some folks out of trouble." The following Sunday, on CBS's *Face the Nation,* he termed Matusow "very well coached."[12]

* * *

Within the Justice Department and the FBI, Matusow's recantation led to a degree of soul-searching, and finger-pointing, concerning the use of "professional witnesses." In a February 12 memorandum to Attorney General Brownell, FBI director Hoover stated, "I feel the utmost care and consideration should be given to the use of professional witnesses in security cases. The necessity to be circumspect in matters of this kind is apparent from [Matusow's] recent action." The director traced a series of apparent perjuries by Matusow, all known to the Justice Department.[13]

Nor was the problem confined to Matusow, the director wrote, for "[a]nother individual who has testified for the Government and concerning whom there was evidence of unreliability is Matthew Cvetic." When in 1950 the Justice Department sought potential witnesses for use in internal security cases, the FBI furnished "background information on Cvetic" and "pointed out certain derogatory information regarding Cvetic and called attention to the fact that the derogatory information should be taken into consideration in determining whether he should be used as a witness." Nonetheless, the department considered him "indispensable for a successful prosecution and he was used" in the Pittsburgh Smith Act case.[14]

Hoover's memorandum continued in this vein, referring to a May 1954 letter to the Justice Department "concerning certain informants and witnesses used by the Immigration and Naturalization Service," some of whom, such as Joseph Mazzei, Cvetic, and Matusow, "had demonstrated their untrustworthiness and unreliability." As to Marie Natvig, the department had been advised, the director stated, before she took the witness stand that she was "of poor reputation," and two FBI memoranda to the department in September 1954 "contain[ed] adverse information bearing upon her character and reliability." Hoover concluded that "unless most careful thought is given to the selection and use of professional witnesses irreparable harm may result."[15]

To be sure, the director's objective in voicing these warnings was not to safeguard the due-process rights of left-wing defendants but rather to avoid further embarrassment to the government—most importantly, the FBI. But whatever his motive, Hoover's memorandum forcefully showed that the Justice Department and its attorneys general, who bore ultimate responsibility for the selection of government witnesses, had been not only imprudent but also ethically blind on repeated occasions.

Brownell, in a press conference on February 17, seemed momentarily chastened. "Asked if he believed that there had been dereliction in the Matusow case," the *New York Times* reported, "the Attorney General answered: 'Why do you think I ordered an investigation?'" But his answer to another question offered a more accurate clue to his thinking. When a reporter inquired about the department's previously announced investigation of Paul Crouch, Brownell responded that the investigation was no longer active, adding that "there was nothing pending in the department on which he could be used." Shortly afterward, Brownell was quoted as saying he had "no reason to believe that Paul Crouch . . . ever gave false testimony."[16]

The Justice Department's attitude was later described by Warren Olney, Brownell's Criminal Division chief. When Matusow "repudiated his testimony," Olney said, "there was a loud to-do, of course, among the lawyers: 'Well, how come we called this guy, anyway?'" The Justice Department's answer: it had relied on the FBI. Because the bureau had initially labeled Matusow's reports as given by an informant "of known reliability," Olney explained, the department's lawyers "went barging right ahead without looking into his character or much else about him as a witness." Brownell's memoirs (in 1993) echoed this rationale.[17]

* * *

When Matusow returned to SISS's witness chair on February 22, the sub-committee, anxious to defend ex-Communist informers, challenged his slur the preceding day on Elizabeth Bentley's credibility. "I want you to tell the committee precisely when and where Miss Bentley told you she lied, and what she told you she lied about," Sourwine began. His open-ended question invited Matusow's extended description of the dinner he shared with Bentley in October 1952:

> Friday, October 3, I met her at the office of her publisher, Devon Adair. It was in the afternoon, and we made a date to have dinner that night. . . .
>
> We had dinner at the Rochambeau Restaurant on Sixth Avenue and, I believe it is, 11th Street in New York City. And during the course of dinner, Miss Bentley cried quite a bit. She was out of work. She said she was a teacher and wanted a job, but nobody would employ her. She said that she had used up all the money she had received from the publication of her book, I forget the title of it, her confessions of some kind. . . .
>
> She said that she didn't have any more information . . . and cried quite a bit.
>
> I believe one thing she said, "Well, you are a man, you are young, you can go out and find a job. I can't. I have to continue doing this sort of thing. It is the only way I can work. I can't get a job as a teacher. I can't get any kind of a job. I just have to continue to find information to testify about."[18]

In response to further probing by Sourwine, Matusow added that his conversation with Bentley at the restaurant "went on for a couple of hours" and that "[a] number of my friends came in during the course of the conversation, at which time Miss Bentley stopped crying, and we went on to other matters; and when they had left the table she went back to crying." Matusow could recall the name of only one of his friends, "a Mr. Llewelyn Watts, a member of the Young Republican Club of New York," with whom he had shared a West 10th Street apartment during the 1952 election campaign, while he "was traveling around the country."[19]

Eastland pursued the subject of Matusow's friends:

> The CHAIRMAN: These people were not known to Miss Bentley?
> Mr. MATUSOW: They were not.

The CHAIRMAN: ... What were they, just in the bar having a drink or two; is that it?

Mr. MATUSOW: Yes, sir.

The CHAIRMAN: ... Now, how close were they standing to you before they would come to the table?

Mr. MATUSOW: Oh, it varied from 10 feet to 5 feet. ...

The CHAIRMAN: Miss Bentley could be plainly seen by those people before they came to your table?

Mr. MATUSOW: Well, if they were looking at her, yes.

The CHAIRMAN: ... and she was sitting there crying, and here is a man standing, oh, 5 or 10 feet; when he would walk up to the table she would turn the tears off?

Mr. MATUSOW: Yes, sir.

The CHAIRMAN: When he stayed there; and when he stepped back 5 feet, she would begin to cry again; is that your testimony?

Mr. MATUSOW: Not on every occasion, but on most; yes, sir. ...

The CHAIRMAN: Well, did she cry while another person was there?

Mr. MATUSOW: She might have.[20]

Senator Jenner chimed in with questions about Matusow's friend Llewelyn Watts:

Senator JENNER: I am speaking about the time you two lived together, you roomed together in an apartment. What kind of a man was Mr. Watts at that time?

Mr. MATUSOW: At the times I knew him he was an honest man.

Senator JENNER: He had to know you rather well living with you, didn't he?

Mr. MATUSOW: He knew me fairly well.

Senator JENNER: There is no way in the world that you can live with a habitual and perpetual liar and not know it, is there?

Mr. MATUSOW: I don't know, sir. I met many people who I lied to, and didn't know it until just recently.

Senator JENNER: You couldn't live with a man and be his roommate and be in his apartment and be a perpetual and habitual liar and he not know it.

Mr. MATUSOW: I was out of town most of the time.[21]

When the questioning turned to Matusow's speeches in Senate races in Montana and Washington state during the 1952 election, the subcommittee's only liberal, Democrat Thomas C. Hennings Jr., became interested. Hennings elicited from Matusow that it was Joe McCarthy who "specifically first asked" him "to go West to take part in these campaigns" and whose office supplied him with the materials he used in making false charges against Representatives (now Senators) Jackson and Mansfield.[22]

McCarthy promptly issued a denial that he had asked Matusow to go to Montana and Washington, stating that "I wouldn't answer a man who confesses he is a liar." But the senator admitted that "[w]hen he's lying and when he's telling the truth you just can't tell."[23]

* * *

For the FBI, even more so than the subcommittee, Matusow's disparaging remarks about Elizabeth Bentley's credibility were a serious matter. Bentley's revelations had long been the foundation for the bureau's case that Soviet espionage networks utilizing American Communists flourished in government agencies during World War II and for its charges against Harry Dexter White and William Remington, among many others. The director had repeatedly and publicly vouched for her. Matusow's testimony about the October 1952 dinner thus triggered an immediate FBI inquiry, overseen by Hoover, with Attorney General Brownell kept closely informed.[24]

On the face of it, an unsupported accusation by a self-proclaimed perjurer should not have been cause for alarm. But headquarters thought otherwise, stating in a communication to local FBI offices: "Matusow's allegations are a serious attack on the Government's whole security program. In attacking Elizabeth Bentley, Matusow appears to have selected a person whose reliability has never seriously been challenged. It is, therefore, of vital importance that this entire matter receive the most thorough investigative attention possible and that all leads are carried out promptly and thoroughly."[25]

There was more to headquarters' concern: it feared Matusow's account might have substance. In Bentley's contacts with the FBI during 1952, the director advised Assistant Attorney General Tompkins, she "on occasions was depressed and emotionally upset." He described a meeting with two FBI agents in September 1952 at which "she cried and claimed she was being mistreated by the State of Connecticut. She later became argumentative and demanding of the agents, claiming her financial and other problems should be taken care of by the FBI." "During 1952," the director wrote, "it appeared she was drinking heavily."[26]

Bentley's grievance against the state of Connecticut stemmed from leaving the scene of an automobile accident, one of three car accidents in which she was involved in less than a month. An FBI report on September 26, 1952, disclosed "that BENTLEY was heavily in debt; that she was apparently drinking excessively; was having an emotional reaction due to shock from an automobile accident, and she was in a highly nervous state." An "airing of that period of BENTLEY's life," the New York office now warned, could cause "more serious embarrassment to the Bureau."[27]

Within hours after Matusow made his initial remark attacking Bentley's credibility, Hoover sent an "URGENT" wire to the FBI's New Orleans office—in 1953 she had obtained employment in nearby Grand Coteau—directing that she be contacted to ascertain the nature of any conversation she may have had with Matusow. Bentley denied to the bureau (and in a statement to United Press) that she ever told Matusow she lied; but otherwise she couldn't give the bureau much help. She recalled no conversation with him, other than at a luncheon with him and Ruth Matthews, which she mistakenly believed took place on October 3—in fact, it occurred two months later.[28]

After the New Orleans office's contact, Bentley tried unsuccessfully to phone Hoover directly to ask the bureau's assistance in ascertaining her whereabouts on the day in question. "We must be careful," the director noted on the message slip, "as we may be charged as coaching her if we give any information." Unable to reach Hoover, Bentley phoned Robert J. Lamphere, an FBI agent long engaged in Soviet counterespionage work whom she knew; Lamphere reported "she was considerably upset by Matusow's allegations and it appeared she probably had been drinking."[29]

While Bentley had no recollection of an October 3 dinner at the Rochambeau restaurant, Matusow's acquaintances did. Watts, Doris Hibbard, his date, and Earl Henry, a friend, all remembered talking with Matusow and Bentley at the restaurant on a Friday evening in the fall of 1952—Watts and Hibbing sat at their table for an extended period. None of the three, however, recalled that Bentley cried or appeared depressed; nor did they hear her mention having to provide new testimony. Henry remembered that Bentley "did not have a chance to say much during the evening because MATUSOW was monopolizing the conversation." Hibbard, who later went out on a few dates with Matusow, termed him "an ego-maniac" and "believe[d] that MATUSOW is glorying in being in the spotlight currently and will make it last as long as possible."[30]

As for Bentley, given her extensive background in espionage, it is unlikely, sober or not, that she would have made significant admissions in a public place to Matusow, whom she barely knew.

Other than a flurry of activity, nothing came of the FBI's inquiry. The bureau had no reason to perpetuate a public debate on Bentley's credibility. Bentley, who was employed at a Catholic women's college, hoped to avoid controversy. And Matusow, under investigation by numerous agencies and with a perjury indictment looming, was in no position to press his charges.

* * *

Matusow's testimony before SISS, interrupted after two days to enable him to appear before the federal grand jury in New York City, continued for three more days the following week. The subcommittee's questioning, if anything, was even less artful than before, allowing Matusow again to clown, to make his questioners appear foolish, and to volunteer information as he chose. He began also to invoke the Fifth Amendment in an erratic fashion. "He was by now a truly remarkable witness," Murray Kempton wrote, "in the *opera bouffe* sense demanded by the inquisitions of the fifties."[31]

Matusow volunteered that he had been paid to escort Arvilla Bentley to the Bahamas in 1952 to evade a Senate committee investigation of her contributions to Joe McCarthy—a trip, he said, arranged by J. B. Matthews. In response, an embarrassed Matthews wrote to Eastland, indignantly denying any role in arranging the trip. His wife Ruth, he said, had simply responded to Arvilla's request "that Matusow accompany her part way on a vacation trip to Nassau in order to assist her with her baggage at transfer points."[32]

Matusow repeatedly and mischievously invoked the Fifth Amendment in testimony about his "stringless yo-yo." This episode commenced when Republican senator Herman Welker of Idaho (a McCarthy ally), seeking to show that Matusow was flat broke when contacted by Cameron & Kahn, asked him if he had any money in the bank. While he admitted to "total cash assets" of only $200 or $300, Matusow mentioned that he expected royalties of several thousand dollars from "a toy that I invented and sold to a manufacturer last year." Welker took the bait, demanding to know the manufacturer's name. But Matusow invoked the Fifth Amendment—not to avoid self-incrimination, he said, but because the amendment provides "that no property can be taken or disturbed in any way without due process of law, and I feel that disclosing the name of the manufacturer, et cetera, would, in effect, be taking property from that manufacturer and have an effect on the sales of that toy." Sourwine interjected: "Is the firm which is to manufacture your toy . . . a Soviet or Communist firm?" Matusow took the Fifth Amendment; "directed and ordered" to answer, he again took the Fifth.[33]

Welker tried a more conciliatory approach, seeking to employ a little humor. "I think all of us are rather interested in this toy," he said. "Could it be a miniature lie detector?" "Well, sir, no; it is not a miniature lie detector," Matusow answered.

Senator WELKER: Would you mind telling us what sort of a toy it is?
Mr. MATUSOW: Well, I call it a stringless yo-yo.

Senator WELKER: A stringless yo-yo?

Mr. MATUSOW: A stringless yo-yo.

Amid audience laughter, Welker again asked "the name of the manufacturer of the stringless yo-yo"; Matusow once more took the Fifth.[34]
Senator Price Daniel, a conservative Texas Democrat, jumped in: "Is he a
member of the Communist Party?" Again, the Fifth Amendment. "I order
and direct you," Daniel demanded, "to answer the question whether or not
the manufacturer of your yo-yo is known to you to be a member of the Communist Party?" Matusow again took the Fifth; but he added brightly, "I will
be glad to send each member of the committee a version of it, sir."[35]
On the last of the three days, Chairman Eastland's clumsy effort to make
him admit that either Tank, Kahn, or Cameron had "protected" (i.e., stood
guard over) him every night for a full month enabled Matusow to pose as a
chivalrous defender of women. After the witness insisted that on some nights
no "protector" was present, Eastland wanted to know where he was on those
nights. "Well, sir, it is a little embarrassing," Matusow responded. He continued:

Mr. MATUSOW: I don't want to embarrass this person; I mean, it was just
    a lady friend.
The CHAIRMAN: Who is that friend?
Mr. MATUSOW: Well, sir, I think I will have to stand here—if you want
    to cite me for contempt for defending the reputation of a lady, I will
    have to take that. . . .
The CHAIRMAN: I think you had a Communist bodyguard each of those
    nights, and we are trying to prove it. . . .
Mr. MATUSOW: I am sorry; I am going to defend the reputation of this
    lady, if it means going to jail for contempt.
The CHAIRMAN: I am ordering you to testify.
Mr. MATUSOW: I will defend her reputation.[36]

Throughout five days of testimony, Matusow had thumbed his nose at a
powerful Senate committee. In the past, as a "friendly" witness, he had viewed
testifying as performing; now, as a hostile witness, with his biggest audience
at hand, he gave a flamboyant performance. But the defiant character of his
testimony perhaps reflected something more: an understanding that he faced
a near certain perjury prosecution and likely would not by his defiance make
his situation any worse.[37]

* * *

The hearing in El Paso on Jencks's motion for a new trial, which began on March 7, bore little resemblance to the thoughtful and deliberate hearing conducted by Judge Dimock in the Smith Act case. Judge Robert E. Thomason, a former Texas congressman appointed to the bench by President Truman, did not analyze whether Matusow's testimony was truthful then or now—he had no doubt the earlier testimony was truthful. And he did not, as Judge Dimock did, issue a carefully written opinion. Rather, at the conclusion of the hearing, on March 12, Judge Thomason simply announced that "the motion for a new trial is in all things overruled and denied."[38]

Most of the five-day hearing was consumed by Matusow's testimony, including another lengthy cross-examination. In his testimony, Matusow went the final mile for Jencks, even expanding on the allegations in his affidavit. Not only did he deny that Jencks admitted Communist Party membership to him in their conversations at the San Cristobal Valley Ranch but denied any conversations with him at all about either the party or Communist activities. Asked whether he had "any conversation" with Jencks "at that time or any other time . . . concerning the Communist Party or its activities," he responded, "No, sir." He denied that his contemporaneous reports to the FBI identified Jencks as a party member and that he had done so only in the later reports "worked up for" HUAC. As to his grand jury testimony that he had "[n]o doubt whatsoever" Jencks was a party member, Matusow now said that this answer "was false." His statements about Jencks on the tapes he and Kahn recorded while writing the book were also false, he said; he made them because he "didn't trust" Kahn at that time.[39]

Judge Thomason listened largely without comment. But immediately upon announcing his denial of the motion, he addressed Matusow: "By recanting your former testimony, given in this court, which I believe in substance was true, you have, in my opinion, deliberately, designedly and maliciously attempted to obstruct the justice of this court." Matusow had done so, the judge said, "for the purpose of furthering your personal gains."[40]

Thomason advised Matusow that, by virtue of his actions, "I am thoroughly convinced that you are in contempt of this court." The judge then asked him whether he wanted a hearing on the contempt charge or "are you ready for me to act?" Matusow asked for a hearing, which was held four days later. The hearing was brief, with Matusow the only witness. He denied that he either lied in his testimony on the new-trial motion or conspired with anyone to change his testimony for money. He sought only, he said, "[t]o try and undo the harm I had done by testifying in the Jencks trial . . . when I testified falsely, and to clear my own conscience." The judge, however, responded that Matusow "used this Court of law as a forum for the purpose of calling public attention to [his] book" and "lent himself to this evil scheme for money and for notoriety." He then found Matusow guilty of contempt and sentenced him to three years' imprisonment.[41]

Commenting on these proceedings, I. F. Stone wrote: "To hold Matusow in contempt is in effect to punish him for recanting without having to take the trouble of proving a charge of perjury. The three-year sentence, imposed on a judge's fiat without jury trial, is a brutal warning to other informers." But Senator Eastland hailed the judge's action as "refreshing and wholly praiseworthy."[42]

Judge Thomason set bail pending appeal at $10,000, and Matusow spent twenty days in the El Paso County jail before it could be raised. "[M]y first time in the cage," he later wrote to Kahn, "locked, penned in a wind-swept desert jail 2000 miles from home." His detention in the government's hands created concern on the part of his publishers that he might have "recanted his recanting"; but their fears proved unwarranted. Sylvia Matusow sent letters of encouragement to her son. And Kahn, after being rebuffed by the Mine-Mill union, obtained the needed bail money from Anita Willcox, the artist wife of a retired Connecticut building contractor, who had never met Matusow. Mrs. Willcox, described by United Press as a "silver-haired grandmother," was shortly afterward hauled before SISS, to be questioned closely about her political affiliations.[43]

A series of appeals and, in the succeeding months, appellate decisions followed Judge Thomason's rulings. In October, the court of appeals in New Orleans affirmed his denial of Jencks's motion for a new trial. The opinion of the three-judge panel, written by Circuit Judge Ben F. Cameron, a conservative Mississippian, found "[i]t was proper for [Judge Thomason] to consider that Matusow had little demonstrable motive for lying at the trial, and the basest of all motives, personal gain, for the recantation."[44]

On the same day, the same three-judge panel affirmed Jencks's conviction for filing a false non-Communist affidavit and his five-year prison sentence. In so doing, the court approved Judge Thomason's refusal to allow the defense access for impeachment purposes to FBI reports containing statements by Matusow and another government witness. However, the Supreme Court in 1957 reversed Jencks's conviction on this issue. With Matusow's testimony no longer available to it, the government did not retry Jencks.[45]

Matusow's summary contempt conviction was a mockery, and in January 1956, the court of appeals—again, the same three-judge panel—set it aside. Even if Matusow had perjured himself when he recanted his trial testimony, the court ruled, "proof of perjury alone will not sustain a conviction for contempt." And Matusow, it held, had been denied fundamental rights, notably the presumption of innocence and a jury trial.[46]

* * *

The publication date for Matusow's book was March 15, 1955, the day before Judge Thomason held him in contempt in El Paso. After the FBI made a round of visits to printers in the New York City area, Cameron & Kahn had difficulty finding anyone who would print the book; but Harvey Satenstein, the self-assured head of a small printing firm, read and decided to print it.[47]

Following the onslaught of publicity that attended the filing of Matusow's affidavits, his testimony at the new-trial hearings, his contempt conviction and sentence, and SISS's hearings, the book's appearance came as an anticlimax. The review in the Sunday *New York Times* said it explicitly: "[t]he reader can learn no more" by buying the book. Nor did it help sales that Cameron & Kahn could only afford "token advertising" and its entire marketing apparatus consisted of a single part-time salesman. Outside the United States, sales of the book, which was translated into a number of foreign languages, were more substantial, particularly in Soviet-bloc countries—which, however, rarely paid copyright royalties. A *Times* advertisement in April claimed a first printing of 50,000 and a second printing of 20,000 copies.[48]

While U.S. sales were modest, the book was widely reviewed. Some reviewers believed that Matusow had been turned around by the Communists. Others used the opportunity to take a swipe at McCarthyism: a reviewer in the *Winston-Salem Journal and Sentinel* wrote that "no one has struck at [McCarthyism] any harder than this opportunistic, calculating, psychopathic liar known as Harvey Matusow." Still others were noncommittal, such as the Sunday *New York Times*'s reviewer, Edward Ranzal (the *Times* reporter who had covered the Smith Act case), who ventured that a "renegade and admitted liar . . . must remain suspect." Herbert Philbrick, writing in the *Herald Tribune*, sought to dissuade would-be buyers of the book, calling it "the most overpublicized and probably the least important book of the year."[49]

* * *

With Matusow absent from its witness stand, SISS, seeking evidence of a Communist plot, turned its attention to Kahn, Cameron, and Tank. All were questioned, in open and closed sessions, about Communist Party membership, and all made liberal use of the Fifth Amendment.[50]

In April, the subcommittee subpoenaed Nathan Witt and questioned him concerning the Mine-Mill union's payments that enabled Matusow's book to be published. Witt answered these questions freely, but he refused to disclose whether he was himself a Communist Party member, asserting the Fifth Amendment.[51]

Harry Sacher, the defense attorney in the Smith Act case, like earlier witnesses, refused to answer SISS's questions about party membership. But unlike the others, Sacher disclaimed reliance on the Fifth Amendment—leading directly to a prosecution for contempt of Congress. He argued, in lieu of the Fifth Amendment, that compelled disclosure of one's political views was "inconsistent with the dignity of any man" and, alternatively, that the questions were "not pertinent to anything with which this committee is concerned." Sacher's alternative contention was sustained three years later by the Supreme Court, which reversed his conviction and six-month prison sentence on the ground that the questions at issue were "not clearly pertinent" to the subject on which the subcommittee had been authorized to take testimony.[52]

Anita Willcox, who posted bail for Matusow when he was jailed for contempt in El Paso, informed the subcommittee that she had never "had any contact with him whatsoever." She said she responded to Kahn's request to furnish Matusow's bail, because he was "a symbol of a sickness that is blighting our beloved country." Most of the subcommittee's questions, however, concerned her visit with her husband to Communist China in 1952, as a result of which her passport had been revoked by the State Department.[53]

SISS's hearings ended (apart from some odds and ends) on April 20, as they had begun, with Matusow in the witness chair. Little had changed. When Chairman Eastland called him "the worst [liar] that I have ever seen," Matusow responded, "I don't think I am. Mr. [Roy] Cohn, I think, tops me in spades." For its part, the subcommittee released a Justice Department letter intended to minimize Matusow's significance as a witness. Ninety percent of the persons named as Communists by Matusow, the letter stated, "have also been identified by other sources." Its hearings complete, the subcommittee began preparation of its report.[54]

"The consensus of opinion among reporters who covered the show," I. F. Stone reported in his newsletter, "was that Harvey was in control of the proceedings." "His voice was strong and loud," Murray Kempton observed, and "if his questioners relaxed, he would leap into a mad filibuster which no television film editor could resist."[55]

* * *

If Brownell's February press conference had suggested to anyone that the Justice Department might assume some blame for its witness practices or provide a remedy for individuals accused by informer-witnesses now found to have committed perjury, the attorney general in March dispelled any such notions. Matusow, he told the Greater Boston Chamber of Commerce in a March 21 speech, was the "focal point" of the "current violent attack" by Communists "against Government witnesses and against the FBI's confidential sources of information." "[W]hile the fight against Communism goes on," Brownell informed his audience, "the tactics of these diabolical conspirators change."[56]

The Justice Department and the FBI mounted an effort to combat adverse media comment. An article ("Can Informers Be Trusted?") in the March 4 issue of *U.S. News & World Report*, for example, recounted the many benefits obtained from the FBI's use of undercover informers placed in the ranks of the Communist Party. "Officials," the article stated in boldface type, "say that Mr. Matusow is the exception, rather than the rule." Another *U.S. News & World Report* article justified monetary payments to informers, a practice "older than trial by jury." "Some informers," the article stated, "are of a very high type, in the opinion of officials of the FBI." The *New York Times* reported on the basis of interviews at the Justice Department that a "number of witnesses," such as Budenz and Bentley, "are regarded as stable witnesses."[57]

Yet the attorney general, in the face of severe criticism of his department's use of professional witnesses, revealed on April 15 that he had disbanded its stable of paid informer-witnesses. The Justice Department, he told a press conference, no longer retained full-time "consultants" on its payroll. "[W]e don't have any consultants," he said, "and haven't had for many, many months." Brownell attributed his decision solely to tactical courtroom considerations: the paid-informer system, he said, "was very foolish from the standpoint of successful prosecution because it would always be brought out in court, and it would look as if this (consultant) was a Government employee." He added, the *Times* reported, "that persons with pertinent knowledge about specific cases were still used as 'expert witnesses' and paid as such."[58]

Brownell parried the reporters' request for a list of the "consultants" and their salaries, promising to supply the information in several days. But the *Times* had "learned" that eighty-seven informer-witnesses received compensation between mid-1952 and mid-1954 and that "[a]mong the top salaries paid last year" were $9,676 to Paul Crouch and $9,096 to Manning Johnson. The *Times*'s information was evidently derived from a list leaked to the press. Matusow, it reported, received only $75. But the salary numbers on the list reflected compensation from the INS only; in addition to his $75 from INS, Matusow received $1,407 from a separate account in the attorney general's office.[59]

When the Justice Department in August released the information Brownell had promised, it did not jibe either with his statements at the April 15 press conference or the *Times*'s report. Although Brownell stated that the "consultant" program had been discontinued "many, many months" earlier, the information released covered the period July 1, 1953, to the day of his press conference. And while the *Times* reported eighty-seven "consultants" on the payroll, the department listed only forty-seven. The department disclosed that John Lautner, the highest-paid "consultant," received over $16,000. An unnamed Justice Department spokesman denied that Lautner was a full-time employee "in the usual sense." "He did use a desk here for a while," the spokesman admitted, "but he never had an office in any sense of the word." Matusow, according to the department, received $2,100 during the period in question.[60]

* * *

Brownell took another, unannounced step to deal with the paid-witness problem. On April 5, he established a "Departmental Committee on Security Witnesses," with representatives from the Justice Department's Criminal and Internal Security divisions and the INS. Its purpose was "to handle problems dealing with ex-Communists as Government witnesses in Departmental cases."[61]

The new committee, when it met behind closed doors the next day, addressed basic concerns. It decided that its functions would include "[d]etermining questions of credibility where raised" and [d]etermining whether action should be taken on past cases in which a discredited witness testified." It recommended that government attorneys who wished to use ex-Communist witnesses be required to check FBI and INS sources for "adverse information." Since contracts to pay witnesses were no longer an option, the committee considered at its April 12 meeting how to assure the continued availability of "the persons whose testimony has been regularly used in the past." Suggested alternatives included "hav[ing] one of the public foundations establish a fund to assure that the persons would have an income when not testifying" and "procur[ing] employment [for them] with public-spirited organizations."[62]

Throughout the spring, the committee reviewed information concerning the credibility of individual witnesses, including Matusow, Matt Cvetic, Joseph Mazzei, and many others, to decide whether they could be used in the future (in all but a handful of cases the answer was yes) and whether the government should reopen proceedings in which they had testified (a course uniformly rejected). In Matusow's case, his recantation rendered moot the question of continued use. But the committee also saw no need to reopen any of the four SACB cases or the Davidoff deportation proceeding in which he had testified. (In the Jencks and Smith Act cases, motions for new trial had already placed the issue before the courts.) As to Mazzei, the committee recommended that he "not be used in the future as a government witness." It ruled that Cvetic not be used "unless in a specific case what he will testify to is essential and is corroborated from independent sources whether admissible or not."[63]

The committee operated in secret, and Brownell admitted nothing publicly. Only after Matusow recanted and public outcry forced the disbanding of the Justice Department's stable of paid witnesses had the attorney general discerned any need for a mechanism to consider witness-credibility questions. The committee's apparent role was to provide an arguable basis for the continued use of as many of the same witnesses as possible.

* * *

Contemporaneously, the work of the grand juries in New York City, Washington, and El Paso, each focused on some aspect of Matusow's recantation, proceeded with dispatch. "The destruction of Matusow," Murray Kempton wrote, "has to be the main focus" of Brownell's effort. The Justice Department, the *New York Times* reported, "plans to have a go at indicting Matusow."[64]

Matusow's own appearances before the New York grand jury, however, did not advance its investigation, for he pleaded the Fifth Amendment in response to virtually every question concerning his book. Moreover, he continued to perform in the manner of a stand-up comic. Questioned during one grand jury appearance about what he did for a living, Matusow said he was an entertainer, thereupon launching into an act that included imitations and his pipe-cleaner routines. He was equally flip with a *Times* reporter following an appearance in late April. "I don't see how they can get me on anything," he said. "The grand jury has called a lot of my old girl friends. But for what, I don't know."[65]

Following a May appearance, Matusow told the press that he had shown the grand jurors several chapters of a novel he was writing, in which the principal character was a "composite" of himself and Roy Cohn. He also disclosed that as a result of his recantation, he had been expelled from the New York Young Republican Club, which he had joined in 1953. The club's action, the *Times* soberly reported, was taken by a unanimous vote of its board of governors, after Matusow personally appeared at the meeting and undertook a twenty-minute defense of his conduct.[66]

The Justice Department, however, would have the last word. In July, the New York City grand jury began returning a series of indictments.

10 Paying the Piper

In June 1955, Matusow remarried. A month later the New York City grand jury indicted him for perjury. His bride, Ellen Raskin, a slender, attractive twenty-seven-year-old commercial artist, lived in Manhattan with her six-year-old daughter. Matusow told Albert Kahn that he sometimes walked a friend's child to the same school attended by Raskin's daughter and met his bride-to-be after she recognized him from newspaper photos and complained to the school's principal that he might be a bad influence on the children. The wedding ceremony, conducted by a rabbi in a room at the Chelsea Hotel, was attended by fewer than a half dozen guests. The Kahns and Angus Cameron were present, seemingly Matusow's only close friends; on the bride's side, her small daughter, who wept loudly throughout, and one friend attended. Matusow invited no family members; his mother later explained to Kahn that "Harvey wanted to keep it as small as possible." Unlike Arvilla Bentley's, Ellen Raskin's politics were not right-wing. But her marriage to Matusow, like his earlier marriage, was neither a lengthy nor successful one.[1]

Matusow's indictment, on July 13, charged six counts of perjury, all relating to his claim that Roy Cohn induced him to testify falsely at the trial in the Smith Act case. The first two counts were directed to allegedly false statements in his affidavit filed with the defendants' new-trial motion, regarding Cohn and the trial testimony linking Alexander Trachtenberg to the Vishinsky book. The final four counts charged he gave false testimony relating to Cohn at the February hearing before Judge Dimock.[2]

Surprisingly, the indictment named only Matusow. The prosecution had labored mightily to find evidence of a conspiracy to bribe or pressure him to recant—the Communist plot of which Brownell and SISS spoke darkly. Kahn, Cameron, the Mine-Mill union, the lawyers, and Tank all appeared to be in jeopardy. But the government came up empty. Bill Dufty, Matusow's friend at the *New York Post,* who testified before the grand jury, offered an explanation. He had described to the grand jury, Dufty said, his own failed efforts to find a publisher for Matusow's book. After this testimony, Dufty believed, a Communist-conspiracy theory was no longer credible. Since Matusow had sought vainly to sell his book to mainstream publishers, the grand jury could find nothing improper in his acceptance of Cameron & Kahn's offer—his only option.[3]

Even the task of prosecuting Matusow alone might have been difficult for the government, if only he had recanted his testimony without making the further claim that Cohn induced his perjury. Had he refrained from this added assertion, the prosecutors could not, as a practical matter, have charged that his original testimony was perjured, for to do so would admit that false testimony had been used against the Smith Act defendants. But if they charged that his later testimony was the perjury, that would not only conflict with Judge Dimock's findings but also require proof that alleged oral statements by Trachtenberg, George Blake Charney, and Pettis Perry, made years earlier—in two of the three instances, privately to Matusow—were in fact made to Matusow as he originally testified.[4]

However, by claiming that Cohn suborned his perjury, Matusow made the prosecutors' task easy, since an array of government witnesses stood ready to controvert his claim. Indeed, his subornation charge had already been denied by Cohn and several other prosecutors in the Smith Act case—denials credited by Judge Dimock. Matusow, on the other hand, had no corroboration for his charge. In El Paso, where his recantation in the Jencks case omitted any claim that prosecutors induced his false testimony, the grand jury did not indict him.[5]

Matusow's bail following the New York indictment was set at three thousand dollars. When he could not raise the money after two weeks, he was jailed at the Federal House of Detention. A few days afterward, Sylvia Matusow posted bail for her son in the form of U.S. Savings Bonds.[6]

Matusow remained free on bail for an extended period, because his trial did not begin until September 1956. Most of the fourteen-month delay resulted from a court order deferring his trial until completion of the retrial of Trachtenberg and Charney, to obviate any claim of prejudice by them stemming from a simultaneous Matusow trial in the same courthouse.[7]

* * *

With his recantation and the writing of his book as their bond, Matusow's friendship with Albert Kahn flourished. On June 11, two days before his wedding, he wrote to Kahn: "I consider you my best friend . . . that is my highest title . . . My conscience convinced me to tell the truth recently in Courts and before the Senate . . . But you showed me the trust which enabled me to believe my conscience." Kahn, in the process of moving with his family to Northern California, responded from Chicago, "I am really proud of that letter, Harvey."[8]

Matusow and his new wife faced substantial everyday obstacles. Initially, they lived with her daughter in cramped quarters in his tiny Greenwich Village apartment. Matusow's notoriety, moreover, made it difficult for him to find and hold a job. For several months he worked for Encyclopedia Britannica selling a children's encyclopedia, before being asked to resign. In early 1956, with his wife's coaching, he obtained a job in Macy's advertising production department. But a few months later, during a strike at Macy's, Matusow was spotted on the picket line by a newspaper reporter, who published a story identifying him—resulting in the loss of his job. Still, he told Kahn, he was very happy.[9]

* * *

The dragnet character of the Justice Department's investigation led to two additional indictments by the New York grand jury, each with only a remote nexus to Matusow's recantation.

In the earlier of the two indictments, handed down the same day as Matusow's, the principal defendant was R. Lawrence Siegel, the New York City attorney who represented *The Nation* and who had met with Matusow to discuss possible investments by his clients in Matusow's book project. Coincidentally or not, *The Nation* had published, in April 1954, an article by attorney Frank Donner sharply condemning the government's use of paid ex-Communist informers. Freda Kirchwey, *The Nation*'s editor and publisher, did not doubt the connection: the Siegel indictment, she told the press, "can only be interpreted as a desire to smear and silence a publication which has played a leading role in attacking the use of political informers."[10]

The charges against Siegel and his associate, Hadassah R. Shapiro, stemmed from the destruction of several memoranda describing his meetings with Matusow and production to the grand jury of altered substitutes. The substituted documents, however, omitted only portions that would have identified Siegel's clients—Gloria Swanson and two others—who, Siegel explained, might be injured in their business or personal affairs if their contacts with Matusow became public knowledge. Siegel and Shapiro were nonetheless convicted by a jury on multiple counts of perjury and obstruction of justice. The sentencing judge, John F. X. McGohey, a tough former prosecutor, was seemingly sympathetic to their plight and imposed only probation and a small fine.[11]

The second of the two indictments, handed down in September 1955, named Paul H. Hughes, an air force veteran and a skilled con man. Falsely claiming to be employed by the McCarthy subcommittee and ready to disclose information damaging to McCarthy, Hughes during 1954 victimized a group of prominent liberals, including Joseph L. Rauh, a civil liberties lawyer and a founder of Americans for Democratic Action. Dropped by the group (which had paid him more than ten thousand dollars), Hughes in early 1955 informed the FBI that Rauh and other influential liberals "might be the motivating force behind Matusow's recanting." The bureau passed his information to Justice Department attorneys, who in turn brought him before the grand jury to repeat his charges. But after Rauh and others accused by Hughes flatly denied to the grand jury any connection with Matusow's recantation, the grand jury indicted Hughes on six counts of perjury.[12]

Hughes's trial, which featured testimony by one of the prosecutors, Thomas A. Bolan (soon to be Matusow's prosecutor and later Roy Cohn's law partner), as a witness for the *defense,* resulted in an acquittal on two counts in the indictment and a hung jury on the remaining counts. Hughes was not retried.[13]

* * *

At the end of December 1955, SISS issued a final report in its investigation of Matusow's recantation—a 104-page document that contained few surprises. The subcommittee, Chairman Eastland stated, "has every reason to believe that Matusow had been telling the truth in his testimony all along until he again fell into the hands of Communists last October and, for thirty pieces of silver—that is, for a little money and notoriety—betrayed his own country to the Communist conspiracy." His book, the subcommittee found, "is a confection of falsehoods" prepared by Witt and Kahn. His recantation "and the campaign around it" were "a collective product of the Communist conspiracy" intended "to discredit Government witnesses, the Department of Justice, the courts, the FBI, and congressional investigating committees." Matusow, it said, "was completely dominated by those participating in this Communist conspiracy, including labor leaders, writers, publishers, lawyers, and a bodyguard, from the moment he was picked up 'destitute' in Taos, N. Mex."[14]

The subcommittee implicitly criticized one aspect of the Justice Department's handling of Matusow's case: its failure to indict his associates. The department, SISS recommended, should "lay before a grand jury the facts relating to the apparent conspiracy to obstruct justice involving Matusow, Witt, Kahn, and others."[15]

The report, however, disregarded any facts inconsistent with its conclusions. It ignored Judge Dimock's reasoned determination that Matusow lied at the 1952 Smith Act trial, necessitating a new trial for Trachtenberg and Charney. It likewise failed to deal straightforwardly with Matusow's false testimony before the subcommittee in October 1952 that the *New York Times* employed over one hundred Communist Party members, characterizing his later affidavit (in which he admitted he could name only six) as "a statement of 'clarification,' *not recantation or retraction*" (emphasis in original).[16]

* * *

About the same time, the government tacitly admitted in the Supreme Court that Matusow's initial testimony, in at least one case, was untruthful. At issue was his testimony before the SACB four years earlier in the proceeding to compel the Communist Party to register under the Internal Security Act. Ordered to register, the party challenged the order on the ground that the board had relied on perjured testimony by Matusow, Paul Crouch, and Manning Johnson. While defending the board's order on appeal, "[t]he Government," the Supreme Court emphasized, "did not deny" the perjury allegations. Holding that "[w]e cannot pass upon a record containing such challenged testimony," the Court reversed the board's order and returned the case to it to be decided on a record that excluded the perjured testimony. At the Court's conference, Chief Justice Earl Warren had told his colleagues, "I have decided to reverse on Matusow's evidence." Several other justices quickly agreed.[17]

In a similar decision a few months later, the Court reversed the Smith Act convictions of Steve Nelson and other Communist Party officials because Joseph Mazzei, a "paid informer of the Government" who testified for the prosecution, had admittedly committed perjury in other tribunals. Finding the convictions "tainted," the Court ruled "there can be no other just result than to accord [the defendants] a new trial."[18]

* * *

Matusow's trial for perjury, presided over by Judge John F. X. McGohey, began on September 17, 1956. It proved to be a one-sided contest.[19]

The central issue was the truth or falsity of Matusow's charge in the new trial proceedings before Judge Dimock that Roy Cohn had induced him to testify falsely at the trial. Matusow's version was contradicted not only by Cohn but also by a procession of five of Cohn's fellow prosecutors and by an FBI agent who had been present at the December 1951 parked-car meeting.[20] Cohn's appearance, on the second and third days of the trial, provided some small element of drama. "Matusow, now a slight 148 pounds, with his black hair crew-cut, never took his eyes off Mr. Cohn's face," the *New York Times* reported. Cohn, the *Times* said, was "calm and confident" and "spoke briskly." Both men—Bronx natives—were twenty-nine years old.[21]

In his testimony, Cohn flatly denied Matusow's claim that he had suggested, at a meeting on February 17, 1952, that Matusow utilize a conversation with Alexander Trachtenberg concerning the Vishinsky book to show Trachtenberg advocated violent overthrow of the government. "Other than exchange of pleasantries," Cohn insisted, he and Matusow had not talked at all that day. "I was walking by and he was standing there waiting for Mr. Blinder [another assistant U.S. attorney]," Cohn said, "and it was hello, hello."[22]

Matusow presented an almost perfunctory defense. Represented by Stanley Faulkner, who had counseled him at the SISS hearings, he testified during his short direct examination that his charges against Cohn were truthful. However, on cross-examination by prosecutor Thomas Bolan, Matusow was a sitting duck: an admitted perjurer facing a charge of perjury. Bolan began as follows:

Q: Mr. Matusow, you have been a vicious liar? Is that correct? . . .
A: I can answer it yes with a qualification, that it refers to the part of my life prior to 1955, parts of 1954, I would say.
Q: You are not a vicious liar now, in other words? Is that correct?
A: No, I am not.
Q: When did you stop being a vicious liar?
A: When I found faith in God.
Q: I said when, Mr. Matusow. . . .
The Court: Can you fix the time? . . .
A: I will answer it as best I can. I don't want to sound evasive, but it took me more than just a few months to undo what 27 years of lying had done.[23]

Asked about a statement in his August 1953 letter to McCarthy that his testimony in the Smith Act case was honest, Matusow testified, "I did lie when I told him I told the truth." He admitted lying to the local police in Amarillo when he was detained at the hotel there and to the two Justice Department attorneys who interviewed him following his return from Taos. His cross-examination continued in this vein well into the following day. He was the only defense witness.[24]

Closing arguments were brief. U.S. Attorney Paul Williams argued that Matusow accused Cohn in order to boost sales of his book and to "discredit" the government's "fight . . . against the Communist menace." Faulkner responded that "[t]o stop [Matusow] from recanting is to stop every person who ever lied under oath from coming forward to admit it."[25]

The jury received the case on September 26, after the lunch recess. It required only ninety minutes of deliberation before returning a guilty verdict on all five counts submitted to it (the sixth had been dismissed by the judge). Matusow, the *New York Times* reported, "sat worried and pale, his head cupped in his hands, as the verdict was announced." But an unnamed "high-ranking" government official was quoted by the *Times* as "express[ing] relief" at the verdict: "It will have a far-reaching effect on informers everywhere."[26]

Judge McGohey set bail at ten thousand dollars and announced that he would sentence Matusow two days later. Unable to make bail, Matusow turned himself in to federal marshals. On September 28, Judge McGohey sentenced Matusow to five years' imprisonment and denied bail pending appeal.[27]

Before sentence was passed, Matusow addressed the court, denying that he had committed perjury. He added, in words the *Times* termed "theatrical": "I feel I've done some good. My past is dead as far as I'm concerned. Harvey Matusow is dead. He died a year ago. I am the individual who took his body and must accept the consequences. I will never have to be ashamed of anything I do from this day forward."[28]

* * *

Matusow appealed his conviction, but he spent three months in the federal penitentiary at Lewisburg, Pennsylvania, before the court of appeals in Manhattan, over the government's objection, allowed him bail pending appeal, which it set at five thousand dollars. His mother again posted bail, and Matusow was released on January 4, 1957.[29]

"I'm job hunting," he wrote optimistically to Kahn a few days later, "and hope to become a breadwinner before weeks end—It seems that my three months at Lewisburg have only made me more determined to move forward, taking only from the past which was good and which was honest." On January 25, he wrote: "Since my last letter I've found work. I'm now the Advertising Production Manager of CASTRO CONVERTIBLE's—the two-purpose sofa that a five-year-old child can operate. . . . If things go well, and I don't return to Lewisburg, I'll probably stay a[t] Castro and someday own the place."[30]

But Matusow's optimism proved unfounded. In February, his father died.

"It me[a]nt a lot to [my mother] having me home when it happ[e]ned," he wrote Kahn, "and I might add, it also me[a]nt a lot to me being home then." By mid-March, he was out of a job. After Castro Convertibles, he had found work at Advance Printing under the name "Harvey Marshall" until, only a day or so later, someone called the owner to identify him. Matusow also separated from his wife. In letters to the Kahns, he described the bitterness that had arisen between him and Ellen, and he expressed particular anger at being separated from his stepdaughter: "Ellen refuses to let me see Susie and there is nothing I can do about it." Once again, he retreated to his mother's Bronx apartment.[31]

In April, Matusow found an advertising-production job with Gussin-Radin Studios where, he wrote Kahn, "I am the straw boss for about fifteen people, artists, paste up people, retouchers and photographers." "We handle some pretty big accounts," he boasted, "and if I were to win the appeal and stay out I could really move in a creative way."[32]

But in May, the court of appeals affirmed his perjury conviction. A unanimous three-judge panel (including Harold R. Medina, promoted to the appellate court as an apparent reward for his services during the 1949 Foley Square Smith Act trial) had little difficulty in rejecting Matusow's appeal. His principal ground for appeal—that prejudicial error occurred when the prosecutor told the jury in his opening statement that Matusow's purpose in recanting was "to release from prison thirteen enemies of the United States Government, thirteen Communist Party leaders"—was, the court said in its short opinion, "so plainly without substance that we shall not discuss it."[33]

* * *

Matusow returned to Lewisburg in June. Initially, he told Kahn, he did "hard time": "I was having all kinds of feelings about why I shouldn't be in prison." But his attitude shifted dramatically in October, he said, when the Soviet Union launched Sputnik:

> [H]ere I was, looking out of my prison cell window at the prison wall which, I believe, was 21 feet high in Lewisburg. And I was thinking of what I was listening to on the head set which was pumping in an outside radio station. . . . I was thinking every hour and a half, the consciousness of humanity is up there. . . . Because we were seeing ourselves for the first time. This little ball became this mirror going around the earth every 90 minutes and I broke up laughing. I started to laugh and thought how ludicrous this stupid prison . . . it was really ludicrous. A 21 foot wall and the consciousness of humanity, which I was part of.

His laughter attracted two guards to his cell and soon an assistant warden. "[Y]ou know," Matusow stated, "I just realized that I'm free."[34]

Thereafter, Matusow's time in prison, at least as he described it to Kahn years later, became "4 magnificent years of study in a cloistered world." He read widely in the prison's library (whose librarian, until his death in prison, was Wilhelm Reich, the eccentric Viennese psychotherapist who ran afoul of the Food and Drug Administration), painted, wrote poetry, gave readings, and produced and directed plays. He told Kahn: "The only time I ever got reviewed for a dramatic work that I did, although I'd been in and out of theatre as you know Albert, for many years, was when I was in prison when the Sunday Herald Tribune reviewed our Mr. Roberts! I thought that was ironical. And mentioned me by name. I got a named review in the Herald Tribune for a play I did in prison." "I did all the things I would have done if I'd gone to a 4 year university," he added. "And I did them much more efficiently."[35]

* * *

Matusow's return to Lewisburg in June 1957 followed by roughly a month Joe McCarthy's death—of liver failure, at age forty-eight. Following his censure over two years earlier, the Wisconsin senator had lived in virtual disgrace, without significant political influence.[36]

On June 3, the Supreme Court reversed Clinton Jencks's conviction, mandating in the future the availability of FBI statements to enable defense counsel to cross-examine government witnesses. Chief Justice Warren had commented at the Court's conference on the need to determine whether the FBI reports "are inconsistent with the testimony of Matusow." "This paid informer," he said, "is testifying to everything he can think of to incriminate a man over a period of years." When John McTernan, arguing for Jencks in the Supreme Court, mentioned Matusow's recantation, Warren leaned forward in his chair: "Yes, Mr. McTernan, tell us about that."[37]

Two weeks later, on June 17, the Court ruled against the government in four "Communist" cases—a day that critics termed "Red Monday."[38]

11 Four Decades of Aftermath

Released from prison on August 8, 1960, Matusow, only thirty-three years old, quite obviously faced a difficult future. His political life was ended, for he was anathema to both left and right. His notoriety and reputation as a perjurer seemingly disqualified him from any position of trust. Yet, in the subsequent years, Matusow displayed energy and versatility in fashioning a life for himself—a decent and productive life, which, if not free of hubris and restlessness, contained none of the destructiveness of his earlier years.[1]

For about six years, Matusow lived in New York City and worked in art publishing ventures. He helped to edit *The New York Arts Calendar*, to compile *The Art Collector's Almanac*, and to found an underground newspaper, the *East Village Other*. He remarried; his new wife, Beatrice Lysander Wolf, was, he said, a spirited young woman of Greek American descent, whom he met in a Greenwich Village bar shortly before returning to Lewisburg in June 1957. She visited and corresponded with him during his prison years and after their marriage gave birth to their daughter, Ann. However, this marriage, like his earlier ones, had a relatively short duration.[2]

While Matusow had hoped that the generally left-of-center individuals active in the art world would, by reason of his recantation, accord him a measure of acceptance, he was instead widely vilified. In the mid-1960s, after performing extensive research on a project to catalog and reproduce the Works Progress Administration art in public buildings, his work came to naught when two large foundations offered funding for the project only on the condition that he withdraw from it. Discouraged and angry, he decided to leave the United States—but for a time had difficulty obtaining a passport.[3]

In 1966, Matusow departed on *The American Veteran*, an ocean freighter

bound for Liverpool. He termed his trip a "self-imposed exile." "I never wanted to see America again," he wrote. He took with him on the ten-day voyage
twenty-two pieces of luggage, containing all of his McCarthy-era papers.[4]

* * *

Arriving in London in 1966 "not knowing a soul," Matusow found a remark-
ably rich life in the arts and journalism. "I just had a very, very full life," he
later told Albert Kahn. He "made a whole new career for himself," Charles
Alverson wrote in *Rolling Stone* in 1972, "as an entrepreneur, broadcaster,
writer, oddball and musician."[5]

Within a year of his arrival, Alverson reported, Matusow "had founded the
London Film Makers' Coop and organized Britain's first underground film
festival." He became an "uncle-figure to the London underground," active
in several underground publications. He formed Harvey Matusow's Jew's
Harp Band, which recorded albums and performed concerts at which hundreds of Jew's harps were given away to the audience. (The Jew's harp, he
explained to Kahn, was "an instrument that I could just play and put my soul
into.") When his Jew's Harp Band dissolved, Matusow organized Naked
Software, a band with an entirely different sound. "If I can find peace in
sound," he told *Rolling Stone,* "it means I can find other types of peace as
well." England was free of McCarthy-era baggage.[6]

Matusow compiled and edited an anticomputer book, published in London in 1968, entitled *The Beast of Business: A Record of Computer Atrocities.*
A German translation of this work was published the following year. He
freelanced for the BBC as a journalist and commentator and served as Euro-
pean editor of an avant-garde music magazine called *Source.* He donated his
private papers from the McCarthy years—he had discarded very little—to
the University of Sussex in Brighton, which he believed had a good American studies program.[7]

Matusow married again in 1967. His new wife, Anna Lockwood, was an
avant-garde composer from New Zealand, whom *Saturday Review* described
as "soft, ethereal . . . one of the most impressive of avant-garde composers."
Some of her compositions consisted of the sounds of broken glass. The couple
lived together in a cottage in Essex County, twenty-two miles from London.[8]

Matusow and Lockwood in 1972 promoted the International Carnival of
Experimental Sound, a sixteen-day, avant-garde music extravaganza—the
highlight of Matusow's years in London. The event, termed "an instant clas-
sic" by *Saturday Review,* was "paid for and played for by the stockholding
composers, choreographers, filmmakers, happening makers, and poets."
Performances were presented in several venues: a nineteenth-century rail-

road roundhouse, refurbished to accommodate three stages, a pub, and a health-food restaurant; a dance center called The Place; and a train, rented by the promoters, between London and Edinburgh.[9] Opening night featured *Hpschd*, a composition by the American composer John Cage utilizing seven harpsichords, electronic sound, and multiscreen projections (the audience of two thousand, according to *Saturday Review*, "didn't seem to know what to do and, being British, fell into a polite if edgy silence"). Another feature was a nude performance, from behind a cello made of ice, by cellist Charlotte Moorman ("a virtuoso performance," *SR* gushed, "legendary in proportion"). But the London-Edinburgh train ride, the magazine said, "found all the artists so bereft of audience and so taken with the English-Scottish countryside that only a few performed their practiced train pieces." It described the promoter, Matusow, as a "portly, forty-five-year-old, ex-Communist American expatriate hustler" who "is himself an avant-garde piece, a walking shock value."[10]

The following year, Matusow returned to the United States. His decision to abandon his full life in England, he told Kahn, stemmed from a 1972 letter he received from Beatrice, his ex-wife, advising, "It's time to stop. Stop, be in one place and be at peace with yourself." He likened himself to a Somerset Maugham character who, he said, "travelled around always seeking the wisdom, always seeking the wisdom. This insatiable hunger that the character had, never fulfilling it." Anna Lockwood came with Matusow to America, but they separated within a few months of their arrival.[11]

* * *

Upon his return to the United States in 1973, Matusow joined the "flower" generation. Asked to assist a western Massachusetts commune in preparing a radio program, he visited the place; "once I came up," he said, "I realized there was something here beyond that which I had ever known." The community of perhaps two hundred persons, most of them much younger than Matusow, located in and around Turners Falls, a tiny, depressed mill town, called itself "The Renaissance Church of Beauty."[12]

For several years, Matusow resided at the Ammal's Garden commune. He lived a "very basic lifestyle," he told Kahn. "Using wood, living without electricity." The members of the community, he said, took "vows of poverty" and gave "everything we have for the betterment of the world around us." He felt "freer in all of the energy that I've lived with": his reference was to "[t]his so-called psychic thing. This ability to read minds or whatever you want to call it. Or see things. You know, like finding my brother's grave."[13]

He met Emily Babbitt, a farmer and ordained minister, who would soon become his wife in a fifteen-year marriage. He assumed the biblical name Job—a change he traces to a bleak day in February 1957 when, temporarily free on bail following his perjury conviction, he learned within a span of hours that his father had died, his wife wished to end their marriage, his employer had fired him, and his lawyer expected the appellate court soon to affirm his conviction. When Matusow's mother died, she left him, after a frugal life, a substantial sum of money—part of which he used to take Emily on an around-the-world trip and the remainder, he said, he gave away to good causes.[14]

When Kahn visited in 1976, to conduct an interview for his book on Matusow's recantation, his friend's lifestyle occasioned puzzlement. Not that Kahn was unfamiliar with utopian societies; but after meeting some of the longhaired young persons in Matusow's commune, he was troubled by what he termed their "separation from the past." They had been "mistaught," he told Matusow, by teachers "afraid to teach the truth" and had "grown up in the shadow of the atom bomb." He contrasted the political impotence of the commune with the power wielded by the Pentagon and "the rulers of this land and the rulers of the system." "The torturers are really in power in this land, still," he said emphatically.[15]

* * *

In 1978, Matusow and his wife, Emily, moved to Tucson—he had come to Arizona in response to an offer to work as a radio disc jockey—and he rejoined the Church of Jesus Christ of Latter Day Saints, from which he had separated in the period following his recantation. Emily elected to join the church and was baptized. The Mormon religion continued to hold appeal for him, Matusow said, because of its communal character and the fact that Mormons, like Jews, had been persecuted by mainstream Christian denominations. He was comfortable in rejoining the Church in 1978, he told an interviewer, because by then it had dropped its ban on blacks serving in the Mormon priesthood.[16]

In Tucson, Matusow became active in children's theater, obtaining funding to organize a theater company that performed in schools. The Associated Press reported in September 1981 that the company, which then numbered about seventeen, "had been performing free near the Tucson zoo but hopes to sell the program to public television stations." Matusow also produced and appeared in a series of five-minute children's programs for National Public Radio.[17]

When a city-run facility was closed, he and Emily opened a kitchen for the homeless called the Natural Balance Cafe. The story was evidently newsworthy: "Ex-McCarthy ally and foe now feeds city's poor," headlined the *Arizo-*

na Daily Star of November 14, 1982. Eight days later, the *Arizona Republic* headlined, "Trials of Job: Folk hero feeds the poor after life filled with exploits." On Christmas Eve 1982, Matusow, "an imposing 230–pound Santa Claus figure with a gray beard," headed a procession of "50 unshaven and bedraggled transients" (the descriptions were by the *National Catholic Reporter*) to Tucson's St. Augustine's Cathedral, which had cancelled midnight mass and locked its doors, and led them in caroling. And he testified once again before a congressional committee in Washington, this one studying homeless issues—an experience he described as "very surreal."[18]

When Emily fell seriously ill, they returned at her request to Massachusetts. Living on a farm outside Orange, near the New Hampshire border, the couple distributed food and clothing from school buses in the town, making regular trips to New York City to raise funds. In 1984, with others, they formed the Gandhi Peace Center as a nonprofit organization to serve as an umbrella for their activities, which now also included ad hoc shipments of clothing to Native American reservations.[19]

Upon Emily's death in 1989, Matusow returned to Tucson, where he remained active in activities for the homeless and produced *Magic Mouse Magazine,* a series of children's television programs in which he appeared as a clown named "Cockyboo." In one unusual *Magic Mouse* episode, the Dalai Lama made a guest appearance—Matusow had earlier voiced support for Tibetan independence—performing with Matusow's clown and a horde of small children.[20]

In the years following Emily's death, he entered into a series of short-lived marriages.[21]

＊ ＊ ＊

Learning that Utah had no public-access cable television station, Matusow in 1995 moved to the tiny town of Glenwood in central Utah (population 450) and in the following year began to operate SCAT-TV (Sevier County Access Television) from an old school bus crammed with equipment parked in his backyard. The station, which later expanded its area of service, served the nearby city of Richfield (population 7,500), the county seat, and towns in several adjoining counties with local-event programming, Mormon religious films, and regular episodes of *Magic Mouse Magazine.*[22]

To the walls of his small home, Matusow attached an eclectic collection of unframed photos and posters—images of Joe McCarthy, Roy Cohn (with whom he said he reconciled in later years), and the Dalai Lama among them. He became active in the largely Mormon community, helping to raise funds for a new health care facility. While local residents "initially may have looked with suspicion" on him, Glenwood's mayor, Glen Warner, told the *Salt Lake Tribune*, "they warmed to him when they saw the talent and energy he was ready to invest in their community." The mayor added that he "lends a little notoriety to the community."[23]

Never one to shun publicity, Matusow in January 1997 was the subject of a laudatory piece ("The World of Job Matusow") in the *Tribune*. Terming him a "humanitarian" and "tireless performer of good works in Sevier County," the newspaper had a simple description of Matusow's McCarthy-era role (presumably provided by Matusow): "By lying so spectacularly when he identified hundreds of 'Communists' during the 1950s, Matusow was actually setting up Joseph McCarthy and his fellow red-baiters. By later publicly admitting to that perjury, Matusow exposed McCarthyism for the hysteria it was." The article closed with his observation that "[w]hen I'm gone, some future generation will do something with the myth of Harvey Matusow. But not in my lifetime. It's not what the Lord wants for me."[24]

Matusow returned to New England in 2001 to take a job with a public-access cable station in Claremont, New Hampshire—selected for the job, he told a caller, over fifteen other applicants. Two months later, Matusow spoke of moving back into the same house in nearby Wendell, Massachusetts, in which he had lived with Emily. It cost him only a dollar, he said, but a lot of fixing-up was necessary. He was at work on a series of three-hour television programs on the rich artistic life of the Connecticut River Valley.[25]

* * *

Matusow died on January 17, 2002, at age seventy-five, of complications from injuries suffered in an automobile accident in Claremont on January 2. The accident was garden variety: Matusow's car, making a left turn, was struck by an oncoming vehicle.[26]

The *New York Times*'s obituary described him harshly as "a paid informer who named more than two hundred people as Communists or Communist sympathizers in the early 1950s, only to recant and say he lied in almost every instance." It repeated a comment about Matusow by Albert Kahn's son, Brian, who said that "[s]how-off is not enough of a word." Matusow's later years were mentioned only in passing.[27]

Epilogue:
A Note on the Historians

A half-century later, with the release of VENONA and KGB materials, historians' views of the McCarthy era remain polarized. The new materials, to be sure, make it vastly more difficult for any historian to deny that a number of American Communists assisted in Soviet espionage prior to and during World War II (and few do deny it); but the debate continues as to "what follows from that?"—that is, the degree of culpability to be assigned these individuals and, more broadly, whether the government's actions in the political sphere during the McCarthy era are thereby legitimized. Historians' evaluations of Matusow's role have been primarily a by-product of their views of the era itself. And because Matusow betrayed both ends of the political spectrum, the final judgments are almost uniformly negative.[1]

Left-of-center historians ("revisionists" to the other side), sharply critical of McCarthy-era practices, condemn Matusow as a reckless informer whose false accusations destroyed lives. They view his recantation as further proof that the Justice Department and congressional investigating committees used any witness, no matter how unreliable, who served their ends. More conservative historians (often termed "traditionalists"), inclined to justify many practices of the era as responsive to a genuine espionage threat, and perhaps embarrassed by Matusow's recantation, prefer to ignore him; but if he is mentioned, they credit the government with discarding him and fault him for having joined "anti-anti-Communists" when he recanted.

Among the former group, Fred J. Cook refers to Matusow as "that ubiquitous agent of the witch hunt who had been passed from hand to hand, from McCarthy to McCarran" but terms his recantation "a declaration of conscience." Victor Navasky presents a similar viewpoint, describing Matusow as having "informed on the informers." Ellen Schrecker, troubled by the harsh impact of Matusow's testimony, "much" of it "false," on Clinton Jencks and the Mine, Mill, and Smelter Workers union, terms him "an unstable character" and "congenitally dishonest." David Caute, in his encyclopedic history of the era, calls Matusow's "spectacular recantation" "[t]he major scandal of the time."[2]

Among "traditionalist" historians, Richard Gid Powers, in his "history of American anticommunism," does not mention Matusow. Nor does Sam Tanenhaus, in his full biography of Whittaker Chambers. Matusow is not mentioned in the Harvey Klehr and John Earl Haynes histories of the CPUSA, presumably due to the insignificance of his role in the party. Haynes's 1996 *Red Scare or Red Menace? American Communism and Anticommunism in the Cold War Era,* which does discuss Matusow, attributes his recantation to prosecutors having "grown uneasy about his reliability" and says that "he quickly became a professional 'anti-anti-Communist.'"[3]

More recently, the work of an unabashedly conservative historian, Arthur Herman's *Joseph McCarthy: Reexamining the Life and Legacy of America's Most Hated Senator,* describes Matusow as an FBI informant and witness who "ma[de] a small name for himself as a lecturer and author" and "even worked for" McCarthy. He suggests that Matusow's article, "Reds in Khaki," in *American Legion Magazine* in 1952 "may have helped steer McCarthy's attention toward the Army." But, Herman writes, after "law enforcement officials began to get leery about Matusow's increasingly sensational claims and his emotional instability," he "lost his audience" and "skipped to the other side," providing fodder for the "anti-anti-Communist left."[4]

Matusow appears more prominently in Kathryn S. Olmsted's biography of Elizabeth Bentley, by reason of his personal friendship with Bentley, albeit a very brief one, and his willingness to offer quotable assessments of her state of mind. Olmsted terms Matusow, who met Bentley during his testifying years, "the Boy Stalinist."[5]

Daniel J. Leab's recent book on Matt Cvetic's life is the first biography of a professional McCarthy-era political informer. While Cvetic never recanted, his career bears obvious parallels to Matusow's. Both were undercover FBI informants dismissed by the bureau under circumstances indicating a lack of trust. Both, however, traded heavily on their FBI connections in pursuing careers as informer-witnesses and became the subject of repeated (and largely unheeded) warnings by the bureau to the Department of Justice. Although unstable in their personal lives and unreliable as witnesses, both were used repeatedly in major cases.[6]

Hoover and the FBI, who suffered mightily at the hands of historians in the intervening years, turn out not to bear primary responsibility for the use of untruthful informer-witnesses. The FBI director, to be sure, merely papered the files with warnings to the Justice Department about Matusow, Cvetic, and others, declining to spend his own vast political capital to insure that unreliable witnesses were, in fact, disqualified. But it was the Justice Department's lawyers who made the ultimate decisions.[7] The historians' portrait of Matusow (it is only fair to add) is oversimplified. While reckless and destructive as an informer-witness, he displayed, at other times, resilience and even courage (as he did following his recantation and during his subsequent imprisonment). If, like Woody Allen's Zelig, he too readily assumed the prevailing political coloration, he was hardly alone. And unlike other McCarthy-era figures bearing equivalent or greater guilt, Matusow paid his dues, serving over three years in prison. The life he led afterward, if peripatetic and at times selfish, was useful and free of the destructive disregard for others that characterized his government-fostered career as an informer.

Notes

Introduction

1. *New York Times,* Feb. 22, 1955 ("No Longer a Liar, Matusow Swears").
2. *New York Times,* Jan. 29, 1955 ("Red Informer Says He Lied at Trial"), Feb. 1, 1955 ("Anti-Red Witness Confesses He Lied"), Feb. 4, 1955 ("Matusow Termed 'Planted' Witness"), Feb 6, 1955 ("Jackson Demands Matusow Inquiry"), and Feb. 6, 1955, sec. 4 ("Role of Informers Now under Inquiry"). See chaps. 8 and 9. His book, published in March, was Harvey Matusow, *False Witness* (New York: Cameron and Kahn, 1955).
3. *New York Times,* Feb. 22, 1955 ("No Longer a Liar, Matusow Swears").
4. *Strategy and Tactics of World Communism: The Significance of the Matusow Case: Hearing before the Subcommittee to Investigate the Administration of the Internal Security Act and Other Internal Security Laws of the Senate Committee on the Judiciary,* 84th Cong., 1st Sess. (1955) (hereafter, Matusow Hearings), 33, 44, 46. Henceforth, the subcommittee will be referred to by its more familiar name, the Senate Internal Security Subcommittee, or SISS.
5. Ibid., 55, 83–84.
6. Ibid., 45. See also chaps. 1 and 7.
7. Matusow Hearings, 87, 207, 289, 447, 969; Senate Internal Security Subcommittee, *Strategy and Tactics of World Communism (Significance of the Matusow Case),* S. Rep. No. 2050, 84th Cong., 1st Sess. (1955) (hereafter, SISS Matusow Report), 87–90.
8. Kempton quoted in Albert Kahn, *The Matusow Affair: Memoir of a National Scandal* (Mt. Kisco, N.Y.: Moyer Bell, 1987), 121.
9. Richard H. Rovere, "The Kept Witnesses," in *The American Establishment and Other Reports, Opinions, and Speculations* (New York: Harcourt, Brace, 1962), 117–20 (quotations), reprinted from *Harper's* magazine, May 1955; Michal R. Belknap, *Cold War Political Justice: The Smith Act, the Communist Party, and American Civil Liberties* (Westport, Conn.: Greenwood Press, 1977), 164–65. David Caute, *The Great Fear: The Anti-Communist Purge under Truman and Eisenhower* (New York: Simon and Schuster, 1978), 116–38; and Frank Donner, "The Informer," *The Nation,* Apr. 10, 1954, 298–309. See also chap. 9, pp. 143–44.

10. Rovere, "Kept Witnesses," 119, 122. Rovere distinguished the use of paid informers by police departments or the Internal Revenue Service to provide evidence of crime, not primarily to testify. A further distinction is the political character of the informers' testimony.

11. John B. Oakes, *New York Times,* Sept. 23, 1951, Sunday Book Review ("Elizabeth Bentley's Own Story").

12. For Bentley's testimony see *Hearings Regarding Communist Espionage in the United States Government, Before the House Committee on Un-American Activities,* 80th Cong., 2d Sess. (1948), 503–62. For Chambers's testimony see ibid., 563–84.

13. On Chambers and Berle see Sam Tanenhaus, *Whittaker Chambers: A Biography* (New York: Random House, 1997), 161–63; Allen Weinstein and Alexander Vassiliev, *The Haunted Wood: Soviet Espionage in America—The Stalin Era* (New York: Random House, 1999), 47–48; and John Earl Haynes and Harvey Klehr, *Venona: Decoding Soviet Espionage in America* (New Haven, Conn.: Yale University Press, 1999), 90–92. On Bentley see Elizabeth Terrill Bentley, 112-page statement to FBI, Nov. 30, 1945 (hereafter, Bentley Nov. 30, 1945, statement), obtained from the FBI via a Freedom of Information Act (FOIA) request; *Interlocking Subversion in Government Departments: Hearings before the Senate Internal Security Subcommittee,* 83rd Cong., 1st Sess. (1953) (hereafter, 1953 White Hearings), 1112–14; Kathryn S. Olmsted, *Red Spy Queen: A Biography of Elizabeth Bentley* (Chapel Hill: University of North Carolina Press, 2002), 97–107, 115; and Curt Gentry, *J. Edgar Hoover: The Man and His Secrets* (New York: W. W. Norton, 1991), 342–44. See also Lauren Kessler, *Clever Girl: Elizabeth Bentley, the Spy Who Ushered in the McCarthy Era* (New York: Harper Collins, 2003).

14. Gentry, *J. Edgar Hoover,* 352, 357–58; Richard Gid Powers, *Secrecy and Power: The Life of J. Edgar Hoover* (New York: Free Press, 1987), 280, 288–89. In Athan Theoharis's view, the FBI, by virtue of its consistent reliance upon illegal wiretaps and break-ins, was itself largely responsible for the near total failure to prosecute the many government employees identified by Bentley (*Chasing Spies: How the FBI Failed in Counterintelligence but Promoted the Politics of McCarthyism in the Cold War Years* [Chicago: Ivan R. Dee, 2002], 43–45, 95–97, 239–40).

15. See sources cited in nn. 12 and 13 (above); and Tanenhaus, *Whittaker Chambers,* 212–335. See also Earl Latham, *The Communist Controversy in Washington: From the New Deal to McCarthy* (Cambridge, Mass.: Harvard University Press, 1966), 159–209; and Herbert L. Packer, *Ex-Communist Witnesses: Four Studies in Fact Finding* (Stanford, Calif.: Stanford University Press, 1962), 21–120.

16. Weinstein and Vassiliev, *Haunted Wood,* 84–109, 153–71, 223–80; Haynes and Klehr, *Venona,* 62–67, 93–163, 339–70; Thomas Powers, "The Plot Thickens," in *Intelligence Wars: America's Secret History from Hitler to Al-Qaeda* (New York: New York Review of Books, 2002), 83–92, 106–7. See also *VENONA: Soviet Espionage and the American Response, 1939–1957,* ed. Robert Louis Benson and Michael Warner (Washington, D.C.: National Security Agency/Central Intelligence Agency, 1996), vii, xxxiii. Athan Theoharis concludes that the VENONA messages "provide conclusive evidence" of the willingness of some American Communists either to spy for the Soviets or to recruit others to do so, but he questions whether the new records provide support for the accusations against Hiss (*Chasing Spies,* 15–21, 28–31, 237). Ellen Schrecker, citing the numerous undeciphered gaps in the

VENONA materials, declines to view them "with complete confidence" (*Many Are the Crimes: McCarthyism in America* [Boston: Little, Brown, 1998], xvii–xviii).

17. Histories of the CPUSA make clear the party's primary reliance on political means. Harvey Klehr and John Earl Haynes, in *The American Communist Movement: Storming Heaven Itself* (New York: Twayne, 1992), wrote: "The party promoted communism and the interests of the Soviet Union through political means; espionage was the business of the Soviet Union's intelligence services. To see the American Communist Party chiefly as an instrument of espionage or a sort of fifth column misjudges its main purpose" (108). In 1999, Haynes and Klehr wrote that "it still remains true that the CPUSA's chief task was the promotion of communism and the interests of the Soviet Union through political means," although they now added that "it is equally true that the CPUSA was indeed a fifth column working inside and against the United States in the Cold War" (*Venona*, 7). The authors counted in the deciphered VENONA messages "349 citizens, immigrants, and permanent residents of the United States" who had a covert relationship with Soviet intelligence (almost all no later than 1945), "many of whom were members of" the CPUSA (ibid., 9). See also Maurice Isserman, *Which Side Were You On? The American Communist Party during the Second World War* (Urbana: University of Illinois Press, 1993); and Schrecker, *Many Are the Crimes*, 3–41.

18. The Truman loyalty program was instituted by Executive Order No. 9835, 12 Fed. Reg. 1935 (Mar. 21, 1947). See Eleanor Bontecou, *The Federal Loyalty-Security Program* (Ithaca, N.Y.: Cornell University Press, 1953); Ralph S. Brown Jr., *Loyalty and Security: Employments Tests in the United States* (New Haven, Conn.: Yale University Press, 1958), 21–91; and Caute, *Great Fear*, 268–72. The Eisenhower program, promulgated in Executive Order No. 10450, 18 Fed. Reg. 2489 (Apr. 27, 1953), merged "loyalty" and "suitability" criteria (Richard M. Fried, *Nightmare in Red: The McCarthy Era in Perspective* [New York: Oxford University Press, 1990], 133). The number of federal employees during the Eisenhower years, substantially all subject to screening under the program, was roughly 2.3 million (*Security and Constitutional Rights: Hearings before the Subcommittee on Constitutional Rights of the Senate Judiciary Committee*, 84th Cong., 2d Sess. [1955] [hereafter, Hennings Hearings], 227, 766).

19. The attorney general's list was, in fact, an expansion of an earlier list of 47 groups, created during World War II. When first published in the *Federal Register*, 13 Fed Reg. 1473 (Mar. 20, 1948), the list included close to 80 organizations; by 1954, it had reached 280. See *Joint Anti-Fascist Refugee Committee v. McGrath*, 341 U.S. 123, 127–29 (1951) (opinion of Burton, J.); Fried, *Nightmare in Red*, 55, 70–71; Frank J. Donner, *The Age of Surveillance: The Aims and Methods of America's Political Intelligence System* (New York: Vintage Books, 1981), 27 and 27 n; and Hennings Hearings, 224–26.

20. Caute, *Great Fear*, 228–30. The constitutionality of the 1950 legislation, §22 of the Internal Security Act, was upheld in *Galvan v. Press*, 347 U.S. 522 (1954).

21. Undated memo re: Davidoff case in materials for June 30, 1955, meeting of the Department of Justice, Departmental Committee on Security Witnesses, file 56363/252, RG 85, National Archives (hereafter, DOJ DCSW minutes); Caute, *Great Fear*, 241.

22. Hennings Hearings, 86–216; Stanley I. Kutler, *The American Inquisition: Justice and Injustice in the Cold War* (New York: Hill and Wang, 1982), 89–117; Caute, *Great Fear*, 245–

51; *San Francisco Chronicle,* Nov. 7, 1997 ("Rehabilitating Robeson"). The Supreme Court decision was *Kent v. Dulles,* 357 U.S. 116 (1958).

23. See Belknap, *Cold War Political Justice,* 82–90, 164–66. On Matusow's recanted testimony see *United States v. Flynn,* 130 F. Supp. 413, 418–19 (S.D.N.Y. 1955). See also chaps. 4 and 8.

24. The registration requirements were enacted as part of the Internal Security Act of 1950, 64 Stat. 987.

25. See Matusow Hearings, 1148–49. See also chap. 6, pp. 96–97.

26. On HUAC see Walter Goodman, *The Committee: The Extraordinary Career of the House Committee on Un-American Activities* (New York: Farrar, Straus and Giroux, 1968); and Athan G. Theoharis and John Stuart Cox, *The Boss: J. Edgar Hoover and the Great American Inquisition* (Philadelphia: Temple University Press, 1988), 215. On SISS and McCarran see Robert P. Newman, *Owen Lattimore and the "Loss" of China* (Berkeley: University of California Press, 1992), 265–86, 314–17, 339–43, 382–83, 450; Kutler, *American Inquisition,* 183–214; and Fred J. Cook, *The Nightmare Decade: The Life and Times of Senator Joe McCarthy* (New York: Random House, 1971), 319–21, 324. On Matusow's testimony see chap. 3, pp. 54–55, and chap. 8, p. 118.

27. Hennings Hearings, 249–329; Caute, *Great Fear,* 70–74. A summary of state and local antisubversive statutes and ordinances, prepared by the Library of Congress, appears on pp. 252–80 of the Hennings Hearings. The Supreme Court in *Pennsylvania v. Nelson,* 350 U.S. 497 (1956), held that state and local criminal enactments were preempted by federal legislation. On teachers see Brown, *Loyalty and Security,* 168–69. On Matusow as a consultant see chap. 3, p. 56.

28. On the film industry blacklist see, generally, John Cogley, *Report on Blacklisting,* vol. 1, *Movies* (New York: Fund for the Republic, 1956); Victor S. Navasky, *Naming Names* (New York: Viking Press, 1980); and Larry Ceplair and Steven Englund, *The Inquisition in Hollywood: Politics in the Film Community, 1930–1960* (Urbana: University of Illinois Press, 2003). On *Red Channels* and *Counterattack* see John Cogley, *Report on Blacklisting,* vol. 2, *Radio-Television* (New York: Fund for the Republic, 1956), 1–21, 59–61; and Richard Gid Powers, *Not without Honor: The History of American Anticommunism* (New York: Free Press, 1995), 247–48. See also chap. 4, pp. 62–65. On "Appendix IX" see Donner, *Age of Surveillance,* 421; Goodman, *Committee,* 160; Robert K. Carr, *The House Committee on Un-American Activities, 1945–1950* (Ithaca, N.Y.: Cornell University Press, 1952), 338–39; and Martin Dies, *Martin Dies' Story* (New York: Bookmailer, 1963), 112, 166.

29. Samuel A. Stouffer, *Communism, Conformity, and Civil Liberties* (New York: Doubleday, 1955), 13–25, 41–45, 105, 234.

30. On McCarthy's speech see *New York Times,* Oct. 28, 1952 ("M'Carthy Terms Stevenson Unfit" and editorial, "The M'Carthy Speech"); Thomas C. Reeves, *The Life and Times of Joe McCarthy: A Biography* (New York: Stein and Day, 1982), 444–47. On Matusow's campaigning see chap. 4, pp. 67–72.

31. Powers, *Not without Honor,* 199–200, 214. Powers wrote: "While liberals believed that discussion and debate would be sufficient to expose the insincerity and disloyalty of the progressive left, countersubversives insisted that Communists and fellow travelers had to be exposed, denounced, and punished, and that the Party's covert activities made it necessary to employ the same law enforcement techniques as against any other criminal con-

spiracy" (214). Schrecker used the term "professional anti-Communists" (*Many Are the Crimes*, 42–45), as did Arthur Herman in *Joseph McCarthy: Reexamining the Life and Legacy of America's Most Hated Senator* (New York: Free Press, 2000): "professional anti-Communists—people who made a living pursuing and exposing Communist penetration of American society" (161).

32. Powers, *Not without Honor*, 229–33, 241–42, 246, 250, 427. See Murray Kempton, "O'er Moor and Fen: J. B. Matthews and the Multiple Revelation," *Part of Our Time: Some Monuments and Ruins of the Thirties* (New York: Dell Publishing, 1967), 151–79. On Matusow as an acolyte see chap. 5, pp. 75–76.

33. Gentry, *J. Edgar Hoover*, 79–105 (second quotation, 81), 338–450; Powers, *Secrecy and Power*, 275–323, 337–52; Theoharis and Cox, *Boss*, 199–300; Schrecker, *Many Are the Crimes*, 143–44, 202–12; Donner, *Age of Surveillance*, 110–25; Caute, *Great Fear*, 113–15 (first quotation, 114). On McCarthy see, generally, David M. Oshinsky, *A Conspiracy So Immense: The World of Joe McCarthy* (New York: Free Press, 1983); and Reeves, *Life and Times of Joe McCarthy*. Hoover repeatedly made covert use of the FBI's resources to promote his brand of anti-Communism. See Theoharis, *Chasing Spies*, 139–69.

34. Rovere, "Kept Witnesses," 124. See also the sources cited in n. 9 (above).

35. Joseph Alsop, "Miss Bentley's Bondage," *The Commonweal*, Nov. 9, 1951, 122.

36. Donner, "Informer," 307; Caute, *Great Fear*, 125–26, 128–29, 217; Philip Jenkins, *The Cold War at Home: The Red Scare in Pennsylvania, 1945–1960* (Chapel Hill: University of North Carolina Press, 1999), 75–77.

37. Caute, *Great Fear*, 122, 131, 217; Frank J. Donner, *The Un-Americans* (New York: Ballantine Books, 1961), 118–19.

38. Donner, "Informer," 307; Caute, *Great Fear*, 126–27; Rovere, "Kept Witnesses," 119–20; Belknap, *Cold War Political Justice*, 164–65; Jenkins, *Cold War at Home*, 77; Daniel J. Leab, *I Was a Communist for the FBI: The Unhappy Life and Times of Matt Cvetic* (University Park: Pennsylvania State University Press, 2000), 73–82, 91, 109; Cedric Belfrage, *The American Inquisition, 1945–1960* (Indianapolis: Bobbs-Merrill, 1973), 198, 268.

39. Donner, "Informer," 307; Caute, *Great Fear*, 123. Budenz was cross-examined at length about his income in Smith Act trials in 1952 and 1954. See *United States v. Elizabeth Gurley Flynn et al.*, C. 136–7, S.D.N.Y., 1952 (trial), 1955 (motion for new trial), transcript (hereafter, Flynn transcript) at 2464–500, 2502–4, 2538–44; and *United States v. Joseph Kuzma et al.*, Crim. No. 17418, E.D.Pa. (1954) trial transcript (hereafter, Kuzma transcript) at 1220–24.

40. Leab, *I Was a Communist for the FBI*, 97; Powers, *Not without Honor*, 252; Jenkins, *Cold War at Home*, 77; Belfrage, *American Inquisition*, 151, 169. See Navasky, *Naming Names*, 12, on Philbrick Day in Boston honoring informer Herbert Philbrick.

41. See Louis Budenz, *This Is My Story* (New York: McGraw-Hill, 1947), *Men without Faces: The Communist Conspiracy in the U.S.A.* (New York: Harper and Bros., 1948), and *The Cry Is Peace* (Chicago: Henry Regnery, 1952); Angela Calomiris, *Red Masquerade: Undercover for the FBI* (New York: Lippincott, 1950); Elizabeth Bentley, *Out of Bondage* (New York: Devon-Adair, 1951); Hede Massing, *This Deception* (New York: Duell, Sloane and Pearce, 1951); Whittaker Chambers, *Witness* (New York: Random House, 1952); and Herbert Philbrick, *I Led Three Lives: Citizen, "Communist," Counterspy* (New York: Grosset and Dunlap, 1952). The television series based on Philbrick's *I Led Three Lives*, which

ran between 1953 and 1956, had 117 episodes (Powers, *Not without Honor,* 253). The Bentley, Massing, and Calomiris books and the first of Budenz's books also "were later converted to radio, television, and movie properties" (Navasky, *Naming Names,* 16–17). Navasky believes that promotion of these works in "the vulgar popular culture of the day . . . was openly dedicated to refurbishing the image of the anti-Communist informer" (17).

42. Donner, "Informer," 299.

43. Whittaker Chambers, *Witness* (Washington, D.C.: Regnery Gateway, 1987), 462–63 (quoting Walter Krivitsky). See also Hannah Arendt, "The Ex-Communists," *The Commonweal,* Mar. 20, 1953, 595–96; and Isaac Deutcher, "The Ex-Communist's Conscience," in *Heretics and Renegades* (1957; reprinted, Indianapolis: Bobbs-Merrill, 1969), 15.

44. Philbrick, *I Led Three Lives,* 59–65; Leab, *I Was a Communist for the FBI,* 11–12; Jenkins, *Cold War at Home,* 75, 188.

45. Caute, *Great Fear,* 119.

46. Ibid., 137.

47. On the Lattimore-Budenz case see Newman, *Owen Lattimore.* On Remington and Bentley see Gary May, *Un-American Activities: The Trials of William Remington* (New York: Oxford University Press, 1994); and Navasky, *Naming Names,* 8–11 (states that government actions in the Remington prosecutions were "comprehensible only in the context of the government's interest in protecting the reputation of one of its more visible informers" [9]).

48. After Matusow charged during the 1952 election campaign that over one hundred Communists were employed at the *New York Times,* a charge never made in earlier FBI interviews or reports, the bureau reinterviewed him in a vain effort to obtain the names of the individuals; but he continued to be used as a government witness. See chap. 4, p. 71, and chap. 5, pp. 78–79, 80.

49. Leab, *I Was a Communist for the FBI,* 98–99. See chap. 6, pp. 88–89, chap. 8, p. 120, and chap. 9, pp. 131–32.

50. On settled principles see *Berger v. United States,* 295 U.S. 78, 88 (1935) (quotation); *Mooney v. Holohan,* 294 U.S. 103 (1935); and *Pyle v. State of Kansas,* 317 U.S. 213 (1942).

51. Melvin Rader, *False Witness* (Seattle: University of Washington Press, 1969); Navasky, *Naming Names,* 38–39; Caute, *Great Fear,* 130, 410; Donner, "Informer," 306.

52. Charles P. Larrowe, *Harry Bridges: The Rise and Fall of Radical Labor in the United States,* 2d ed. (New York: Lawrence Hill, 1977), 310–12; Caute, *Great Fear,* 126–28; Donner, "Informer," 298, 304–5; Rovere, "Kept Witnesses," 121–22, 125–27; Navasky, *Naming Names,* 14; Sherman Labovitz, *Being Red in Philadelphia: A Memoir of the McCarthy Era* (Philadelphia: Camino Books, 1998), 83–86.

53. Kuzma transcript, 781–87, 792–802 (quotation, 796), 814; Rovere, "Kept Witnesses," 126.

54. Internal Security Division submission, Apr. 21, 1955 (quotations), INS submission, Apr. 28, 1955, and minutes of meeting, May 19, 1955, in DOJ DCSW minutes; Caute, *Great Fear,* 129; Donner, "Informer," 305–6; Rovere, "Kept Witnesses," 129–30; Navasky, *Naming Names,* 14–15, 39; Murray Kempton, *America Comes of Middle Age: Columns, 1950–1962* (Boston: Little, Brown, 1963), 14; *I. F. Stone's Weekly,* Mar. 18, 1957, 2.

55. *Mesarosh v. United States,* 352 U.S. 1, 3–4 (1956). See also Asst. Atty. Gen. William F. Tompkins to Director, FBI, May 5, 1955, 2–3, in DOJ DCSW minutes.

56. Edward Lamb, *"Trial by Battle": The Case History of a Washington Witch-Hunt* (Santa

Barbara, Calif.: Center for the Study of Democratic Institutions, 1964), 12, 14–15, *No Lamb for Slaughter: An Autobiography* (New York: Harcourt, Brace and World, 1963), 123–62, and "The High Cost of Winning," in *It Did Happen Here: Recollections of Political Repression in America*, ed. Bud Schultz and Ruth Schultz (Berkeley: University of California Press, 1989), 379–80, 283–91; Caute, *Great Fear*, 132–33; Rovere, "Kept Witnesses," 114–15; Belfrage, *American Inquisition*, 210–11; *New York Times*, Oct. 5, 1954 ("Article by Lamb Cited"), Oct. 6, 1954 ("Lamb Accused of Red Aid").

57. Lamb, "*Trial by Battle*," 9–11, 13–14, *No Lamb for Slaughter*, 164–69, and "High Cost of Winning," 386–90; Caute, *Great Fear*, 132–33; *New York Times*, Mar. 8, 1955 ("U.S. Jury Indicts a False Witness"), Mar. 13, 1955 ("Recanters Pose a Problem for Government"), May 17, 1955 ("Witness Guilty in Red-Link Case").

58. Murray Kempton, "The Achievement of Harvey Matusow," *The Progressive*, Apr. 1955, 7.

59. On the events leading up to and surrounding Matusow's recantation, see chaps. 6–9.

60. *New York Times*, Apr. 16, 1955 ("Brownell Drops Informant Plan"). See also chaps. 9–10.

61. John Steinbeck, "The Death of a Racket: An Editorial," *Saturday Review*, Apr. 2, 1955, 26.

62. See chap. 10.

63. *New York Times*, Feb. 4, 2002 ("Harvey Matusow, 75, an Anti-Communist Informer, Dies"). See also chap. 11.

Chapter 1: Birth of a Party Member

1. Lloyd Ultan, *The Beautiful Bronx, 1920–1950* (New Rochelle, N.Y.: Arlington House, 1979), 14, 27–30, 37–38.

2. Ibid., 14 (quotation); Lloyd Ultan and Gary Hermalyn, *The Bronx in the Innocent Years, 1890–1925* (New York: Harper and Row, 1985), 140–41 (photo of the Grand Concourse, circa 1925, showing a wide boulevard lined with recently built five- and six-story apartment houses); Harvey Matusow, "Cockyboo: A Saga of Our Time," ms., 1992, chap. 1, pp. 5–6 (copy in the possession of the authors). On his parents see ibid., chap. 1, p. 2.

3. Matusow, "Cockyboo," chap. 1, pp. 2, 9 (quotation); Harvey Matusow, telephone conversation with Lichtman, Sept. 28, 1999.

4. Matusow, "Cockyboo," chap. 1, pp. 2–3, 5, 8–10; SAC NY [special agent in charge, New York] to Director, Apr. 7, 1950, FBI 100-375988-1, 12–13 (personal history given the FBI by Matusow at the time he approached them); Matusow, *False Witness*, 69–70; Kahn, *Matusow Affair*, 88–92. Matusow's headquarters file (100-375988) was obtained from the FBI in response to an FOIA request. The bureau withheld portions of the voluminous file, including all materials after February 1955, and often redacted parts of pages.

5. Matusow, "Cockyboo," chap. 1, pp. 2 (quotation), 8–9, and *False Witness*, 19.

6. Matusow, "Cockyboo," chap. 1, pp. 4–5 (first quotation), and *False Witness*, 20 (second quotation); Milnes to Director, Feb. 7, 1955, FBI 100-375988-271.

7. Matusow Hearings, 28–29; Matusow, *False Witness*, 19–20.

8. Matusow, "Cockyboo," chap. 1, p. 7, chap. 2, p. 1 (quotation).

9. Ibid., chap. 1, p. 10, chap. 2, p. 1; SAC NY to Director, Apr. 7, 1950, 12.

10. Matusow, "Cockyboo," chap. 1, p. 5, chap. 2, p. 1, and *False Witness,* 21; SAC NY to Director, Apr. 7, 1950, 12; Milnes to Director, Feb. 7, 1955.

11. Milnes to Director, Feb. 7, 1955; Matusow, "Cockyboo," chap. 1, p. 9, chap. 2, pp. 1–2, and *False Witness,* 21–22; SAC NY to Director, Apr. 7, 1950, 13.

12. Matusow, "Cockyboo," chap. 2, p. 2; SAC NY to Director, Apr. 7, 1950, 12; Matusow Hearings, 347.

13. Matusow, "Cockyboo," chap. 2, p. 2. On his medical condition see Matusow Hearings, 1114–15, 1117 (quotation); and Scheidt to Director, June 7, 1950, FBI 100-375988-3, 4.

14. Matusow, "Cockyboo," chap. 2, p. 2, and *False Witness,* 25; Matusow Hearings, 349.

15. Matusow, "Cockyboo," chap. 2, p. 4; Matusow Hearings, 347.

16. Matusow, *False Witness,* 22–23, and "Cockyboo," chap. 1, p. 9, chap. 3, p. 6. As the result of a fall in Germany, he incurred, according to military records, "strain, lumbo-sacral chronic" and later was awarded a 10 percent disability allowance. See Matusow Hearings, 1111–12; Scheidt to Director, June 7, 1950, 4; and SAC NY to Director, Apr. 7, 1950, 8.

17. Matusow, "Cockyboo," chap. 2, pp. 4–5; Matusow Hearings, 347, 1122.

18. Kelly to Director, Feb. 9, 1955, FBI 100-375988-359.

19. Matusow, *False Witness,* 22–23, and "Cockyboo," chap. 3, p. 1; SAC NY to Director, Apr. 7, 1950, 12.

20. Matusow, "Cockyboo," chap. 3, p. 3 (quotation); Scheidt to Director, June 7, 1950, 4–5; Kelly to Director, Feb. 10, 1955, FBI 100-375988-604.

21. Matusow, "Cockyboo," chap. 3, pp. 4–6.

22. Ibid., 6–7.

23. Ibid., 7–8; SAC NY to Director, Apr. 7, 1950, 2–3; Matusow Hearings, 349; *Communist Activities among Youth Groups (Based on Testimony of Harvey M. Matusow): Hearings before the House Committee on Un-American Activities,* 82nd Cong., 2d Sess. (1952) (hereafter, 1952 HUAC Youth Hearings), 3274–75, 3277; Matusow, *False Witness,* 23.

24. Matusow, "Cockyboo," chap. 3, pp. 8–10 (quotation); Matusow Hearings, 349; 1952 HUAC Youth Hearings, 3274; William K. Klingaman, *Encyclopedia of the McCarthy Era* (New York: Facts on File, 1996), 14.

25. Matusow, "Cockyboo," chap. 3, pp. 9–10, chap. 4, pp. 1–2; Matusow Hearings, 349; 1952 HUAC Youth Hearings, 3275–76.

26. Matusow Hearings, 350; 1952 HUAC Youth Hearings, 3275; Matusow, "Cockyboo," chap. 4, pp. 3–4.

27. Matusow, "Cockyboo," chap. 4, pp. 3–4; SAC NY to Director, Apr. 7, 1950, 3, 12; Kelly to Director, Feb. 10, 1955; Matusow Hearings, 350–51; 1952 HUAC Youth Hearings, 3275.

28. 1952 HUAC Youth Hearings, 3277, 3282, 3338; SAC NY to Director, Apr. 7, 1950, 3; Matusow, "Cockyboo," chap. 4, p. 4.

29. Matusow, *False Witness,* 25–26 (quotations); 1952 HUAC Youth Hearings, 3277; Matusow, "Cockyboo," chap. 4, pp. 4–5, chap. 5, p. 3.

30. SAC NY to Director, Apr. 7, 1950, 3.

31. Matusow Hearings, 351–52; Matusow, "Cockyboo," chap. 5, p. 1 (quotation); Kempton, "Achievement of Harvey Matusow," 7; Kahn, *Matusow Affair,* 62–63.

32. Matusow, "Cockyboo," chap. 4, p. 5.

33. Matusow, *False Witness,* 26, and "Cockyboo," chap. 4, p. 5; *Dennis v. United States,* 339 U.S. 162 (1950); Caute, *Great Fear,* 96.

34. Matusow, "Cockyboo," chap. 4, pp. 5–6.

35. Matusow, *False Witness*, 26, and "Cockyboo," chap. 4, pp. 7–8 (quotation).

36. Matusow, "Cockyboo," chap. 4, pp. 3–7.

37. Ibid., chap. 5, pp. 8, 11 (quotation); SAC NY to Director, Apr. 7, 1950, 3, 12; 1952 HUAC Youth Hearings, 3304.

38. Matusow, "Cockyboo," chap. 5, p. 11 (quotation); SAC NY to Director, Apr. 7, 1950, 3; 1952 HUAC Youth Hearings, 3303.

39. 1952 HUAC Youth Hearings, 3286, 3288–89; SAC NY to Director, Apr. 7, 1950, 4; Testimony of Harvey M. Matusow, of Dayton, Ohio, Feb. 25, 1952, in *Report of the Un-American Activities Commission, State of Ohio, 1951–1952* (hereafter, Ohio Commission testimony), 103–10; Matusow Hearings, 352, 357.

40. On the HUAC hearings see Goodman, *Committee*, 207–25 (quotation, 207), 244–67. On the Dennis indictment see Belknap, *Cold War Political Justice*, 52–53; and Caute, *Great Fear*, 31–32.

41. Matusow, "Cockyboo," chap. 5, pp. 11–14.

42. Ibid., 14–15; Harvey Matusow, interviewed by Lichtman, Glenwood and Salt Lake City, Utah, Dec. 23–24, 1996. On the election see Klehr and Haynes, *American Communist Movement*, 122.

43. Matusow, "Cockyboo," chap. 5, pp. 16–18 (quotation). According to M. J. Buhle, P. Buhle, and D. Georgakas, eds., *Encyclopedia of the American Left* (Urbana: University of Illinois Press, 1992), the Progressive Party's "failure to win over significant numbers of New Deal coalition voters from the Democrats served . . . as a signal to the Truman administration and the conservative coalition in Congress to broaden and deepen their anticommunist campaign" (600–601). Schrecker, in *Many Are the Crimes*, wrote: "American Communism . . . was revealed as a marginal force within the United States. Its obvious isolation was to make it increasingly vulnerable to attack" (36).

44. Caute, *Great Fear*, 212–14; Klehr and Haynes, *American Communist Movement*, 136–39; Belknap, *Cold War Political Justice*, 193–95; Schrecker, *Many Are the Crimes*, 24–25 (states "For a time, in the early fifties, roughly one-third of the CP's cadres had gone underground").

45. Matusow, "Cockyboo," chap. 5, pp. 24–25.

46. Ibid., 25–27; SAC NY to Director, Apr. 7, 1950, 4. Matusow told the FBI in 1950 that when he learned during the contest that his lead was threatened, he contributed $100 of his own money to purchase subscriptions for persons who could not otherwise afford them.

47. Matusow Hearings, 361–62, 996–1006; Matusow, "Cockyboo," chap. 5, pp. 27–29 (quotation); 1952 HUAC Youth Hearings, 3290–95; SAC NY to Director, Apr. 7, 1950, 4.

48. Matusow Hearings, 362; Matusow, "Cockyboo," chap. 5, p. 30; SAC NY to Director, Apr. 7, 1950, 4; Belknap, *Cold War Political Justice*, 90.

49. Matusow, "Cockyboo," chap. 5, pp. 30–36 (quotation, 36).

50. Ibid., 41 (quotation); SAC NY to Director, Apr. 7, 1950, 4.

51. Caute, *Great Fear*, 164–65; Pete Seeger, "Thou Shall Not Sing," in *It Did Happen Here*, ed. Schultz and Schultz, 15; Buhle et al., *Encyclopedia of the American Left*, 572–73; Matusow, "Cockyboo," chap. 5, p. 41.

52. Caute, *Great Fear*, 164–65; Seeger, "Thou Shall Not Sing," 15–17; Buhle et al., *Ency-*

clopedia of the American Left, 573; "Job Matusow" (radio broadcast), *This American Life,* WBEZ-FM, Chicago, Mar. 14, 1998; hearing transcript, *Brownell v. Veterans of the Abraham Lincoln Brigade,* SACB Dkt. 108-53, June 7–8, 1954, 1719–24; Matusow, telephone conversation with Lichtman, Sept. 28, 1999. Paul Jr.'s recollection differed from Matusow's: he did know Matusow at Camp Unity, he later said, but had no contact with him at the Peekskill concert (Paul Robeson Jr., telephone conversation with Cohen, Feb. 10, 2002).

53. SAC NY to Director, Apr. 7, 1950, 4–5, 7; hearing transcript, *Brownell v. Labor Youth League,* SACB Dkt. 102-53, Dec. 9–10, 1953, 530, 540–41. Matusow told the SACB that his "white chauvinism" offense also included selling advertising for the *Amsterdam News,* which carried ads for skin lighteners and hair straighteners.

54. SAC NY to Director, Apr. 7, 1950, 8; Matusow, "Cockyboo," chap. 5, pp. 43–48 (quotations, 46); Matusow telephone conversation, Sept. 28, 1999.

55. On the Wheeling speech and subsequent changes in the numbers see *Report of the Senate Committee on Foreign Relations Pursuant to S. Res. 231,* S. Rep. No. 2108, 81st Cong., 2d Sess. (July 20, 1950), 2–3 (hereafter, Tydings Report); Reeves, *Life and Times of Joe McCarthy,* 223–29; Cook, *Nightmare Decade,* 148–54; and Oshinsky, *Conspiracy So Immense,* 108–14.

56. See chap. 4, pp. 67–68.

57. Matusow, *False Witness,* 27.

58. Ibid.; Matusow Hearings, 39.

59. Matusow, *False Witness,* 29.

60. Charles Alverson, "I Led Twelve Lives: Adventures of Comrade Harvey Matusow, Hustler Supreme," *Rolling Stone,* Aug. 17, 1972, 20; Navasky, *Naming Names,* 41 n; Matusow, "Cockyboo," chap. 5, pp. 39–40 (second quotation), chap. 6, pp. 1–5; Fariello, *Red Scare,* 99, 100. Jeff Kisseloff, in *The Box: An Oral History of Television, 1920–1961* (New York: Viking, 1995), quotes Matusow: "[I]t was my fantasy that Cockypoo [*sic*] was infiltrating the McCarthyites and would wipe them out. This was my fantasy, not reality, but that is how I justified what I was doing" (407).

61. Matusow affidavit, Jan. 21, 1950, box 7, file 7, Matusow Papers, University of Sussex, Brighton, Eng. (hereafter, Matusow Papers). No document purporting to be an original appears in the file.

62. Presumably because *False Witness* does not mention the affidavit, Matusow told *Rolling Stone* that the book "was a load of bullshit" (Alverson, "I Led Twelve Lives," 20).

63. Kempton, "Achievement of Harvey Matusow," 8; *United States v. Flynn,* 130 F. Supp. 413, 415 (S.D.N.Y. 1955).

64. Kahn, *Matusow Affair,* 62. Bill Dufty, a former *New York Post* journalist and his close friend since 1953, speculated that Matusow chose to go undercover as an informer because he was "always trying to do something heroic, like his brother." That "his brother died and he didn't," Dufty believed, was "crucial" (William Dufty, telephone conversation with Lichtman, Dec. 21, 1999). On Chambers's belief in a "duty to inform" see Chambers, *Witness* (1987 ed.), 455–57, 463.

65. Matusow, *False Witness,* 28. Matusow claimed that he flipped a coin before calling: "Heads I do. Tails I don't. Heads it was."

Chapter 2: The Making of an Informer

1. SAC NY to Director, Apr. 7, 1950, 1 (quotations); Matusow, *False Witness*, 28.

2. SAC NY to Director, Apr. 7, 1950, 1–2; Matusow, *False Witness*, 28–29. Several paragraphs in the review of Matusow's file by the agents who interviewed him were redacted by the bureau's FOIA censors.

3. SAC NY to Director, Apr. 7, 1950, 1–8 (quotations, 8).

4. Ibid., 6–7.

5. Ibid., 7–9.

6. Ibid., 13–14.

7. Ibid.

8. Ibid., 9–10, 13. In 1952 testimony before SISS, Matusow gave a litany of names of Communist Party members who he said held positions in the union (*Subversive Control of Distributive, Processing, and Office Workers of America: Hearings before the Senate Internal Security Subcommittee*, 82nd Cong., 1st and 2d Sess., 1951–52 [hereafter, DPOWA Hearings], 153–64).

9. Scheidt to Director, Apr. 14, 1950, FBI 100-375988-2.

10. Hoover to SAC NY, Apr. 17, 1950, FBI 100-375988-2.

11. Scheidt to Director, June 7, 1950, FBI 100-375988-3, 1–2, 6, 20; Matusow, *False Witness*, 30.

12. Scheidt to Director, June 7, 1950, 6, 7, 20–21.

13. Director to SAC NY, June 22, 1950, FBI 100-375988-3.

14. Ibid.

15. *New York Times*, Aug. 9, 1950 ("Wallace Deserts Progressive Party in Split on Korea").

16. Klehr and Haynes, e.g., in *American Communist Movement*, wrote that "War coarsens a people. . . . [m]any became impatient with the tedious legalisms of America's constitutional order and developed a preference for rough-and-ready justice toward domestic Communists" (132).

17. Matusow's written reports are listed in Kelly to Bureau, Feb. 3, 1955, FBI 100-375988-376; his report containing diagrams of party headquarters appears in Matusow Hearings, 1034–44; Flynn transcript, 17232–34; Matusow, *False Witness*, 30–32; Matusow interview, Dec. 23–24, 1996.

18. Matusow, *False Witness*, 32.

19. Scheidt to Director, July 25, 1950, FBI 100-375988-5, 1–2 (quotation); Matusow, *False Witness*, 32, and "Cockyboo," chap. 6A, pp. 1–2.

20. Scheidt to Director, July 25, 1950, 1; Matusow, "Cockyboo," chap. 6A, pp. 4, 7.

21. SAC Albuquerque to Director, Aug. 11, 1950, FBI 100-375988-7, 1 (quotations); Scheidt to Director, Aug. 11, 1950, FBI 100-375988-6; Matusow Hearings, 174–76, 184; Matusow, *False Witness*, 32, and "Cockyboo," chap. 6A, pp. 8, 11; transcript of hearing on motion for new trial in *United States v. Clinton E. Jencks*, Crim. No. 54013 (W.D.Tex., El Paso Div., 1955) (hereafter, Jencks motion transcript), 109. Schrecker, in *Many Are the Crimes*, describes the ranch as "a resort that catered to a multiracial, left-wing clientele from all over the United States" (309); and James J. Lorence, in *The Suppression of Salt of the Earth: How Hollywood, Big Labor, and Politicians Blacklisted a Movie in Cold War America* (Albuquerque: University of New Mexico Press, 1999), terms it "a vacation ranch that advertised in the liberal journal *PM* and

attracted a leftist clientele" (56). Matusow told the SACB that he met Jenny Vincent in 1949 at a Communist Party meeting "at People's Artists, and she told me that when and if I were in New Mexico I would be welcome at the ranch" (hearing transcript, *McGrath v. CPUSA,* SACB Dkt. 51-101, Mar. 10, 1952, 11004).

Jenny Vincent's recollection, however, is that she never "met" Matusow in New York; rather, she talked about her ranch in the course of performing at a People's Songs folk music event for children, stating that persons in the audience would be welcome. Matusow was present, she remembered, selling raffle tickets at the door (J. Vincent to Lichtman, May 20, 2000).

22. SAC Albuquerque to Director, Aug. 11, 1950, 1–2.

23. Ibid., 2–3 (first quotation); SAC Albuquerque to Director, Oct. 10, 1950, FBI 100-375988-12, 2; Matusow Hearings, 176–79, 181–82; trial transcript in *United States v. Clinton E. Jencks,* Crim. No. 54013 (W.D.Tex., El Paso Div., 1954) (hereafter, Jencks trial transcript), 583–96; Schrecker, *Many Are the Crimes,* 310–13; Clinton Jencks, interviewed by Lichtman, San Diego, Calif., May 3, 2000; Clinton Jencks, interviewed by Albert Kahn, July 26, 1977, 13–14 (second quotation, 14), 24–25, Albert E. Kahn Papers, Wisconsin Historical Society, Madison (hereafter, Kahn Papers); Kahn, *Matusow Affair,* 14.

24. SAC Albuquerque to Director, Oct. 10, 1950, 2–4 (quotation, 3); SAC Albuquerque to Director, Aug. 11, 1950, 3; Hoover to SAC Albuquerque, Oct. 24, 1950, FBI 100-375988-14; Bryce to Director, Feb. 4, 1955, FBI 100-375988-211, 2. See Caute, *Great Fear,* 134–35.

25. SAC Albuquerque to Director, Oct. 10, 1950, 1; Matusow, "Cockyboo," chap. 6A, pp. 11–13 (quotation, 12); Matusow Hearings, 176. Among other books, Mabel Dodge Luhan wrote *Lorenzo in Taos* (1932), about D. H. Lawrence, and *Taos and Its Artists* (1947).

26. Tydings Report, 1–3, 54–57; Oshinsky, *Conspiracy So Immense,* 115–17, 150–53; Newman, *Owen Lattimore,* 281–84; Robert Griffith, *The Politics of Fear: Joseph R. McCarthy and the Senate,* 2d ed. (Amherst: University of Massachusetts Press, 1987), 87, 101, 107–8; Kutler, *American Inquisition,* 197; I. F. Stone, "Budenz: Portrait of a Christian Hero," in *The Truman Era, 1945–52* (Boston: Little, Brown, 1953), 191; *New York Times,* Apr. 20, 1950 ("Budenz Testimony Awaited Intently"), Apr. 21, 1950 ("Lattimore Accused by Budenz as a Red; Backed by General"). For the "rescuer-in chief" comment see Joseph Alsop, "The Strange Case of Louis Budenz," *Atlantic Monthly,* Apr. 1952, 30.

27. On the Rosenbergs' arrest see Ronald Radosh and Joyce Milton, *The Rosenberg File,* 2d ed. (New Haven: Yale University Press, 1987), 2–3. On the Internal Security Act of 1950 see Reeves, *Life and Times of Joe McCarthy,* 329–31; Caute, *Great Fear,* 38–39; and Klingaman, *Encyclopedia of the McCarthy Era,* 194–96.

28. SAC Albuquerque to Director, Oct. 10, 1950, 1 (first quotation); SAC Albuquerque to Director, Oct. 19, 1950, FBI 100-375988-14 (second quotation); SAC Albuquerque to Director, Jan. 11, 1951, FBI 100-375988-17, 1 (final quotation); SAC NY to Director, Jan. 17, 1952, FBI 100-375988-38, 2 (states "He returned to New York upon learning the Party was considering expelling him"). Nora deToledano, in her article "The Harvey Matusow Story" (*American Mercury,* June 1955), wrote that "Craig Vincent told Harvey he had received word through the New Mexico Party that Harvey was being expelled. . . . Harvey went haring back to New York to try to patch things up" (145).

29. Scheidt to Director, Dec. 26, 1950, FBI 100-375988-18; SAC NY to Director, Dec. 29, 1950, FBI 100-375988-19; Baumgardner to Belmont, Jan. 22, 1951, FBI 100-375988-20, 1; Matusow Hearings, 132; Matusow, "Cockyboo," chap. 6B, pp. 1–2.

30. Scheidt to Director, Dec. 26, 1950 (first quotation); SAC NY to Director, Dec. 29, 1950; Director to SAC NY, Jan. 10, 1951, FBI 100-375988-19 (other quotations); Baumgardner to Belmont, Jan. 22, 1951, 1.

31. *Daily Worker*, Jan. 19, 1951 ("H. Matisow [*sic*] Expelled by Communists"), Jan. 29, 1951 ("Harvey Matisow [*sic*] Expelled by CP," which includes photo); Scheidt to Director, Jan. 19, 1951, FBI 100-375988-21; Matusow, *False Witness*, 33. The FBI curiously interpreted the "enemy agent" charge not to mean that Matusow was deemed a government informant but rather as "a blanket charge to cover the offenses" of which he had been accused (Baumgardner to Belmont, Jan. 22, 1951, 1–2).

32. Matusow Hearings, 1083–87; SAC NY to Director, Jan. 24, 1951, FBI 100-375988-23; Matusow, *False Witness*, 33–34.

33. Matusow Hearings, 1085, 1087; Scheidt to Director, Mar. 8, 1951, FBI 100-375988-26 (quotation); Matusow, *False Witness*, 35, and "Cockyboo," chap. 6B, pp. 3–5.

34. Matusow Hearings, 128–29, 211, 220–26e; Matusow, *False Witness*, 36 (quotation), and "Cockyboo," chap. 6B, p. 6. Matusow evidently filled out two personal history forms, one at Kirtland AFB, Albuquerque, on February 13, shortly before he was called to active duty, and a second at Brooks AFB on March 7.

35. Baumgardner to Liaison, Mar. 13, 1951, FBI 100-375988-27 (quotation); Baumgardner to Belmont, Mar. 13, 1951, FBI 100-375988-28; Matusow Hearings, 221.

36. SAC San Antonio to Director, Apr. 14, 1951, FBI 100-375988-29, 1–2.

37. Ibid., 2–3. The remainder of the report (much of it redacted by the FBI's FOIA censors) dealt largely with Bresler's left-wing political associations. On the Abraham Lincoln Brigade see Buhle et al., *Encyclopedia of the American Left*, 2–4.

38. Director to SAC San Antonio, Apr. 23, 1951, FBI 100-375988-29.

39. Matusow Hearings, 1085; SAC San Antonio to Director, May 11, 1951, FBI 100-375988-31; SAC NY to Director, May 23, 1951, FBI 100-375988-32 (quotation); Matusow, "Cockyboo," chap. 6B, p. 6.

40. Matusow, "Cockyboo," chap. 6B, pp. 6–7; Matusow Hearings, 1085; Matusow, *False Witness*, 36.

41. Matusow, *False Witness*, 37 (quotation); Matusow Hearings, 30; Matusow, "Cockyboo," chap. 6B, pp. 8, 10.

42. SAC NY to Director, Nov. 30, 1954, FBI 100-375988-140, 1–2 (quotation); Matusow Hearings, 497; Matusow, "Cockyboo," chap. 6B, p. 8. A lengthy medical report, reflecting a two-week hospital stay during August 1951, states this diagnosis: "schizoid personality, chronic moderate, manifested by nomadism, eccentricity, seclusiveness, moderate stress of break with Communist Party, moderate predisposition with schizoid features since childhood, minimal impairment" (McFarlin to Director, Feb. 15, 1955, FBI 100-375988-620, 4).

43. Matusow Hearings, 106–8, 495; Matusow, *False Witness*, 37.

44. Matusow Hearings, 107, 495; Matusow, *False Witness*, 37–38.

45. Matusow, *False Witness*, 37–38 (quotations), and "Cockyboo," chap. 6B, p. 10. Matusow later told SISS that Ed Edmiston "was a habitual drunkard, and you could not get along with him—it is just that simple—never stayed sober" (Matusow Hearings, 500).

46. Matusow, *False Witness*, 38 (quotation); Matusow Hearings, 107, 503; Matusow, "Cockyboo," chap. 6B, p. 10.

47. Matusow Hearings, 495–96; SAC Cincinnati to Director, Oct. 20, 1951, FBI 100-375988-36, 1; Matusow, *False Witness*, 37–38, 40–41, 47.

48. Matusow Hearings, 495 (quotations); Matusow, *False Witness*, 38.

49. Matusow Hearings, 496; Matusow, *False Witness*, 38 (quotations).

50. Matusow Hearings, 496.

51. Ibid., 496–97; Tanenhaus, *Whittaker Chambers*, 254, 302; Chambers, *Witness* (1987 ed.), 538–39, 754; Matusow, *False Witness*, 38–39.

52. Matusow Hearings, 496–97; Matusow, *False Witness*, 39–40.

53. Matusow Hearings, 497; Matusow, *False Witness*, 39–40.

54. Matusow, *False Witness*, 40.

55. Ibid., 41.

56. On the McCarran subcommittee see Cook, *Nightmare Decade*, 319–21, 324; Newman, *Owen Lattimore*, 314–17, 337–39; Kutler, *American Inquisition*, 199–200; and Packer, *Ex-Communist Witnesses*, 158–60. On Budenz's testimony see *Institute of Pacific Relations: Hearings before the Senate Internal Security Subcommittee*, 82nd Cong., 1st and 2d Sess. (1951–52), 513–91, 593–701 (hereafter, IPR Hearings). See also *New York Times*, Aug. 23, 1951 ("Sorge's Spy Ring Held Copied in U.S."), and Aug. 24, 1951 ("Currie Is Linked to Reds' Smearing").

57. *Dennis v. United States*, 341 U.S. 494 (1951). "So far as the present record is concerned, what [the defendants] did was to organize people to teach and themselves teach the Marxist-Leninist doctrine contained chiefly in four books: Foundations of Leninism by Stalin (1924); The Communist Manifesto by Marx and Engels (1848); State and Revolution by Lenin (1917); History of the Communist Party of the Soviet Union (B.) (1939)" (341 U.S. at 582 [Douglas, J., dissenting], footnote omitted). Belknap, in *Cold War Political Justice*, wrote: "This dated literary evidence was the guts of [the prosecution's] case. . . . As for proof that Communist theory was about to translate itself into revolutionary action, the U.S. attorney would not offer any—because he had none" (82–83).

58. Belknap, *Cold War Political Justice*, 152–57 ("A nationwide assault, it would produce repeat performances of the Foley Square trial in cities from New Haven to Honolulu" [152]).

59. Matusow, *False Witness*, 42.

60. Matusow Hearings, 345–65 (Matusow quotations, 345), 403, 497 (Edmistons quotations). A seventy-five-page typed version of the document, titled "Report of Communist Activities of Harvey Marshall Matusow" and introduced as an exhibit at a February 1955 court hearing following Matusow's recantation, is found in box 8, file 5, Matusow Papers. A second, untitled version is printed in the 1955 SISS hearings; it was derived from "a 71 page statement" and ends with Matusow's expulsion from the party in January 1951 (Matusow Hearings, 347–65, 403). The final four pages of the seventy-five-page version relate to an October 1951 meeting of the "National Negro Labor Council" in Cincinnati (not mentioned in the other version), after Matusow was "recalled to active duty [by the air force] on 21 Feb 1951" (72).

61. Matusow Hearings, 497 (quotation), 1074–76. Unlike the larger document, virtually all of which appears to be reprinted in the record of the 1955 Senate subcommittee hearings, only a short excerpt from the list of names appears in the Senate record.

62. SAC Cincinnati to Director, Oct. 20, 1951, 1; Matusow Hearings, 832, 1074–75.

63. SAC Cincinnati to Director, Oct. 20, 1951, 1 (quotations). The longer report was received by the bureau on November 5, 1951 (McFarlin to Director, Feb. 2, 1955, FBI 100-375988-344).

64. SAC Cincinnati to Director, Oct. 20, 1951, 1–2.

65. Matusow, *False Witness,* 43–44 (quotation); Matusow Hearings, 497.

Chapter 3: Hitting the Big Time

1. Matusow, *False Witness,* 44; Director to SAC NY, Dec. 28, 1951, FBI 100-375988-35.

2. Matusow, *False Witness,* 44, 46 (quotations); transcript of Matusow-Kahn tape recordings, Nov. 16–Dec. 14, 1954 (hereafter, Matusow-Kahn tape transcript), reel 7, pp. 85–88, Kahn Papers; Matusow, "Cockyboo," chap. 6B, pp. 15–16.

3. Matusow Hearings, 497 (quotation); Matusow, *False Witness,* 46–47.

4. Baumgardner to Belmont, Dec. 11, 1951, FBI 100-375988-41, 2; Baumgardner to Belmont, Dec. 20, 1951, FBI 100-375988-NR.

5. Matusow Hearings, 215; Matusow, *False Witness,* 47.

6. Director to SAC NY, Dec. 28, 1951; Director to SAC NY, Jan. 23, 1952, FBI 100-375988-47; Hoover to SACs NY/Albuquerque/San Juan, Feb. 7, 1952, FBI 100-375988-48 (quotation).

7. SAC NY to Director, Feb. 15, 1952, FBI 100-375988-55; Director to SAC NY, Feb. 27, 1952, FBI 100-375988-55. The New York office's response was almost entirely redacted by the bureau's FOIA censors; see SAC NY to Director, Apr. 11, 1952, FBI 100-375988-56.

8. On the campaign against the Mine-Mill union see Schrecker, *Many Are the Crimes,* 338–40, 355–58.

9. Boardman to Director, Feb. 2, 1955, FBI 100-375988-425, 1–2, 8 (quoting Matusow); Schrecker, *Many Are the Crimes,* 342, 526 n. 82. Matusow repeated in his December 29 statement: "As I have stated before, from my conversation with Jencks, there is no question in my mind but that Jencks is a Communist, although he has never admitted to me that he was a member of the Communist Party." The statement was obtained by a Dayton agent at the request of the Albuquerque office (Shaw to Baumgardner, Feb. 10, 1955, FBI 100-375988-616).

10. During a vacation at the San Cristobal Valley Ranch in the late summer of 1951, Jencks interested a group of blacklisted Hollywood filmmakers in making a motion picture about an ongoing bitter Mine-Mill union strike in Hanover, New Mexico; the filming of *Salt of the Earth* in 1953 gave rise to crude government interference and a subsequent industry boycott. See Lorence, *Suppression of* Salt of the Earth, 56–62, 80–84, 87–88, 113–47; and Schrecker, *Many Are the Crimes,* 331–36. Jencks's role in the project—he and his wife even appeared in the film—doubtless whetted the government's interest in him and may well have led to his indictment in 1953: "Since Jencks was a relatively minor functionary, it was clear that the furor about *Salt of the Earth* had prompted his arraignment" (Schrecker, *Many Are the Crimes,* 336).

11. Hoover to SAC NY, Dec. 20, 1951, FBI 100-375988-NR.

12. Flynn transcript, 16678–82; Matusow, *False Witness,* 60–62 (quotation); *United States v. Flynn,* 130 F. Supp. at 414; Matusow Hearings, 974; Nicholas vonHoffman, *Citizen Cohn* (New York: Doubleday, 1988), 88–89; *New York Times,* Feb. 11, 1955 ("53 Matusow Note Cites 'Dishonesty'"); Baumgardner to Belmont, Dec. 20, 1951; SAC NY to Director, enclosing

(name-deleted) SA to SAC NY, Feb. 8, 1955 (agent's account of interview), FBI 100-375988-579; SAC NY to Director, Jan. 30, 1952, box 3, folder 2, Kahn Papers (another FBI account of the interview with Matusow referred to as "former NY-570-S").

13. Matusow, *False Witness*, 61; vonHoffman, *Citizen Cohn*, 51–52, 75–76, 88–92, 95–101; Radosh and Milton, *Rosenberg File*, 148–49, 153–54, 428; May, *Un-American Activities*, 217–60, 271–74; *United States v. Remington*, 191 F. 2d 246 (2d Cir. 1951). *New York Times*, Aug. 23, 1951 ("Remington Verdict Is Upset on Appeal; New Trial Studied"), Oct. 26, 1951 ("Remington Named in New Indictment").

14. Matusow, *False Witness*, 61–62; Matusow Hearings, 974; *United States v. Flynn*, 130 F. Supp. at 414. FBI agent McCarthy, who was also present, did not recall in 1955 any reference to the Vishinsky book during the interview ([name deleted] SA to SAC NY, Feb. 8, 1955, 1). Matusow was asked about the details of his expulsion from the party and "OTHER FACTS WHICH MIGHT BE USED BY DEFENSE FOR ATTACKING HIS CREDIBILITY ON CROSS EXAMINATION" (Scheidt to Director, July 16, 1952, FBI 100-375988-62).

15. Matusow, *False Witness*, 62.

16. Baumgardner to Belmont, Dec. 20, 1951, 2 (Cohn described as "favorably impressed by" Matusow and "expect[s] to use him as a witness"); Hoover to SAC NY, Dec. 20, 1951. On benefits to prosecutors see *New York Times*, Oct. 15, 1949 ("11 Communists Convicted of Plot"), Oct. 16, 1949 ("McGohey Is Named Federal Judge" and "Communists Act to Salvage Party"); Belknap, *Cold War Political Justice*, 67, 113, 136; and May, *Un-American Activities*, 274.

17. Scheidt to Director, Jan. 3, 1952, FBI 100-375988-44; Matusow, *False Witness*, 64. When, during his HUAC testimony on February 7, Matusow was asked by one of the committee members about Communist Party advocacy of forceful overthrow of the government, HUAC counsel persuaded the member to withdraw his question (1952 HUAC Youth Hearings, 3325–26).

18. Matusow Hearings, 975.

19. Ibid., 974–85 (quotations, 976, 984).

20. Cogley, *Report on Blacklisting*, 2:1–21; Caute, *Great Fear*, 521; Powers, *Not without Honor*, 247.

21. Matusow, *False Witness*, 48–52; Belmont to Baumgardner, Dec. 7, 1951, FBI 100-375988-40; Baumgardner to Belmont, Dec. 11, 1951 ("no comment"); Matusow Hearings, 974; *Counterattack* to "Salesman," Dec. 10, 1951, box 14, file 3, Matusow Papers. See chap. 4, pp. 62–65.

22. Matusow, *False Witness*, 53–54 (quotation); Matusow Hearings, 978–79.

23. Matusow, *False Witness*, 53–54, 57.

24. Ibid., 54–55. See Nora Sayre, *Previous Convictions* (New Brunswick, N.J.: Rutgers University Press, 1995), 400–405.

25. Matusow, *False Witness*, 55–60, 81–86; Matusow Hearings, 994. The commission also obtained lists of signers of Communist Party nominating petitions in Akron and Columbus. See materials in box 21, file 3, Matusow Papers.

26. Matusow, *False Witness*, 81–82. Matusow in January 1952 submitted a number of reports on left-wing organizations in Ohio, including the Dayton Women for Peace and Dayton Negro Labour Council; each of his reports named names. See box 21, file 2, Matusow Papers.

27. Matusow, *False Witness*, 65. In Matusow's manuscript "Blacklisting Was My Business" (Apr. 1954, box 3, folder 1, Kahn Papers), he wrote: "we planned a public relations campaign for my testimony. It was I who was behind it because I wanted the publicity" (61). See Brown to Director, Feb. 4, 1951 (FBI 100-375988-51), advising of an article and photograph on Matusow's HUAC appearance in the *Dayton Daily News.*

28. Matusow, *False Witness*, 65–67 (quotations); Matusow Hearings, 986–87. See *United States v. Flynn*, 130 F. Supp. at 415 ($750 fee).

29. Matusow, *False Witness*, 68; Matusow Hearings, 987. See J. B. Matthews, *Odyssey of a Fellow Traveler* (New York: Mount Vernon Publishers, 1938); and Kempton, "O'er Moor and Fen," 151–79. Kempton describes Matthews as one of "the odd new entrepreneurs to whom the letterhead of a dead subversive organization is at once a weapon and a commodity" (*Part of Our Time*, 4). On the Matthews-Hearst relationship see Berlin to Clements (undated note) and Berlin to Matthews, Feb. 18, 1948, Apr. 1 and 5, 1949, Sept. 1951, and Mar. 31, 1952, box 652, file: Berlin, Richard E., 1945, Feb.–1955, Jan., J. B. Matthews Collection (hereafter, JBM Collection), Rare Book, Manuscript, and Special Collections Library, Duke University, Durham, N.C.

30. Matusow, *False Witness*, 68–69; Matusow Hearings, 1021; *United States v. Flynn*, 130 F. Supp. at 415. See Rushmore to Matthews, July 13, 1954, and numerous newspaper articles following Rushmore's murder of his estranged wife and suicide on Jan. 4, 1958, box 678, file: Rushmore, Howard, 1939–1963 and n.d., JBM Collection. See also *New York Times*, Dec. 22, 1939 ("Daily Worker Critic Forced Out of Job on Refusal to Attack 'Gone with the Wind'"). Rushmore, according to a recent source, left *Confidential* in 1957 when Robert Harrison, its founder and publisher, refused to publish a false and scurrilous Rushmore piece on Eleanor Roosevelt (Neal Gabler, "The Scandalmonger: *Confidential*'s Reign of Terror," *Vanity Fair*, Apr. 2003, 190, 202).

31. Matusow, *False Witness*, 69–70.

32. Matusow Hearings, 1021; Matusow, *False Witness*, 67. See the reprinted articles in Matusow Hearings, 1022–33; and Matusow, *False Witness*, 71.

33. Hennrich to Belmont, Feb. 5, 1952, FBI 100-988375-50.

34. 1952 HUAC Youth Hearings, 3273–3339. Matusow's testimony about Clinton Jencks appears on 3314, and the deferential question, from Rep. Clyde Doyle, on 3322.

35. 1952 HUAC Youth Hearings, 3282, 3338 (quotations). See also *New York Times*, Feb. 8, 1952 ("'Passport Dodge' of Reds Disclosed").

36. 1952 HUAC Youth Hearings, 3327–28. See Matusow, *False Witness*, 74, 76–77.

37. *New York Daily Mirror*, Feb. 7, 1952 ("FBI Aide Says Reds Employ Sex as Snare"); *Columbus (Ohio) Citizen*, Feb. 7, 1952 ("Says Reds Used Sex to Lure Members"); *New York Times*, Feb. 8, 1952 ("'Passport Dodge' of Reds Disclosed"). See Matusow, *False Witness*, 75.

38. Matusow, *False Witness*, 70, 73 (headline and final quotation); Matusow Hearings, 987 (diary quotations).

39. Belmont to Ladd, Feb. 6, 1952, FBI 100-375988-53, 2.

40. IPR Hearings, 3056–62 (February 13 executive-session testimony), 3823–47 (March 13 public testimony); Matusow, *False Witness*, 102–6. Lattimore testified on February 26–29 and March 1, 3–6, 10, 14, and 21, 1952, and his interrogation, testimony, and related exhibits (including the executive-session Matusow testimony) cover pp. 2897–3674 of the

published hearings. Cook, *Nightmare Decade*, 369–73 (quotation, 370); Newman, *Owen Lattimore*, 365–77.

41. On Budenz's testimony before SISS see IPR Hearings, 513–701. For contrary evidence see Tydings Report, 57–60, 63, 72–74, 152–67; and Newman, *Owen Lattimore*, 288–91. See also Packer, *Ex-Communist Witnesses*, 125–77.

42. IPR Hearings, 3058–59 (February testimony quotations), 3829, 3831 (March testimony quotations); *New York Times*, Mar. 14, 1952 ("Former Red Says Party Sold Lattimore's Books").

43. IPR Hearings, 3054–64 (quotations, 3063).

44. *United States v. Lattimore*, 127 F. Supp. 405, 408–10 (D.D.C. 1955) (dismissing indictment), 232 F. 2d 334 (D.C. Cir. 1955) (affirming by equally divided court).

45. *Communist Tactics in Controlling Youth Organizations: Hearings before the Senate Internal Security Subcommittee*, 82nd Cong., 1st and 2d Sess. (1951–52) (hereafter, SISS Youth Hearings), 199–260; Matusow, *False Witness*, 97–100 (quotation, 97); Matusow Hearings, 990; Matusow, "Cockyboo," chap. 6B, p. 22.

46. SISS Youth Hearings, 207–9.

47. Ibid., 209–17 (quotations). See Paul C. Mishler, *Raising Reds: The Young Pioneers, Radical Summer Camps, and Communist Political Culture in the United States* (New York: Columbia University Press, 1999), 41–61.

48. SISS Youth Hearings, 217–20, 223–24 (quotation, 224).

49. Arthur A. Schuck to "Scout Executives Only," Aug. 14, 1952, box 12, file 8, Matusow Papers; Matusow, *False Witness*, 98.

50. Matusow Hearings, 1074 (quotations). The *New York Journal-American* reported on March 10, 1952, that SISS had recently been furnished executive-session testimony regarding efforts by a Czech UN delegate to recruit young persons for atomic espionage; the FBI believed "the source of the information appearing in the article" was Matusow (Director to SAC NY, Apr. 22, 1952, FBI 100-375988-63). Matusow returned very briefly to the subject in public testimony before SISS in October 1952 and before the McCarthy subcommittee in 1953. See *Communist Domination of Union Officials in Vital Defense Industry— International Union of Mine, Mill, and Smelter Workers: Hearings before the Senate Subcommittee on Internal Security*, 82nd Cong., 2d Sess. (1952) (hereafter, Mine-Mill Hearings), 152; and *State Department Information Program—Information Centers: Hearings before the Senate Permanent Subcommittee on Investigations*, 83rd Cong., 1st Sess. (1953) (hereafter, Overseas Libraries Hearings), 371. When Matusow first approached the FBI in March 1950, he told the agents that "[t]hrough his contact with a Czechoslovakian delegate to the United Nations he could possibly furnish information of intelligence value"; his December 29, 1951, interview (which resulted in his written statement concerning Jencks) also addressed the Czechs. See SAC NY to Director, Apr. 7, 1950, 14; Director to SAC NY, Apr. 22, 1952; and Matusow Hearings, 976.

51. Matusow Hearings, 991.

52. Matusow, *False Witness*, 88–93; Saul Moskoff memo of Matusow interview, Feb. 14, 1955, box 20, file 5, Matusow Papers; Caute, *Great Fear*, 438–39; Kempton, *America Comes of Middle Age*, 321, 324; Matusow Hearings, 989, 990, 992; Kelly to Director, Feb. 11, 1955, FBI 100-375988-603; *New York Times*, Feb. 16, 1955 ("Matusow Admits Faking Blacklist")

(quotation). Matusow sold Moskoff a $24 subscription to *Counterattack* (Moskoff to Matusow, June 3, 1952, box 20, file 5, Matusow Papers).

53. Clark Getts to Matusow, Feb. 7, 1952, letter agreement, Feb. 14, 1952, and undated promotional circular, box 13, file 3, Matusow Papers.

54. *New York Times,* Mar. 11, 1952 ("Reds Burned Papers, F.B.I. Informer Says") (quotations); Matusow, *False Witness,* 100–102. See hearing transcript, *McGrath v. CPUSA,* 11002–23, 11055–63. "Communist-action organization" was defined in Section 13(e) of the Internal Security Act.

55. 1952 HUAC Youth Hearings, 3289–90; Matusow, *False Witness,* 87–88; Matusow Hearings, 992; Kempton, *America Comes of Middle Age,* 321. Matusow evidently had a photograph of the strike, which some months later he loaned to the FBI (Leland Boardman to Matusow, Feb. 4, 1953, box 20, file 5, Matusow Papers).

56. Matusow Hearings, 988; Matusow, *False Witness,* 81–83.

57. Ohio Commission testimony, 119–21; Matusow, *False Witness,* 80–81; *New York Times,* Aug. 16, 1952 ("Red Charge Denied by Antioch College"), Aug. 20, 1952 ("Ex-Red Cites Letter").

58. Ohio Commission testimony, 103–16; *New York Times,* Feb. 8, 1952 ("Singers' Contract Cancelled") (quotation), Feb. 26, 1952 ("Agent Calls Singers Reds"); Sayre, *Previous Connections,* 401.

59. *Subversive Infiltration of Radio, Television, and the Entertainment Industry: Hearings before the Senate Internal Security Subcommittee,* Pt. 2, 82nd Cong., 2d Sess. (1952) (hereafter, SISS Radio-TV Hearings), 127–40; Matusow Hearings, 992. On the *Journal-American* article see ibid., 1028. See also Sam Levenson to Paul M. Hahn (American Tobacco Co.), May 5, 1952, and Matusow to Ohio Un-American Commission, Mar. 17, 1952, box 14, file 2, Matusow Papers. On Jack Wren see Cogley, *Report on Blacklisting,* 2:115–21; and Caute, *Great Fear,* 521–22.

60. SISS Radio-TV Hearings, 137–39.

61. Flynn transcript, 17316–17; Kisseloff, *Box,* 413 (quotation).

62. Matusow to Ed Sullivan, Mar. 21, 1952, box 14, file 2, Matusow Papers.

63. Belmont to Ladd, Apr. 29, 1952, FBI 100-375988-NR.

64. Caute, *Great Fear,* 449; Powers, *Not without Honor,* 252; Leab, *I Was a Communist for the FBI,* 92–94.

65. Tanenhaus, *Whittaker Chambers,* 461–63.

66. *New York Times,* Apr. 29, 1952 ("Budenz Is Witness at Trial of 16 Reds"), May 17, 1952 ("Budenz' Testimony Ends after 14 Days"); Louis Budenz to Hoover, July 25, 1952, FBI 100-63-463; Hoover to Budenz, July 30, 1953, FBI 100-63-463; Baumgardner to Belmont, July 29, 1952, FBI 100-63-462 (Hoover quotation). Budenz's headquarters FBI file (100-63) was obtained via an FOIA request.

67. Matusow, *False Witness,* 86; Matusow Hearings, 982, 987, 988, 993.

68. SAC Cincinnati to Director, June 3, 1952, FBI 100-375988-59.

Chapter 4: Blacklists and Election Campaigns

1. Matusow Hearings, 989, 990, 992; Harry Morgan to Matusow, Apr. 24, 1952, box 14, file 2, Matusow Papers.

2. Ted Kirkpatrick to Matusow, Feb. 14, 1952, and Matusow to John Marbach (D.A.'s office), Feb. 16, 1952, box 14, file 2, Matusow Papers. See chap. 1, pp. 26–27.

3. Harvey Matusow (as told to Howard Rushmore), "Reds in Khaki," *American Legion Magazine,* Oct. 1952, 14; Flynn transcript, 17240–50.

4. Matusow, *False Witness,* 108–10, 113 (quotations); Flynn transcript, 6694–716.

5. Cogley, *Report on Blacklisting,* 2:6–8.

6. Ibid., 2:2–3; Matusow, *False Witness,* 109–10.

7. Cogley, *Report on Blacklisting,* 2:60–62, 89–99, 112–14; *New York Post,* June 25, 1956 ("Fund for the Republic Reports: Blacklist a Part of TV and Films; Reveals 'High Court' of Clearance"); Kisseloff, *Box,* 413 (Matusow quotation). Sokolsky had a central role in the operation of the motion picture industry blacklist, performing what John Cogley termed (without irony) an "extra-legal judiciary function" (*Report on Blacklisting,* 1:127). The Hearst columnist, accorded life-or-death power over careers, claimed to have rehabilitated some 300 blacklistees. Cogley's fawning 1956 tribute to Sokolsky—"a court of last resort, an almost universally accepted father figure"—illustrates the enormous power he possessed (ibid., 1:127–32, 168–69; quotation, 128). See also Navasky, *Naming Names,* 87–96; and Caute, *Great Fear,* 505–7.

8. Matusow, *False Witness,* 116–18; Matusow-Kahn tape transcript, reel 8, pp. 100–101, Kahn Papers.

9. Cogley, *Report on Blacklisting,* 2:100–109; Matusow, *False Witness,* 115, 119–25; Matusow-Kahn tape transcript, reel 8, pp. 96–111 ("very jovial," 101), 106; Kisseloff, *Box,* 404–5, 413 ("Johnson . . . took a liking").

10. Cogley, *Report on Blacklisting,* 2:101; Matusow, *False Witness,* 122 (quotations); Matusow-Kahn tape transcript, reel 8, pp. 98–99; Kisseloff, *Box,* 404. Johnson's threats were also communicated in the name of the "Veterans Action Committee of Syracuse Super Markets," a paper organization that did not list him on its letterhead but that he controlled. See *New York Post* articles in the series commencing January 26, 1953 ("The Veto Power in TV-Radio," "How the Blacklist Works in TV-Radio"), box 14, file 7, and letters of "Veterans Action Committee," box 14, file 6, Matusow Papers.

11. Kisseloff, *Box,* 413 (Matusow quotation); Matusow, *False Witness,* 115 (photocopy of letter).

12. Matusow, *False Witness,* 123–25; Matusow to Mr. Keesely (of Lennen & Mitchell), Sept. 30, 1952, box 14, file 2, Matusow Papers (quotations); Kisseloff, *Box,* 410.

13. Flynn transcript, 17105–11 ("was thinking of somebody else"), 17204–7; Kelly to Director, Feb. 9, 1955, FBI 100-375988-419; Soucy to Director, Feb. 14, 1955, FBI 100-375988-421; Foster to Director, Feb. 11, 1955, FBI 100-375988-525; Director to Asst. Atty. Gen. Tompkins, Feb. 11, 1955, FBI 100-375988-461, 2; Matusow-Kahn tape transcript, reel 8, pp. 103–4 ("accepted reluctantly"). George Sokolsky informed the FBI that, in the summer of 1953, he advised Johnson that he had information "that Matusow was receiving 'kickbacks' for clearing individuals whom he had been hired to investigate by Johnson" (Director to Asst. Atty. Gen. Tompkins, Feb. 16, 1955, FBI 100-375988-574, 2).

14. Cogley, *Report on Blacklisting,* 2:107.

15. John Henry Faulk, *Fear on Trial* (New York: Simon and Schuster, 1964), 41–49, 229–30, 264–65 (quotation), 385, 390; Kisseloff, *Box,* 407; Matusow, *False Witness,* 123–24; Matusow-Kahn tape transcript, reel 8, p. 107; John Henry Faulk, "The High Cost of Winning,"

in *It Did Happen Here,* ed. Schultz and Schultz, 402–3, 406. Nizer did receive a $10,000 retainer for out-of-pocket costs, of which amount Edward R. Murrow advanced $7,500 to Faulk. After the verdict, Matusow received a thank-you phone call from Faulk. See Matusow to Stanley Faulkner, July 2, 1962, box 18, file 2, Matusow Papers. On Vincent Hartnett see Cogley, *Report on Blacklisting,* 2:92–99.

16. *New York Times,* July 22, 1952 ("War Sabotage Aim of Reds Described"), July 23, 1952 ("Vishinsky Quoted in Trial of 15 Reds"), July 24, 1952 ("Red Trial Witness Cites 'Violent' Ice"), July 25, 1952 ("Admission of Data Argued at Red Trial"), July 26, 1952 ("Data Fail to Jar Red Trial Witness"), July 29, 1952 ("Judge Warns U.S. on Red Trial Data"); Matusow, *False Witness,* 126–30.

17. *United States v. Flynn,* 130 F. Supp. at 413.

18. Ibid., 419.

19. Flynn transcript, 6645–71; *United States v. Flynn,* 130 F. Supp. at 419 (quotations); Matusow, *False Witness,* 131–34.

20. *New York Times,* July 23, 1952 ("Vishinsky Quoted in Trial of 15 Reds").

21. *United States v. Flynn,* 130 F. Supp. at 417; Flynn transcript, 6630–38 (quotations).

22. *United States v. Flynn,* 130 F. Supp. at 418; Flynn transcript, 6626–29 (quotations).

23. *United States v. Flynn,* 130 F. Supp. at 417.

24. Ibid., 413, 422 (quotations). On the acquittal of two defendants see *United States v. Flynn,* 216 F.2d 354, 358 n. 1 (2d Cir. 1954).

25. *New York Times,* Feb. 3, 1953 ("Convicted Communists Snub Offer to Go to Russia Instead of Prison") (quotations); Belknap, *Cold War Political Justice,* 159; Caute, *Great Fear,* 198.

26. Flynn transcript, 16584; *New York Times,* Feb. 4, 1953 ("13 Secondary Reds Get Their Wish: Jail Sentences Instead of Russia"); Caute, *Great Fear,* 198 (Flynn quotation).

27. Matusow Hearings, 993; Matusow interview, Dec. 23–24, 1996.

28. Ladd to Belmont, Aug. 12, 1952, FBI 100-375988-67 (quotation); Matusow, *False Witness,* 135–38; Matusow interview, Dec. 23–24, 1996.

29. Oshinsky, *Conspiracy So Immense,* 231–34; Reeves, *Life and Times of Joe McCarthy,* 401–2, 420, 430–32.

30. Matusow, *False Witness,* 138–42, 144–45; Reeves, *Life and Times of Joe McCarthy,* 430 (quotations).

31. Matusow, *False Witness,* 142–43 (quotation); Matusow interview, Dec. 23–24, 1996.

32. Matusow, *False Witness,* 148–49.

33. Ibid., 149.

34. Mine-Mill Hearings, 5–25 (Matthews testimony), 150–63, 175 (Matusow testimony); Matusow, *False Witness,* 152–53. Matthews, using his extensive files, testified to "subversive" affiliations on the part of Mine-Mill officials.

35. Mine-Mill Hearings, 153.

36. Ibid., 153, 175 (quotations); Boardman to Director, Feb. 4, 1955, FBI 100-375988-505.

37. Mine-Mill Hearings, 162.

38. Ibid., 158–61.

39. Matusow, *False Witness,* 160–61; Matusow interview, Dec. 23–24, 1996; Eva B. Adams (McCarran asst.) to Matusow, Oct. 15, 1952, and enclosures, box 16, file 6, Matusow Papers. The employee list was accompanied by a typed May 1952 HUAC report stating that

its files did not "contain anything concerning" Hank Greenspun (but setting forth a bumper crop of information on a "Jack Greenspan").

40. Matusow, *False Witness*, 154, 162; Matusow-Kahn tape transcript, reel 11, p. 152, Kahn Papers. See J. Howard Andrews (of Clark H. Getts, Inc.) to Matusow, Sept. 12, 1952, and Getts's undated "Details of Engagement Form" to Matusow, box 13, file 3, Matusow Papers. Unlike subsequent speeches, Matusow's October 5 talk to the Libertyville Community Sunday Evening Club, titled "It Can Happen Here," was booked by his agent, Clark H. Getts, Inc.

41. Matusow Hearings, 307 (quoting article in *Idaho State Journal*, Oct. 10, 1952); Matusow, *False Witness*, 162–66 (Matusow quotation, 164).

42. Wyly to Director, Oct. 15, 1952, FBI 100-375988-NR; Hoover to SAC Butte, Oct. 15, 1952, FBI 100-375988-NR (quotation); Director to SAC NY, Nov. 12, 1952, FBI 100-375988-76, 1–2. Matthews's best-known statement of his charges against liberal Protestant clergy is contained in his article "Reds and Our Churches," *American Mercury*, July 1953, which led directly to his removal in August 1953 from the position of executive director of the McCarthy investigating subcommittee. See chap. 5, n. 5. On Cvetic see Leab, *I Was a Communist for the FBI*, 18, 24–26, 98–99.

43. Cook, *Nightmare Decade*, 382; newspaper clipping, "Speaker Contends Montana Heavily Communistic," and newspaper ad for Matusow speech at Great Falls High School Auditorium, "Communist Spy for the F.B.I," enclosed in G. Bromley Oxnam to Hoover, Oct. 31, 1952, FBI 100-375988-75; Hosteny to Director, Feb. 16, 1955, FBI 100-375988-588 (Matusow's Pocatello speech charging 76 Communists worked at *Time* and 126 on the Sunday *New York Times* was also broadcast); Matusow, *False Witness*, 166–70.

44. Boedecker to Hoover, Oct. 23, 1952, FBI 100-375988-74; Hoover to Boedecker, Oct 27, 1952, FBI 100-375988-74; Quinn Tamm to Tracy, Oct. 21, 1952, FBI 100-375988-72; Oxnam to Hoover, Oct. 31, 1952; Hoover to Oxnam, Nov. 7, 1952, FBI 100-375988-75.

45. Matusow, *False Witness*, 170–71. Even prior to Matusow's arrival in Utah, the FBI received inquiries about him; the bureau advised an associate of Congressman Walter Granger, Watkins's opponent, that Matusow "was paid as an informer several years ago, [but] that we have no connection with him whatever at this time" (Tracy to Tolson, FBI 100-375988-70, Oct. 17, 1952).

46. SAC Seattle to Director, Oct. 29, 1952, FBI 100-375988-76; SAC Seattle to Director, Nov. 20, 1952, FBI 100-375988-81 (quotation). On McCarthy and Pearson see Oshinsky, *Conspiracy So Immense*, 179–82.

47. Matusow, *False Witness*, 161; SAC NY to Director, Dec. 3, 1952, FBI 100-375988-82.

48. *New York Times*, Oct. 28, 1952 ("Text of Address by McCarthy," "M'Carthy Terms Stevenson Unfit," and editorial, "The M'Carthy Speech"); Reeves, *Life and Times of Joe McCarthy*, 444–47. McCarthy's speech ran longer than the allotted broadcast time, and his introduction of Matusow evidently was not televised.

49. Cook, *Nightmare Decade*, 391; Matusow, *False Witness*, 172.

50. Matusow, *False Witness*, 172–74, and "Cockyboo," chap. 8, pp. 1, 8.

51. Nichols to Tolson, Nov. 4, 1952, FBI 100-375988-76; Director to SAC NY, Nov. 12, 1952.

52. Jencks motion transcript, 210–11; Matusow, *False Witness*, 177–78; Reeves, *Life and Times of Joe McCarthy*, 407–14; Cook, *Nightmare Decade*, 355–57. See also Kahn, *Matusow Affair*, 281–84 (reprint of Drew Pearson's column in the *Washington Post and Times-Her-*

ald, Feb. 5, 1955); and Ruth Matthews's handwritten list of dates (including "Thanksgiving . . . Billie and Harvey to Nassau"), box 673, file: Matusow, Harvey, 1952–56 and n.d., JBM Collection.

53. Matusow, *False Witness*, 178–82; SAC NY to Director, Dec. 3, 1952.

54. Matusow to Matthews, Dec. 5 and 6, 1952, box 673, file: Matusow, Harvey, 1952–56 and n.d., JBM Collection; Matusow, *False Witness*, 172.

55. Matusow, *False Witness*, 182.

56. SAC NY to Director, Dec. 3, 1952.

57. Matusow, *False Witness*, 106–7; Matusow interview, Dec. 23–24, 1996 (quotation); Director to Asst. Atty. Gen. Tompkins, Feb. 16, 1955, 1.

Chapter 5: Fruits of Triumph

1. Alfred Kohlberg to J. B. Matthews, Dec. 19, 1952, box 119, file: J. B. Matthews 1950, Alfred Kohlberg Collection, Hoover Institution Archives, Stanford University, Palo Alto, Calif.

2. Martin S. Matthews, interviewed by Lichtman, Whidbey Island, Wash., Jan. 14–16, 1997; N. Dawson, "From Fellow Traveler to Anticommunist: The Odyssey of J. B. Matthews," *Register of the Kentucky Historical Society* 84:3 (1986): 280, 299, 303–4; "Biographical Note," JBM Collection; Matusow interview, Dec. 23–24, 1996. See envelope labeled "1953 Parties"; file: June 5, 1954, and other parties; and envelope labeled "1955 Parties," Martin S. Matthews Papers, Whidbey Island, Freeland, Wash.

3. Ruth I. Matthews's handwritten list of dates of contacts between the Matthewses and Matusow, Oct. 6, 1952–Mar. 2, 1954 (evidently prepared following his recantation), box 673, file: Matusow, Harvey, 1952–56 and n.d., JBM Collection.

4. Matusow Hearings, 88–89, 253–56; Matusow, "Cockyboo," chap. 7, pp. 27–28. See chap. 9, pp. 130, 133–36. Nearly a half century afterward, Matusow told Bentley's biographer, Kathryn S. Olmsted, that he had been Bentley's boyfriend, lover, "the new 'quasiman' in her life" (Olmsted, *Red Spy Queen*, 6, 68, 181–85 [quotation, 184], 193–94, and notes thereto). His claim, however, made in a July 11, 2001, phone interview with Olmsted, is doubtful. Not only did the FBI's 1955 investigation, directed specifically to Bentley's contacts with Matusow, evidently fail to discover such a relationship but also the chronology of their lives is inconsistent with anything more than the most abbreviated friendship. Immediately after their initial dinner on October 3, 1952, Matusow went on the campaign trail in the West; he met Arvilla Bentley on election night and left with her for the Bahamas on Thanksgiving Day (see chap. 4, pp. 72–73); during January and February 1953, he commuted regularly to Washington to see Arvilla (Matusow, "Cockyboo," chap. 8, p. 2); and the couple were married on March 6, 1953 (see chap. 5, p. 77). At about the same time, Elizabeth Bentley took a teaching job in Louisiana. See *New York Times*, Feb. 5, 1953 ("Ex-Communist Is Joining Catholic College Faculty"); SAC Washington to Director, Mar. 9, 1953, FBI 134-435-NR (saying that Bentley is to "depart within the next few days"); and Olmsted, *Red Spy Queen*, 184–85. Elizabeth Bentley's FBI file (134-435) was obtained via an FOIA request.

5. Box 700, file: Testimonial dinner, 1952–53, JBM Collection; dinner list, and Matthews to Sokolsky, Feb. 18, 1953, box 87, file 3 ("Matthews, J. B., Mr. and Mrs., 1950–61"), George Sokolsky Collection, Hoover Institution Archives, Stanford University, Palo Alto, Calif.; file:

J. B. Matthews Dinner (2-13-53), Martin S. Matthews Papers; Cook, *Nightmare Decade*, 426–28; Kempton, "O'er Moor and Fen," 172 (Dies "anointed him with the nickname 'Doc,' an honorary degree reflecting the semi-literate's awe of the scholar"), 178–79; Murray Kempton column, *New York Post*, Feb. 16, 1953 ("A Rose for the Doc"). Matthews's appointment in June to the top staff position on McCarthy's subcommittee turned into a fiasco when a magazine article written by him, which appeared simultaneously with the appointment, charged that "[t]he largest single group supporting the Communist apparatus in the United States today is composed of Protestant clergymen." In the ensuing dispute, Matthews was forced to resign (after only three weeks), and McCarthy suffered a political defeat. See McCarthy press release, "P.M. Thursday," June 18, 1953, box 621, file: McCarthy, Joseph R., 1953–1959, JBM Collection; J. B. Matthews, "Reds and Our Churches," *American Mercury*, July 1953, 3–13 (quotation above, 3); *New York Times*, June 19, 1953 ("Veteran Red Hunter Joins M'Carthy Unit"); *Newsweek*, July 20, 1953 ("Joe Stubs Toe"), 29; Goodman, *Committee*, 335–37; Oshinsky, *Conspiracy So Immense*, 318–20; Reeves, *Life and Times of Joe McCarthy*, 498–502; and Griffith, *Politics of Fear*, 229–33.

6. Dinner list ("Matthews, J. B., Mr. and Mrs., 1950–61"), George Sokolsky Collection.

7. Nixon's message is in box 700, file: Testimonial dinner, 1952–53, JBM Collection.

8. Cook, *Nightmare Decade*, 428 (quotation). Dean Acheson, secretary of state in the Truman administration, was a favorite McCarthy target.

9. Matusow to Matthews, Mar. 1953, box 673, file: Matusow, Harvey, 1952–56 and n.d., JBM Collection (quotation); Matusow interview, Dec. 23–24, 1996; Matusow, "Cockyboo," chap. 8, p. 2, and *False Witness*, 211. A brief article on the marriage in the *Charlotte Amalie (V.I.) Daily News*, Mar. 6, 1953, describes Matusow as "a writer."

10. Matusow, *False Witness*, 172–73, 211–13, and "Cockyboo," chap. 8, p. 8; Matusow interview, Dec. 23–24, 1996 (quotation).

11. Matusow, *False Witness*, 183, and "Cockyboo," chap. 8, pp. 7, 9. A newspaper article at the time of their divorce, over six months later, states his age as twenty-seven and hers as forty-one (*New York News*, Sept. 27, 1953 ["Rich Wife Tosses Out Ex-Red As He Asks Her to Drop Suit"]).

12. Murphy to Director, Feb. 8, 1955, FBI 100-375988-333; SAC Dallas to Director, Feb. 9, 1955, FBI 100-375988-444; Matusow, *False Witness*, 184–87; Wm. R. McDowell to Matthews, Jan 28, 1953, box 673, file: Matusow, Harvey, 1952–56 and n.d., JBM Collection. In fact, the Communist Party was hostile to the national committee (Radosh and Milton, *Rosenberg File*, 327–28).

13. Kohlberg to Budenz, Paul Crouch, and Matusow, Jan. 19, 1953, box 21, file: Budenz, Louis F., 1947–1954, Alfred Kohlberg Collection; Matusow, *False Witness*, 220–22.

14. Matusow, *False Witness*, 190–94 (quotation, 191); Matusow's grand jury testimony in Jencks motion transcript, 672–84; Boardman to Director, Feb. 4, 1955. The Taft-Hartley Act, enacted in 1947, required officials of all international and local unions to file non-Communist affidavits as a condition to utilizing important rights of unions under existing labor laws. Filing a false affidavit was punishable by imprisonment. See *American Communications Assn. v. Douds*, 339 U.S. 382 (1950).

15. Jencks motion transcript, 672–84 (quotations, 679, 683). See Matusow, *False Witness*, 241.

16. Undated memo re Davidoff case in materials for June 30, 1955 meeting, in DOJ DCSW minutes; Flynn transcript, 17255–57; Caute, *Great Fear*, 241.

17. SAC NY to Director, Dec. 3, 1952; SAC NY to Director, Apr. 24, 1953, FBI 100-375988-92.

18. SAC NY to Director, May 15, 1953, FBI 100-375988-91, 5–7; Hood to Director, May 14, 1953, FBI 100-375988-93 (quotation); Boardman to Bureau, May 8, 1953, FBI 100-375988-95; Belmont to Ladd, May 19, 1953, FBI 100-375988-96.

19. Nichols to Tolson, May 13, 1953, FBI 100-375988-94 (quotations); Matusow, *False Witness*, 217 (mentions "a lavish party with a few hundred guests"). Sokolsky also told Nichols that "Matusow is now trying to make money out of fighting the Communists"— a most hypocritical complaint.

20. Matusow, *False Witness*, 206–9; Matusow, telephone conversation with Lichtman, June 20, 1997. In 1954 testimony, Matusow described his status with the subcommittee as "semi-volunteer" (House Un-American Activities Subcommittee, *Communist Activities among Youth Groups [Based on Testimony of Harvey M. Matusow]: Hearings before the House Committee on Un-American Activities*, Pt. 2, 83rd Cong., 2d Sess. [1954], [hereafter, 1954 HUAC Youth Hearings], 5847).

21. Overseas Libraries Hearings, 393; Matusow, *False Witness*, 216–20; James A. Wechsler, *The Age of Suspicion* (New York: Random House, 1953), 245–46, 262–64.

22. *New York Times*, May 7, 1953 ("M'Carthy Asks List of Reds on Papers").

23. Boardman to Bureau, May 8, 1953; Belmont to Ladd, May 19, 1953, 3.

24. Hood to Director, May 29, 1953, FBI 100-375988-100 (May 29 quotation); Director to SAC WFO [Washington Field Office], June 9, 1953, FBI 100-375988-98; Belmont to Ladd, June 9, 1953, FBI 100-375988-101; Belmont to Ladd, June 22, 1953, FBI 100-375988-102 (June 15 quotations); SAC WFO to Director, June 17, 1953, FBI 100-375988-103; Acting SAC WFO to Director, Aug. 26, 1953, FBI 100-375988-109; SAC NY to Director, Nov. 30, 1954, 2–3; Director to Asst. Atty. Gen. Tompkins, Dec. 6, 1954, FBI 100-375988-140; (name deleted) WFO agent to Bureau, Feb. 9, 1955, FBI 100-375988-600, 10–11.

25. Overseas Libraries Hearings, 367–73, 385, 392–93; Matusow, *False Witness*, 215–16.

26. Richard H. Rovere, *Senator Joe McCarthy* (New York: Harcourt, Brace, 1959), 199–205; Reeves, *Life and Times of Joe McCarthy*, 489–90; Cook, *Nightmare Decade*, 411–13. The quoted observation is from Griffith, *Politics of Fear*, 214.

27. Oshinsky, *Conspiracy So Immense*, 277–79, 280 n. Budenz's testimony appears in Overseas Libraries Hearings, 41–59 (quotations, 50, 51).

28. Overseas Libraries Hearings, 367–73 (quotation, 369), 385, 392–93.

29. Ibid., 374–85 (quotations, 379, 380). For Aptheker's descriptions of American society, see Harvey Klehr, John Earl Haynes, and Kyrill M. Anderson, *The Soviet World of American Communism* (New Haven, Conn.: Yale University Press, 1998), 272.

30. Cook, *Nightmare Decade*, 413–17, 419–21; Oshinsky, *Conspiracy So Immense*, 284–85.

31. Cook, *Nightmare Decade*, 421–23; Stephen E. Ambrose, *Eisenhower*, vol. 2, *The President* (New York: Simon and Schuster, 1984), 82 (quotation).

32. Matusow interview, Dec. 23–24, 1996; Matusow, "Cockyboo," chap. 8, p. 10.

33. SAC Salt Lake City to Director, Aug. 4, 1953, FBI 100-375988-108 (quotation); SAC Salt Lake City to Director, Aug. 14, 1953, FBI 100-375988-107.

34. Matusow's typed report, July 25, 1953, box 621, file: McCarthy, Joseph R., 1953–1959, JBM Collection (quotations); Flynn transcript, 17251–53; *New York Herald Tribune,* Feb. 17, 1955 ("Matusow Offer to Spy for McCarthy Alleged"); *New York Times,* Feb. 17, 1955 ("Matusow Admits Lie about Oxnam").

35. SAC Salt Lake City to Director, Aug. 4, 1953; Director to Asst. Atty. Gen. Warren Olney III, August 19, 1953, FBI 100-375988-NR.

36. Matusow Hearings, 373–74 (quotation); Bryce to Director, Feb. 16, 1955, FBI 100-375988-585; Cornelius to Director, Feb. 15, 1955, FBI 100-375988-452; Keay to Belmont, Feb. 16, 1955, FBI 100-375988-622. In connection with his efforts in early August to reconcile with Arvilla, Matusow wrote a letter to Joseph Rafferty, her attorney, admitting to having stolen $1,780 from her and to having received $250 from Drew Pearson for the story of their Bahamas trip (Laughlin to Director, Feb. 7, 1955, FBI 100-375988-380, and attached letter, Matusow to Rafferty, August 3, 1953).

37. Matusow Hearings, 374–77, 386–88; SAC Albuquerque to Director, Sept. 23, 1953, FBI 100-375988-110, also containing clipping from *Albuquerque Journal,* Sept. 20, 1953 ("Matusow Asks Divorce, $20,000 from His Wife"); Cornelius to Director, Feb. 15, 1955; (name-deleted) WFO agent to Bureau, Feb. 9, 1955, 1, 9; Laughlin to Director, Feb. 7, 1955, and attached $20,000 promissory note dated Sept. 4, 1953.

38. See Sokolsky comments reported in Nichols to Tolson, May 13, 1953; and Matusow, "Cockyboo," chap. 8, pp. 2–12.

39. Matusow to Joseph McCarthy, Aug. 24, 1953, box 621, file: McCarthy, Joseph R., 1953–1959, JBM Collection; Matusow, *False Witness,* 224; *New York Times,* Feb. 11, 1955 ("'53 Matusow Note Cites 'Dishonesty'"). More than one version of the letter exists. The version in the text utilizes a photocopy with pen-and-ink signature in the Matthews Collection at Duke. In Matusow, *False Witness,* the printed letter states that Matusow's upcoming birthday is his twenty-*seventh* (a correct computation). A version submitted by defense counsel at the 1955 new-trial hearing in the Smith Act case, quoted in part in the *Times* article, bears an August 23 date and refers to Matusow's twenty-eighth birthday.

40. Matusow to McCarthy, Aug. 24, 1953, JBM Collection.

Chapter 6: Mixed Messages

1. Kahn, *Matusow Affair,* 30–32 ("implicitly," "When I was working"); SAC Salt Lake City to Director, Sept. 30, 1953, FBI 100-375988-117 ("to write a book"); Matusow, "Cockyboo," chap. 8, p. 18.

2. Dufty telephone conversation, Dec. 21, 1999; Matusow Hearings, 483, 491.

3. Dufty telephone conversation, Dec. 21, 1999.

4. Matusow Hearings, 481–83. In a 1955 interview, Marquis Childs told the FBI that Matusow "MENTIONED" to him that "HE COULD USE FIFTEEN HUNDRED OR TWO THOUSAND DOLLARS TO GIVE HIM TWO OR THREE MONTHS TO EASILY FINISH HIS BOOK" (Laughlin to Director, Feb. 15, 1955, FBI 100-988375-567).

5. Matusow Hearings, 498–99 (quotations); SAC Cincinnati to Director, Feb. 7, 1955, FBI 100-375988-390, enclosing affidavit of the Edmistons. Matusow's falling out with the Edmistons stemmed in large part from a debt he owed them when he left Dayton in May 1952. A subsequent letter, in February 1954, again attempting a reconciliation, was evidently

ignored. See M. Edmiston to Matusow, May 16, 1952, and Matusow to Edmistons, Feb. 11, 1954, box 21, file 1, Matusow Papers.

6. Julius Ochs Adler to Hoover, Oct. 1, 1953, FBI 100-375988-114, and attachments (quotations); Matusow Hearings, 137–38, 386; *New York Times,* Feb. 12, 1955 ("Matusow Sought Anti-Reds' Favor"), Feb. 23, 1955 ("Matusow Blames M'Carthy for Lies").

7. The text of the affidavit is found in Adler to Hoover, Oct. 1, 1953, and is also printed in Matusow Hearings, 139–40. The five names are found in Nichols to Tolson, Oct. 2, 1953, FBI 100-375988-113.

8. Matusow Hearings, 124–26 ("dice game"), 140–43 (other quotations); Flynn transcript, 16878.

9. Nichols to Tolson, Oct. 2, 1953; Adler to Hoover, Oct. 1, 1953; Hoover to Adler, Oct. 6, 1953, FBI 100-375988-114.

10. Belmont to Ladd, Oct. 8, 1953, FBI 100-375988-NR (quotations, 1, 4).

11. Director to Olney, Oct. 9, 1953, FBI 100-375988-113.

12. SAC Albuquerque to Director, Oct. 6, 1953, FBI 100-375988-115; SAC WFO to Director, Oct. 8, 1953, FBI 100-375988-116 (quotations). On October 26, FBI headquarters advised its Washington field office, "According to latest information, Matusow is employed on a part-time basis as a consultant by the Department of Justice"; it asked to be kept advised of any information obtained concerning "his present or future plans" (Director to SAC WFO, Oct. 26, 1953, FBI 100-375988-116).

13. Hearing transcript, *Brownell v. Labor Youth League,* 489–729; Matusow Hearings, 1148.

14. Matusow, *False Witness,* 227, 229 (quotation); hearing transcript, *Brownell v. Labor Youth League,* 545, 547, 655–57, 670–71; *New York Times,* Dec. 10, 1953 ("200 Declared Reds in Jefferson Staff"), Dec. 11, 1953 ("Judge Asks Delay on Red Front Move").

15. SAC WFO to Director, Dec. 16, 1953, FBI 100-375988-123.

16. Chiles to Director, Dec. 2, 1953, FBI 100-375988-NR; Belmont to Ladd, Dec. 4, 1953, FBI 100-375988-NR (first quotation); Hoover to SAC San Antonio, Dec. 4, 1953, FBI 100-375988-NR (second quotation).

17. Transcript of Testimony of Harvey M. Matusow, Meeting of the Texas Industrial Commission to Investigate Alleged Communist Domination of Certain Labor Organizations in the State of Texas, Austin, Tex., Dec. 4, 1953 (hereafter, Matusow Texas transcript), 63–105, box 1, file 3, Matusow Papers; Matusow, *False Witness,* 186, 188. Although the state advised the FBI that Louis Budenz, not Lautner, would testify, Matusow recalled clearly in 1955 that Lautner was the witness.

18. Matusow Texas transcript, 67–68 (quotations); Matusow, *False Witness,* 186; Chiles to Director, Dec. 2, 1953. DPOWA was a successor to the United Office and Professional Workers of America and the Food, Tobacco, and Agricultural Workers Union, both expelled by the CIO in 1950 (Buhle et al., *Encyclopedia of the American Left,* 196). Matusow had testified against DPOWA in 1952 before SISS (DPOWA Hearings, 153–64). See chap. 2, n. 8.

19. Matusow Texas transcript, 85–88.

20. Ibid., 89–90 (quotations, 90), 94–97.

21. Flynn transcript, 17591–93; Burton to Director, Feb. 17, 1955, FBI 100-375988-639.

22. Matusow, *False Witness,* 194–96 ("El Paso," 196), 204 (quotations about rehearsing).

Matusow later testified that his work as stand-up comic paid him "maybe a couple of hundred dollars, maybe a little less," because he "didn't work every night" (Matusow Hearings, 474). But the FBI could confirm only that during one all-night spree with a group of uniformed air force men he "had been an 'M.C.' at three shows in Juarez" (Murphy to Director, Feb. 14, 1955, FBI 100-375988-610). Years later, Jencks remembered that he had seen Matusow at an El Paso restaurant entertaining a group of children by fashioning animals from pipe cleaners (C. Jencks interview, May 3, 2000).

23. *Jencks v. United States*, 226 F. 2d 540, 544, 546–47, 549 (5th Cir. 1955); Jencks trial transcript, 579–99 (Matusow direct examination); Matusow, *False Witness*, 204.

24. Jencks trial transcript, 596; Matusow, *False Witness*, 196.

25. Jencks trial transcript, 584–96 (quotations). The Asociación Nacional México-Americana (ANMA), a Denver-based organization, was formed in 1949 as an outgrowth of the Henry Wallace for President campaign (Lorence, *Suppression of* Salt of the Earth, 9–10).

26. Jencks trial transcript, 599–703 (cross-examination), 659–62 (answers concerning FBI reports), 663–75 (motion for production of FBI statements); Matusow, *False Witness*, 197–204. The defense's motion, in deference to then-prevailing procedure, sought to have the FBI reports produced for inspection by the trial judge, who would then select and provide to the defense those portions of the reports that he believed impeached Matusow's courtroom testimony. When the Supreme Court decided the case three years later, it held that the reports must be given directly to the defense, without any prior showing that the witness's statements contradicted his in-court testimony (*Jencks v. United States*, 353 U.S. 657, 666–69 [1957]).

27. *Jencks v. United States*, 226 F. 2d at 542, 544; Jencks trial transcript, 1036 (defense case), 1065 (jury verdict), 1193 (judgment and sentence). A DOJ attorney wrote Matusow that "[t]he jury was out only 22 minutes" (Joseph Alderman to Matusow, Jan. 29, 1954, box 22, file 4, Matusow Papers). By McTernan's account, the jury returned its verdict before he could finish stating on the record his objections to the judge's jury instructions (John McTernan, interviewed by Lichtman, Pacific Palisades, Calif., Nov. 14, 2002).

28. Matusow Hearings, 121–23.

29. Matusow affidavits, Mar. 24, 1954, box 20, file 6, Matusow Papers (quotations); Kelly to Director, Feb. 12, 1955, FBI 100-375988-462, 6; Flynn transcript, 16882–84; *New York Times*, Feb. 12, 1955 ("Matusow Sought Anti-Reds' Favor"); Kahn, *Matusow Affair*, 155. The same day, he sent a more than five-page, single-spaced letter to Henry R. Luce, *Time*'s chief, containing, he said, "The reflection of a guy who has just learned that in the past he knew nothing about too many things" (Matusow to Luce, Mar. 24, 1954, box 20, file 6, Matusow Papers).

30. (Name deleted) WFO agent to Bureau, Feb. 9, 1955, 12–15. The text of the letter appears on pp. 13–15 of the agent's report.

31. Ibid., 12.

32. SAC WFO to Director, June 9, 1954, FBI 100-375988-125, 2 (quotations); (name deleted) WFO agent to Bureau, Feb. 9, 1955, 15.

33. Oshinsky, *Conspiracy So Immense*, 405–71; Reeves, *Life and Times of Joe McCarthy*, 595–637; Griffith, *Politics of Fear*, 243–69.

34. *Special Senate Investigation on Charges and Countercharges Involving Secretary of the Army Robert T. Stevens, etc.: Hearings before the Special Subcommittee on Investigations,*

83rd Cong., 2d Sess. (1954), 2427–29; Reeves, *Life and Times of Joe McCarthy*, 628–32; Oshinsky, *Conspiracy So Immense*, 457–65.

35. Oshinsky, *Conspiracy So Immense*, 464; Cook, *Nightmare Decade*, 534; Reeves, *Life and Times of Joe McCarthy*, 584.

36. Jencks motion transcript, 260–63.

37. Donner, "Informer," 298–309; Matusow Hearings, 149–51 (quotation).

38. *United States v. Siegel*, 263 F. 2d 530, 532 (2d Cir. 1959); *New York Times*, Jan. 19, 1958 ("2 Lawyers Guilty in Matusow Case"). See chap. 10, pp. 148–49.

39. Laughlin to Director, Feb. 4, 1955, FBI 100-375988-294, and attached Brown memorandum; *New York Times*, Oct. 28, 1954 ("Matusow Is Accused of Doubting Himself"); Matusow Hearings, 146–47, 149, 151 ("probably could help"). Matusow told SISS that he had accused Lamb of being "a Communist-fronter" in a speech in North Canton, Ohio, before the Keep America Free Council. On Lamb see the introduction, p. 14.

40. Brown memorandum attached to Laughlin to Director, Feb. 4, 1955; Matusow Hearings, 146–47.

41. Matusow Hearings, 341–42, 454–59, 1142; Jencks motion transcript, 298–301; Goodman, *Committee*, 337–41. Walter Goodman wrote that the "worst [Oxnam] had done was to allow the use of his name by a few organizations to whose activities he did not pay sufficient attention" (ibid., 338). Matusow said he assumed Oxnam "didn't like the committees, and would be anxious to see a book of mine, of that nature, out" (Matusow Hearings, 458). On Matusow's election speeches see chap. 4, pp. 70–72. Oxnam's book is *I Protest* (New York: Harper and Bros., 1954).

42. Matusow Hearings, 341–45, 454–56, 1142 (quotations); Oxnam to Atty. Gen. Herbert Brownell, Oct. 19, 1954, FBI 100-375988-133; Jencks motion transcript, 684–88; *United States v. Flynn*, 130 F. Supp. at 416.

43. Matusow Hearings, 460 ("For Whom the Boom Dooms"), 462, 1143–46 (other quotations); Jencks motion transcript, 689–95; Kahn, *Matusow Affair*, 17–18.

44. Matusow Hearings, 457–58, 1144–45 (quotations); Jencks motion transcript, 301–2.

45. SAC WFO to Director, June 9, 1954. The owner of the night club, Matt Windsor's Lounge, told the FBI eight months later that Matusow made a single appearance "as a guest artist," "laid an egg," and was not hired (report of [name deleted] WFO agent to Bureau, Feb. 18, 1955, FBI 100-375988-660, 2).

46. Matusow, *False Witness*, 231–32, and "Cockyboo," chap. 8, pp. 18–19; Matusow interview, Dec. 23–24, 1996.

47. SAC WFO to Director, June 9, 1954, 1; Flynn transcript, 16898–906 (quotation), 16966–69; Brownell to Oxnam, Nov. 8, 1954, FBI 100-375988-NR; Jencks motion transcript, 292–94; Matusow Hearings, 1148–49; Kahn, *Matusow Affair*, 24. See hearing transcripts, *Brownell v. National Council of American-Soviet Friendship, Inc.*, SACB Dkt. 104-53, June 3, 1954, 1636–749, and *Brownell v. Veterans of the Abraham Lincoln Brigade*, SACB Dkt. 108-53 June 7–8, 1854, 1690–744, 1745–852, box 2, files 4–6, Matusow Papers. In the latter hearing, Matusow testified that VALB members received instruction in street fighting in preparation for Robeson's Peekskill concert in 1949 (1719–24). See chap. 1, pp. 26–27 and chap. 4, p. 61.

48. *Evening Star* article quoted in 1954 HUAC Youth Hearings, 5844; Hoover to Olney, July 6, 1954, FBI 100-375988-127.

49. 1954 HUAC Youth Hearings, 5839–43.

50. Ibid., 5843–46, 5848; *Washington Post and Times-Herald,* July 13, 1954 ("Ex-Red Disputes Oxnam on 'Lies'"); *New York Herald Tribune,* July 13, 1954 ("Matusow Denies He Lied or Said to Oxnam He Did"). Oxnam issued an immediate rebuttal. See *Washington Evening Star,* July 13, 1954 ("Bishop Oxnam Insists Former Red Admitted False Testimony"); and *Washington Post and Times Herald,* July 14, 1954 ("Matusow Admitted Lying about Alleged Reds, Oxnam Says").

51. 1954 HUAC Youth Hearings, 5840 (first quotation); Matusow Hearings, 344 (second quotation); Flynn transcript, 16910–22.

Chapter 7: Matusow's Odyssey

1. Matusow, *False Witness,* 234–35 (quotation); Murphy to Director, Feb. 4, 1955, FBI 100-375988-227, 1; Murphy to Director, Feb. 9, 1955, FBI 100-375988-342; Matusow interview, Dec. 23–24, 1996; Matusow, "Cockyboo," chap. 9, first page (unnumbered). Louis (Lucky) Lapp, a union official and a friend of Matusow's father, arranged the job at his father's request (Kelly to Director, Feb. 11, 1955, FBI 100-375988-545).

2. Murphy to Director, Feb. 3, 1955; Mumford to Bureau, June 29, 1953, FBI 100-375988-128 (quotation); SAC Dallas to Director, Feb. 9, 1955, 4; J. H. Gipson, The Caxton Printers, Inc., to Matusow, July 12 and 19, Oct. 23, 1954, box 13, file 1, Matusow Papers; Matusow interview, Dec. 23–24, 1996; Matusow, interviewed by Albert Kahn, ca. 1976, 24/90, Kahn Papers. On the employee-discharge case see chap. 5, p. 77.

3. Jencks motion transcript, 288–89 (second quotation, 289), 302–3; Murphy to Director, Feb. 3, 1955; Matusow to "Dear People," July 11, 1954, box 673, file: Matusow, Harvey, 1952–56 and n.d., JBM Collection (third quotation); Matusow, "Cockyboo," chap. 9, first page (first quotation).

4. Matusow to "Dear People," July 11, 1954. The Matthewses apparently did not respond to the letter.

5. Matusow interview, Dec. 23–24, 1996 ("convert," "expanded"); Flynn transcript, 17020 ("I go to church"), 17438–43, 17457–65 ("leaders of the Dallas Stake," 17461); *United States v. Flynn,* 130 F. Supp. at 415–16; Jencks motion transcript, 290–91, 391–410 ("leaders of the Dallas Stake," 406). On Watkins see Oshinsky, *Conspiracy So Immense,* 478 ("Mormon elder").

6. SAC Denver to Director, Aug. 11, 1954, FBI 100-375988-NR; Director to Asst. Atty. Gen. Tompkins, Aug. 18, 1954, FBI 100-375988-NR; C. Jencks interview, July 26, 1977, 45, Kahn Papers.

7. Jencks motion transcript, 844–46, 869 (quotation); McTernan interview, Nov. 14, 2002. Witt's testimony was given before a federal grand jury in Manhattan in February 1955 and a few weeks afterward was introduced into the record of the proceedings on Jencks's motion for a new trial in El Paso. McTernan was a graduate of Amherst and the Columbia Law School. On Chambers's charges against Witt see Tanenhaus, *Whittaker Chambers,* 93, 97, 162; Chambers, *Witness* (1987 ed.), 334–35, 465–67; and Latham, *Communist Controversy in Washington,* 107–8, 129.

8. Jencks motion transcript, 845, 847–48, 869–72 (quotations); *Jencks v. United States,* 226 F. 2d at 553, 556–57.

9. Jencks motion transcript, 840–43, 848–51; Matusow Hearings, 767; Kahn, *Matusow Affair,* 13–16; C. Jencks interview (Lichtman), May 3, 2000; C. Jencks interview (Kahn), July 26, 1977, 10, 43–44, Kahn Papers; Virginia Jencks, interviewed by Albert Kahn, Mar. 13, 1977, 4–5, Kahn Papers. Kahn's recollection of the events differs slightly from Witt's. Kahn recalls meeting with Jencks in early September, meeting with Witt the next day when the Jenckses were not present, and receiving Witt's answer concerning the union's book order several days later. Jencks remembered that Kahn was conspicuous at the San Cristobal Valley Ranch because he drove a big, showy Buick convertible.

10. Bentley Nov. 30, 1945, statement, 28–29; Matusow, "Cockyboo," chap. 10, p. 4. Haynes and Klehr describe Kahn as "a left-wing journalist and secret CPUSA member" and speculate that he is the "unidentified KGB asset with the cover name Fighter" referred to in VENONA messages (*Venona,* 254–55, 349, 375–76). Kahn was cofounder in 1939 of *The Hour,* an "anti-Nazi newsletter" (Albert Kahn, introduction to Matusow, *False Witness,* 7). His books include *Sabotage! The Secret War against America* (New York: Harper and Bros., 1942) and *High Treason: The Plot against the People* (New York: Lear Publishers, 1950).

11. Kahn, *Matusow Affair,* 23–24; IPR Hearings, 649–50 (Budenz testimony); Kahn, introduction to Matusow, *False Witness,* 10; Angus Cameron, introduction to Kahn, *Matusow Affair,* xix; Rovere, "Kept Witnesses," 115; Matusow interview, Dec. 23–24, 1996.

12. Jencks motion transcript, 849–51 (quotations), 873; Kahn, *Matusow Affair,* 16.

13. Jencks motion transcript, 851–52, 871–72 (quotation).

14. Matusow, *False Witness,* 234 ("simplicity of their attitude"); Flynn transcript, 13444–46; Jencks motion transcript, 285–86; *New York Times,* Feb. 18, 1955 ("Matusow's Reform Is Laid to Children") ("performed puppet and magic shows"); Kisseloff, *Box,* 428 ("Do justice," "became a mantra"); Fariello, *Red Scare,* 106; Matusow interview, Dec. 23–24, 1996.

15. Matusow, *False Witness,* 233–34 ("my conscience"); Jencks motion transcript, 287–88 ("man at the copy desk"); SAC Dallas to Director, Oct. 13, 1954, FBI 100-375988-132; Belmont to Boardman, Feb. 15, 1955, FBI 100-375988-586; Murphy to Director, Feb. 3, 1955, 2–3; Matusow Hearings, 411, 1058–59; Kahn, *Matusow Affair,* 20.

16. Oxnam to Brownell, Oct. 19, 1954, 4 (second quotation); *New York Times,* Oct. 19, 1954 ("Witness Admitted Lies, Oxnam Says") (first quotation).

17. Baumgardner to Belmont, Oct. 25, 1954, FBI 100-375988-133 (quotations); *New York Times,* Oct. 26, 1954 ("Matusow Is Accused of Doubting Himself").

18. Flynn transcript, 17512; Jencks motion transcript, 304–5, 327–29; "Job Matusow" (radio broadcast). In the 1955 SISS hearings, Matusow testified that two of his associates in the uranium-prospecting plan had experience as radio announcers, and the plan contemplated that one would work in radio in Salt Lake City to support the others. Cardell, he said, also held a priesthood in the Mormon church and discussed spiritual matters with him (Matusow Hearings, 278–79).

19. Matusow, "Cockyboo," chap. 9, pp. 2, 3; Matusow interview, Dec. 23–24, 1996; Dufty telephone conversation, Dec. 21, 1999; Murphy to Director, Feb. 9, 1955, FBI 100-375988-342; Flynn transcript, 17298–301, 17503–4, 17530; Matusow Hearings, 64–65.

20. Murphy to Director, Feb. 3, 1955; Murphy to Director, Feb. 9, 1955; Matusow, "Cockyboo," chap. 9, p. 3; Flynn transcript, 17542–44.

21. Oshinsky, *Conspiracy So Immense,* 472–82 (quotation, 482); Reeves, *Life and Times of Joe McCarthy,* 639–53; Griffith, *Politics of Fear,* 294–304; Cook, *Nightmare Decade,* 520–

24. McCarthy's vulnerability was underscored on July 20 by the forced resignation, over his objection, of Roy Cohn as counsel to his subcommittee.

22. Griffith, *Politics of Fear*, 305–6. Nixon is quoted in Oshinsky, *Conspiracy So Immense*, 482–83.

23. Act of August 24, 1954, 68 Stat. 775 (Communist Control Act); 100 Cong. Rec. 14208–36 (Aug. 12, 1954); Griffith, *Politics of Fear*, 292–94; Klingaman, *Encyclopedia of the McCarthy Era*, 82–83. See 50 U.S.C. §§841–42. Humphrey's proposal, offered as "an amendment in the nature of a substitute" to Republican John Marshall Butler's bill to create a new category of "Communist-infiltrated" organizations that would be required to register under the Internal Security Act, was adopted without a dissenting vote (100 Cong. Rec. at 14234). The Communist Control Act's mischievous character was well illustrated a few years later, when a decision of the U.S. Supreme Court was needed to clarify that the statute did not require New York state to exclude the Communist Party from its unemployment compensation system (*Communist Party, U.S.A. v. Catherwood*, 367 U.S. 389 [1961]).

24. Jencks motion transcript, 306–7, 308–9. See Flynn transcript, 17542–44 (departure from Dallas on a Saturday night).

25. Flynn transcript, 17468–71 (quotation, 17470–71), 17491–92; Jencks motion transcript, 309–12, 316–17, 325; Matusow interview, Dec. 23–24, 1996; Matusow, "Cockyboo," chap. 9, pp. 4, 5. Testifying more than once, Matusow also gave this inventory of his load: "I had thirty hand puppets, a marionette, a recorder, a musical instrument, two harmonicas, a typewriter, my poetry, change of blue jeans, two changes of T-shirts, change of turtle-neck sweater, a jacket, two blankets, a frying pan, a couple of cooking utensils, and well, I had a trench knife, and canteen, and cartridge belt, and I had my beret, and I believe that was all" (Jencks motion transcript, 325–26).

26. Jencks motion transcript, 309–10, 313–18 (quotations), 329–30; Flynn transcript, 17471–85; Matusow interview, Dec. 23–24, 1996; Matusow, "Cockyboo," chap. 9, p. 5.

27. Jencks motion transcript, 318–20; Flynn transcript, 17485–89.

28. Flynn transcript, 17499–501; Jencks motion transcript, 329–30, 333–40 (quotation, 334); Matusow interview, Dec. 23–24, 1996; Matusow, "Cockyboo," chap. 9, pp. 5–6; SAC Dallas to Director, Nov. 15, 1954, FBI 100-375988-137; Murphy to Director, Feb. 14, 1955, FBI 100-375988-582.

29. Jencks motion transcript, 341–47 (quotation, 343); Flynn transcript, 17510; Matusow Hearings, 64. After the hotel incident, Matusow recalled years later, he stopped at a Baptist revival meeting in another section of Amarillo; the Baptist "preacher" put him up for the night; he worked for two days on the maize harvest; and there he met a young scientist working on "cross-pollinization of pot" (Matusow, "Cockyboo," chap. 9, pp. 6–7).

30. Jencks motion transcript, 346, 349–54; Flynn transcript, 17513; Matusow Hearings, 65; (name deleted) agent to Bureau, Feb. 9, 1955, FBI 100-375988-601, 2–3.

31. Jencks motion transcript, 354–55 (quotation); Flynn transcript, 17567–71; Bryce to Director, Feb. 4, 1955, 3; (name deleted) agent to Bureau, Feb. 9, 1955, 5.

32. (Name deleted) agent to Bureau, Feb. 9, 1955, 2; Jencks motion transcript, 363, 667–69 ("fit of temper," 669); *Albuquerque Journal*, Oct. 23, 1954 ("Harvey Matusow Asserts Bishop Told Half Truths," AP dispatch).

33. (Name deleted) agent to Bureau, Feb. 9, 1955, 2; J. Vincent to Lichtman, May 20, 2000.

34. (Name deleted) agent to Bureau, Feb. 9, 1955, 5–6 (quotations); Director to Asst. Atty. Gen. Tompkins, Feb. 7, 1955, FBI 100-375988-287, 1; Flynn transcript, 16962, 17282–83, 17542–44, 17548–59, 17563–66; Jencks motion transcript, 742–43.

35. Fariello, *Red Scare,* 107 (quotation); Matusow interview, Dec. 23–24, 1996; Kahn, *Matusow Affair,* 21; Matusow to Kahn, May 17, 1957, box 1, folder 12 (hereafter, Matusow-Kahn correspondence, 1955–57), Kahn Papers. In an interview with Albert Kahn (ca. 1976, Kahn Papers), Matusow told him "I got out of Taos about 6 hours or so before the FBI arrived or within a few hours" (27/99).

36. Malone to Director, Oct. 9, 1954, FBI 100-375988-NR; Director to Asst. Atty. Gen. Tompkins, Oct. 12, 1954, FBI 100-375988-131; Boardman to Director, Nov. 10, 1954, FBI 100-375988-134; Keay to Belmont, Jan. 26, 1955, FBI 100-375988-NR (describes the director's Oct. 12, 1954, memorandum in the words quoted in text). See Belmont to Boardman, Jan. 25, 1955, FBI 100-375988-NR ("Department was advised by memorandum 10-12-54 of a report that Matusow was dickering with IUMMSW for a fee to provide the union with a statement admitting false testimony on his part in the Jencks trial").

37. SAC Dallas to Director, Nov. 15, 1954.

38. Kahn, *Matusow Affair,* 24 (quotation); Flynn transcript, 16989; Jencks motion transcript, 415.

39. Kahn, *Matusow Affair,* 24–28.

40. Ibid., 30–36; Matusow, "Blacklisting Was My Business," 4, 9, 41, 45, Kahn Papers.

41. Kahn, *Matusow Affair,* 36–37 (quotations); Flynn transcript, 17087–88, 17573–76; Jencks motion transcript, 251, 415.

42. Kahn, *Matusow Affair,* 39–40, 45–46; Flynn transcript, 16962–66, 17001–3; Jencks motion transcript, 429, 432, 464–65; Matusow Hearings, 268; SISS Matusow Report, 73. The letter agreement appears in Matusow Hearings, 5–6 (quotation), and in Jencks motion transcript, 421–22. Although it specifies a $350 (rather than $250) immediate payment, $100 was deducted for Matusow's airline fare. See Jencks motion transcript, 417.

43. Matusow, "Cockyboo," chap. 10, p. 3 (quotation), and *False Witness,* chap. 18: "Stirrings of Conscience"; Matusow interview, Dec. 23–24, 1996. The *New York Times* report (its reporter was Russell Baker) on Matusow's February 21, 1955, appearance before SISS illustrates the skepticism with which his professions of religious faith were received. See *New York Times,* Feb. 22, 1955 ("No Longer a Liar, Matusow Swears"). On his later embrace of the Mormon faith, see chap. 11, p. 158.

44. Kempton, "Achievement of Harvey Matusow," 8; Judge Dimock's statement in *United States v. Flynn,* 130 F.Supp. at 416; Matusow, "Blacklisting Was My Business," 61. FBI aide Leland Boardman, in a February 1955 memo, concluded that "Matusow appears to have been motivated by an extreme desire for publicity" and when he "ran out" of "publicity, money, and glamour . . . probably sold himself back to Communist elements" (Boardman to Director, Feb. 7, 1955, FBI 100-375988-512).

45. Kempton, "Achievement of Harvey Matusow," 9.

Chapter 8: Writing and Recanting

1. Jencks motion transcript, 465. Matusow's medical problem was not fanciful; a VA hospital in the Bronx examined him on October 26 and found "[w]eakness of left leg"

and "[c]lot in vein of left leg—recommend hospitalization" (SAC NY to Director, Nov. 30, 1954, 3).

2. Jencks motion transcript, 465–69 (quotations); Flynn transcript, 17287–94.

3. Boardman to Director, Nov. 10, 1954.

4. Ibid.

5. Ibid.

6. Director to Asst. Atty. Gen. Tompkins, Nov. 10, 1954, FBI 100-375988-136.

7. Jencks motion transcript, 436–37; Kahn, *Matusow Affair,* 47–48 (quotations).

8. Kahn, *Matusow Affair,* 48–53 (quotation, 52); Matusow, *False Witness,* 201 (same quotation).

9. SAC NY to Director, Dec. 4, 1954, FBI 100-375988-141.

10. Jencks motion transcript, 438–39 (Matusow quotation, 438); Kahn, *Matusow Affair,* 53–55 (Kahn quotations, 53–54).

11. Kahn, *Matusow Affair,* 55–56 (Kahn quotation, 56), 60–61; Matusow Hearings, 767–68, 773; Jencks motion transcript, 438, 851–52 (Witt quotation, 852).

12. Kahn, *Matusow Affair,* 56–60.

13. Matusow-Kahn tape transcript, reel 2, p. 20, reel 6, pp. 64–69, reel 8, pp. 117–18, reel 10, pp. 137, 138, Kahn Papers.

14. Jencks motion transcript, 760 (first quotation); Kahn, *Matusow Affair,* 64–66 (second quotation, 65).

15. Matusow Hearings, 774; Jencks motion transcript, 756; Kahn, *Matusow Affair,* 67–69; *Jencks v. United States,* 226 F. 2d at 557; Matusow-Kahn tape transcript, reel 12, p. 171, Kahn Papers.

16. Jencks motion transcript, 760–62 ("the whole story," "he will not use any"); Kahn, *Matusow Affair,* 69–71 (other quotations), 82 ("Matusow suspected at first that Angus and I really didn't intend to publish his book. He thought we might only be trying to trick him into admitting he'd lied in the Flynn and Jencks cases"); *Jencks v. United States,* 226 F. 2d at 557.

17. Matusow Hearings, 76 (second quotation), 163, 167–68; Jencks motion transcript, 761 (first quotation); Kahn, *Matusow Affair,* 69. See Matusow testimony in Jencks motion transcript, 441: "I don't recall specifically saying to Mr. Kahn on [December 14] I was going to write an affidavit in behalf of Jencks. It might have been that date."

18. Flynn transcript, 17026–27; *Jencks v. United States,* 226 F. 2d at 557; Kahn, *Matusow Affair,* 73–77. After publication, the book title itself would draw fire from the conservative press as "an impudent communist device to cast doubt on the veracity of Whittaker Chambers' biography, Witness" (*Saturday Evening Post,* Mar. 26, 1955 ["Reds Now Undertake to Brainwash America!"], 10).

19. Griffith, *Politics of Fear,* 306; Oshinsky, *Conspiracy So Immense,* 483; Reeves, *Life and Times of Joe McCarthy,* 654.

20. Oshinsky, *Conspiracy So Immense,* 483–88, 492 (quotation); Griffith, *Politics of Fear,* 307–11; Reeves, *Life and Times of Joe McCarthy,* 658.

21. Oshinsky, *Conspiracy So Immense,* 489–91; Cook, *Nightmare Decade,* 283–87; Reeves, *Life and Times of Joe McCarthy,* 662. John F. Kennedy of Massachusetts, hospitalized for spinal surgery, was neither recorded nor paired.

22. Kahn, *Matusow Affair,* 75, 77–80.

23. Ibid., 81–86.

24. Ibid., 64, 82 (first quotation), 86–88 (second quotation, 87), 97–98; Flynn transcript, 17028–37; C. Jencks interview, July 26, 1977, 53, Kahn Papers; Jencks to Matusow, Feb. 15, 1955, box 22, file 4, Matusow Papers. The two-year deadline for motions based on newly discovered evidence posed no immediate problem in the Jencks case; but Matusow was agreeable to supplying an affidavit presently, and Jencks's lawyers undoubtedly preferred to have it in hand.

25. Jencks motion transcript, 857–58 (quotation); Flynn transcript, 17003–7; *Jencks v. United States*, 226 F. 2d at 558; Kahn, *Matusow Affair*, 97–98.

26. Jencks motion transcript, 382–88 ("it would be difficult," 387), 866–67 ("analyzed all the possibilities," 867); Matusow Hearings, 109 (SISS testimony). Matusow added that he was "prepared to take any consequences I have to take . . . but in actuality I felt that the Government and the Justice Department would feel the fact that I am now telling the truth and maybe swallow its pride and accept the truth" (Jencks motion transcript, 389).

27. Kahn, *Matusow Affair*, 93–96; Jencks motion transcript, 863–66 (quotation, 864); Matusow to Sullivan, Mar. 21, 1952, Matusow Papers; Matusow Hearings, 548–60, 642; SISS Matusow Report, 75–76. See chap. 3, pp. 58–59.

28. Kahn, *Matusow Affair*, 99–103 (Stewart Alsop quotation, 103); Matusow, *False Witness*, 104 ("complete falsehood"); Stewart Alsop column, *New York Herald Tribune*, Jan. 28, 1955 ("Legal Lying"). The Alsops in January 1953 questioned the credibility of Matusow, Louis Budenz, and Paul Crouch (see chap. 5, pp. 77–78); in October 1951, Joseph Alsop appeared as a witness before SISS to contradict Budenz's testimony concerning a wartime trip to China by Lattimore and Vice President Henry Wallace, about which Alsop had firsthand knowledge (IPR Hearings, 1403–89).

29. Matusow Hearings, 160–62 (text of affidavit), 778; *False Witness*, 237–41 (same); *New York Times*, Jan. 29, 1955 ("Red Informer Says He Lied at a Trial"). Unlike his affidavit in the Smith Act case, a few days later, Matusow did not claim that prosecutors in the Jencks case knew of, or cooperated in, his false testimony (Matusow Hearings, 194).

30. Matusow Hearings, 156–59 (text of affidavit); Matusow, *False Witness*, 242–50 (same); *New York Times*, Feb. 1, 1955 ("Anti-Red Witness Confesses He Lied"). As to the fourth defendant, Arnold Johnson, Matusow disavowed testimony that Johnson, in a 1949 speech, spoke of the need to place Communist Party members in trade unions in "'basic industries,'" so that "'we would then have people on our side'" in the event of a war with the Soviets.

31. Matusow Hearings, 6–9, 263, 268–71; Flynn transcript, 17007–10, 17040–43; SISS Matusow Report, 75; *New York Times*, Feb. 15, 1955 ("Matusow Admits Recantation Pays"). Matusow testified that although the contract was signed on February 1, terms were agreed upon in early January, before he signed the affidavits. One contract change was in Cameron & Kahn's favor: under the October letter agreement, Matusow retained all film, radio, and television rights, while in the February agreement he assigned these rights to the publisher, subject to a 75 percent royalty. He denied he got "a better contract," contending it was "basically the same contract" (Matusow Hearings, 4, 8, 268–69).

32. S. Alsop column, "Legal Lying"; Chuck [Allen], interviewed by Albert Kahn, 1976–77, pp. 1–8, 14–17, and Angus Cameron, interviewed by Albert Kahn, 1976, Angus #5, pp. 2–3, Kahn Papers.

33. S. Alsop column, "Legal Lying."

34. Belmont to Boardman, Feb. 1, 1955, FBI 100-375988-163 (states "The Phoenix Office by teletype dated January 25, 1955, furnished the first specific information regarding the probability of Matusow's retraction").

35. Belmont to Boardman, Jan. 25, 1955. Belmont apparently overlooked the bureau's warning in October 1953, at the time Matusow gave his affidavit to the *New York Times*, that he may have committed perjury in the SISS Salt Lake City hearings a year earlier. See chap. 6, pp. 88–89.

36. Belmont to Boardman, Jan. 25, 1955.

37. Director to Asst. Atty. Gen. Tompkins, Jan. 25, 1955, FBI 100-375988-NR.

38. Hoover to SAC NY, Jan. 28, 1954, FBI 100-375988-142; Kelly to Bureau, Feb. 1, 1955, FBI 100-375988-312; Kelly to Bureau, Feb. 3, 1955, FBI 100-375988-322; Kelly to Director, Feb. 3, 1955, FBI 100-375988-365; Kelly to Director, Feb. 5, 1955, FBI 100-375988-300 ("REVIEW OF APPROXIMATELY EIGHTY-SIX THOUSAND REFERENCES AND FILES COMPLETED. . . . ABOUT FIVE HUNDRED REFERENCES AND FILES TO BE LOCATED AND REVIEWED TO COMPLETE CORRECTION OF CHARACTERIZATION OF MATUSOW AS OF KNOWN UNRELIABILITY"); Bryce to Director, Feb. 5, 1955, FBI 100-375988-326 ("REVIEW OF APPROXIMATELY TWENTY SIX THOUSAND FIVE HUNDRED FILES").

39. *New York Times*, Feb. 5, 1955 ("The Professional Informer"), Feb. 6, 1955, sec. 4 ("Role of Informers Now under Inquiry").

40. Kahn, *Matusow Affair*, 109 (quoting *Milwaukee Journal*); *The Worker*, Feb. 6, 1955 ("Full Text of Matusow's Statement—'I Lied for the FBI to Jail Communists'"), reprinted in Matusow Hearings, 1242–43; Herbert Philbrick column, *New York Herald Tribune*, Feb. 6, 1955 ("Matusow 'Confessions' Signal New Campaign").

41. Kahn, *Matusow Affair*, 112–14 (Movietone News quotation); Kelly to Bureau, Feb. 3, 1955, FBI 100-375988-352 (containing a transcript of CBS interview); Director to Asst. Atty. Gen. Tompkins, Feb. 5, 1955, FBI 100-375988-160, 3; Kelly to Bureau, Feb. 8, 1955, FBI 100-375988-613 (containing a transcript of ABC interview).

42. Kahn, *Matusow Affair*, 113.

43. *New York Times*, Feb. 4, 1955 ("Matusow Termed 'Planted' Witness"), Feb. 6, 1955, sec. 4 ("Repentant Matusow"); Director to Asst. Atty. Gen. Tompkins, Feb. 5, 1955, 2–3; Nichols to Tolson, Feb. 2, 1955, FBI 100-375988-199; Kelly to Director, Feb. 3, 1955, FBI 100-375988-241 (FBI source quotation); Nichols to Tolson, Feb. 3, 1955, FBI 100-375988-357; Kahn, *Matusow Affair*, 117–21 (Kahn quotation, 117); Rovere, "Kept Witnesses," 113–15.

44. Kelly to Director, Feb. 5, 1955, FBI 100-375988-201, 2; Kahn, *Matusow Affair*, 118–20 ("How do we know" and quotations about Communist sponsorship); transcript of press conference, Feb. 3, 1955, M93-264, box 1, folder 47, Kahn Papers ("had a nervous breakdown," 7); *New York Times*, Feb. 6, 1955, sec. 4 ("Repentant Matusow") ("type of glamor," "right some of the wrongs").

45. Matusow Hearings, 44.

46. Kahn, *Matusow Affair*, 120–21.

47. Director to indicated officials, Feb. 10, 1955, with attached Riesel column dated Feb. 4, 1955, FBI 100-375988-286.

48. *New York Times*, Feb. 4, 1955 ("Matusow Termed 'Planted' Witness"), Feb. 6, 1955 ("Jackson Demands Matusow Inquiry") (Jackson quotation); Nichols to Tolson, Feb. 10,

1955, FBI 100-375988-466 (Nixon quotation); Jones to Nichols, Feb. 14, 1955, FBI 100-275988-546.

49. *New York Times*, Feb. 6, 1955 ("Role of Informers Now under Inquiry" and "Jackson Demands Matusow Inquiry"), Feb. 8, 1955 ("Red Motion Is Due for Hearing Today") ("vigorous"); Nichols to Tolson, Jan. 31, 1955, FBI 100-375988-247 ("felt obligated").

50. See Director to Attorney General, Feb. 2, 1955, FBI 100-375988-144.

51. Belmont to Boardman, Feb. 1, 1955.

52. Ibid. (quotations); Hennrich to Belmont, Feb. 1, 1955, FBI 100-375988-146; Keay to Belmont, Feb. 1, 1955, FBI 100-375988-149; Kelly to Director, Feb. 2, 1955, FBI 100-375988-153.

53. Belmont to Boardman, Feb. 1, 1955, FBI 100-375988-NR (headed "COMMUNIST PARTY, USA-BRIEF") (quotations in second sentence); Belmont to Boardman, Feb. 1, 1955, FBI 100-375988-NR (headed "COMPROS-NEW YORK INTERNAL SECURITY-C"); Belmont to Boardman, Feb. 2, 1955, FBI 100-375988-NR ("review of the Bureau files"); Boardman to Director, Feb. 2, 1955 (Boardman quotations); Boardman to Director, Feb. 4, 1955. Boardman passed Belmont's conclusions to Hoover on February 3 (Boardman to Director, Feb. 3, 1955, FBI 100-375988-262).

54. Director to Attorney General, Feb. 3, 1955, FBI 100-375988-202.

55. Hoover to SACs NY et al., Feb. 1, 1955, FBI 100-375988-161; McFarlin to Director, Feb. 5, 1955, FBI 100-375988-216; Kelly to Director, Feb. 2, 1955, FBI 100-375988-185; Bryce to Director, Feb. 4, 1955; Murphy to Director, Feb. 5, 1955, FBI 100-375988-219; Murphy to Director, Feb. 4, 1955, FBI 100-375988-227; Hawkins to Director, Feb. 4, 1955, FBI 100-375988-229; Brown to Director, Feb. 2, 1955, FBI 100-375988-258; Director to Asst. Atty. Gen. Tompkins, Feb. 7, 1955, 4–5.

56. Kelly to Director, Feb. 6, 1955, FBI 100-375988-267 (Matthews quotation, 3); Director to Asst. Atty Gen. Tompkins, Feb. 5, 1955, FBI 100-375998-160, 4–8 (Arvilla Bentley quotation, 7). In her interview, Kay Kerby, with whom Matusow lived in 1950, stated that he "would do anything to direct publicity to himself" (Director to Asst. Atty. Gen. Tompkins, Feb. 15, 1955, FBI 100-375988-507, 3). Matthews also told of a late-night phone call from Matusow in August 1953, during which he reportedly stated, "I am such a double crosser that I double cross myself twice a day to keep in practice" (Kelly to Director, Feb. 6, 1955, 2).

57. Director to Attorney General, Feb. 2, 1955; Belmont to Boardman, Feb. 2, 1955, FBI 100-375988-167; Keay to Belmont, Feb. 2, 1955, FBI 100-375988-175; Keay to Belmont, Feb. 2, 1955, FBI 100-375988-184; Keay to Belmont, Feb. 4, 1955, FBI 100-375988-178; Kelly to Director, Feb. 4, 1955, FBI 100-375988-200; Kelly to Director, Feb. 8, 1955, FBI 100-375988-389; *New York Times*, Feb. 8, 1955 ("Red Motion Is Due for Hearing Today"), Feb. 9, 1955 ("Matusow Hearing by Jury Delayed") (quotation).

58. *United States v. Flynn*, 130 F. Supp. at 414–15.

59. Flynn transcript, 16674–922; *New York Times*, Feb. 11, 1955 ("'53 Matusow Note Cites 'Dishonesty'") (quotation), Feb. 12, 1955 ("Matusow Sought Anti-Reds' Favor"); Kahn, *Matusow Affair*, 153–56.

60. Flynn transcript, 16962–17593; *New York Times*, Feb. 11, 1955 ("'53 Matusow Note Cites 'Dishonesty'") (quotation), Feb. 12, 1955 ("Matusow Sought Anti-Reds' Favor"), Feb. 13, 1955, sec. 4 ("'False Witness'"), Feb. 15, 1955 ("Matusow Admits Recantation Pays"), Feb. 16, 1955 ("Matusow Admits Faking Blacklist"), Feb. 17, 1955 ("Matusow Admits Lie about

Oxnam"), Feb. 18, 1955 ("Matusow's Reform Is Laid to Children"), Feb. 20, 1955, sec. 4 ("More on Matusow"), Mar. 26, 1955 ("Matusow Switch Is Laid to Greed"); Kahn, *Matusow Affair,* 157–59.

61. *United States v. Flynn,* 130 F. Supp. at 414–16.

62. Ibid., 416, 420.

63. Ibid., 420–22; *New York Times,* Apr. 23, 1955 ("Matusow Lies Get 2 Reds New Trial") (quotation), Apr. 24, 1955, sec. 4 ("New Trial"), Apr. 26, 1955 ("Speedy New Trial of 2 Reds Sought"), Aug. 5, 1958 ("U.S. Court Frees 6 Convicted Reds"). See *United States v. Jackson,* 257 F. 2d 830 (2d Cir. 1958), reversing the convictions of Trachtenberg, Charney, and four other defendants and dismissing the indictment.

64. *New York Times,* Feb. 9, 1955 ("Matusow Hearing by Jury Delayed"), Feb. 10, 1955 ("Publisher of a Book by Matusow Gets Six-Month Contempt Term"), Feb. 11, 1955 ("53 Matusow Note Cites 'Dishonesty'"), Feb. 13, 1955, sec. 4 ("'False Witness'"); *New York Herald Tribune,* Feb. 10, 1955 ("Matusow's Publisher Sentenced to 6 Months"); Kahn, *Matusow Affair,* 125–44, 146–51.

65. *New York Times,* Feb. 18, 1955 ("Matusow Study Widened by U.S.").

66. *New York Times,* Feb. 21, 1955 ("U.S. 'Risk' Policy under Wide Fire").

Chapter 9: At Center Stage

1. See the introduction, pp. 1–2.

2. *New York Times,* Feb. 22, 1955 ("No Longer a Liar, Matusow Swears"); *New York Herald Tribune,* Feb. 22, 1955 ("Matusow Backs Book Even If It Helps Reds"); Russell Baker to Lichtman, Apr. 9, 2000. On Faulkner see Matusow Hearings, 464–66.

3. Matusow Hearings, 1–2.

4. Ibid., 2.

5. Ibid., 26, 30; *New York Times,* Jan. 6, 1956 ("Strategist for Inquiry").

6. Matusow Hearings, 39–40.

7. Ibid., 41–42, 45.

8. Ibid., 41 ("and wasn't with me"), 53–62 (other quotations, 56). Charles Allen later told Kahn that Tank had indeed "started to write a play about the whole incident" and "the opening passages were powerful" but that the work was not finished (Chuck [Allen] interview, 1976–77, 19, Kahn Papers).

9. Matusow Hearings, 55.

10. Ibid., 60–61.

11. Ibid., 83–84.

12. *New York Herald Tribune,* Feb. 22, 1955 ("Matusow Backs Book Even If It Helps Reds") (first quotation); *New York Times,* Feb. 22, 1955 ("No Longer a Liar, Matusow Swears") (same quotation), Feb. 28, 1955 ("Two Call Matusow Truthful at First") (second quotation).

13. Director to Attorney General, Feb. 12, 1955, FBI 100-375988-642, 1–2.

14. Ibid., 2. See Leab, *I Was a Communist for the FBI,* 98–99.

15. Director to Attorney General, Feb. 12, 1955, 3.

16. *New York Times,* Feb. 18, 1955 ("Matusow Study Widened by U.S."); *Saturday Evening Post,* Mar. 26, 1955 ("Reds Now Undertake to Brainwash America!"), 10 (quoting *Herald Tribune*).

17. Warren Olney III oral history interviews, 1970–77, "Law Enforcement and Judicial Administration in the Earl Warren Era," 364, Regional Oral History Office, Bancroft Library, University of California, Berkeley; Herbert Brownell with John Burke, *Advising Ike: The Memoirs of Herbert Brownell* (Lawrence: University Press of Kansas, 1993), 235.

18. Matusow Hearings, 88.

19. Ibid., 88–90.

20. Ibid., 102.

21. Ibid., 103.

22. Ibid., 184–93 (quotation, 188). Hennings was chairman of the Judiciary Committee's three-member Subcommittee on Constitutional Rights, which in late 1955 conducted informed and critical hearings, unique during the period, on the government's loyalty-security programs. See Hennings Hearings. The hearings were provocatively styled "A SURVEY OF THE EXTENT TO WHICH THE RIGHTS GUARANTEED BY THE FIRST AMENDMENT ARE BEING RESPECTED AND ENFORCED IN THE VARIOUS GOVERNMENT LOYALTY-SECURITY PROGRAMS."

23. *New York Times*, Feb. 23, 1955 ("Matusow Blames McCarthy for Lies").

24. On Bentley's revelations see Bentley Nov. 30, 1945, statement; see also introduction, pp. 3–4. On Hoover's vouching see Statement of J. Edgar Hoover on Harry Dexter White case, Nov. 17, 1953, 1953 White Hearings, 1145.

25. Director to SAC NY, Mar. 15, 1955, FBI 134-435-NR, 3.

26. Director to Asst. Atty. Gen. Tompkins, Mar. 4, 1955, FBI 134-435-134.

27. SAC NY to Director, Mar. 24, 1955, FBI 134-182-66, 5; SAC NY to Director, Sept. 26, 1952, FBI 134-435-66. The New York office's lengthy September 26 report stated that the U.S. attorney's office in Manhattan was "kept constantly apprised" of Bentley's condition, so that "these facts might be borne in mind at such times as Miss BENTLEY is being considered as a witness" (ibid., 9). About four months later, Bentley appeared as a government witness in the second trial of William Remington (as she had at his first trial), which resulted in his conviction and imprisonment. See *New York Times*, Jan. 16, 1953 ("Ex-Red Is a Witness at Remington Trial"); and May, *Un-American Activities*, 285–86.

28. Hoover to SAC New Orleans, Feb. 21, 1955, FBI 134-435-129; Chiles to Director, Feb. 22, 1955, FBI 134-435-130; *New York Times*, Feb. 24, 1955 ("Miss Bentley Issues Denial").

29. Message of Bentley call to Director, Feb. 24, 1955, FBI 134-435-131 (Hoover notation); Belmont to Boardman, Feb. 25, 1955, FBI 134-435-132 (Lamphere quotation); Nichols to Tolson, Feb. 24, 1955, FBI 134-435-135. Lamphere was a Bentley expert at the bureau. See Robert J. Lamphere and Tom Shachtman, *The FBI-KGB War: A Special Agent's Story* (New York: Random House, 1986), 182, 279. Bentley phoned Lamphere at the suggestion of Joseph M. Kelly, a former FBI agent, whom she knew well and called after failing to reach Hoover.

30. Browne to Bureau, Mar. 9, 1955, FBI 134-435-NR, 8–13 (Henry quotation, 10; Hibbard quotation, 13); Kelly to Bureau, Mar. 1, 1955, FBI 134-182-61; Kelly to Bureau, Mar. 2, 1955, FBI 134-182-65. The second Elizabeth Bentley FBI file (134-182) was also obtained via an FOIA request.

31. Kempton, "Achievement of Harvey Matusow," 10.

32. Matusow Hearings, 261–64, 1152 (quotation).

33. Ibid., 377, 379–84; *New York Times*, Mar. 2, 1955 ("Matusow Says Ex-Wife Told Him She Gave $70,000 to McCarthy"), July 12, 1955 ("Senate Group Cites Three in Contempt"). For other assertions of the Fifth Amendment see Matusow Hearings, 313–20, 346.

34. Matusow Hearings, 384. The parent Judiciary Committee voted in July to cite Matusow for contempt with respect to his stringless yo-yo (and other) testimony (S. Rep. No. 823-25, July 12, 1955, at 7–13), and the full Senate concurred. See *New York Times,* July 12, 1955 ("Senate Group Cites Three in Contempt"), and Mar. 30, 1956 ("Matusow Trial Urged"). But no prosecution for contempt of Congress was brought against him.

35. Matusow Hearings, 384–85; *New York Times,* Mar. 2, 1955 ("Matusow Says Ex-Wife Told Him She Gave $70,000 to McCarthy").

36. Matusow Hearings, 509–10.

37. In the radio broadcast "Job Matusow," Matusow said, "I knew they were going to put me in jail, so what could they do?"

38. Jencks motion transcript, 890–91; *New York Times,* Mar. 17, 1955 ("Matusow Receives 3-Year Prison Term"); Kahn, *Matusow Affair,* 198–203.

39. Jencks motion transcript, 13, 36 ("any conversation"), 87–88 ("didn't trust"), 722–23 ("worked up for"), 732–33 ("was false"); *New York Times,* Mar. 8, 1955 ("Matusow Recants in Texas").

40. Jencks motion transcript, 892–93.

41. Ibid., 892–96; *Matusow v. United States,* 229 F. 2d 335, 338 (5th Cir. 1956); Judge Thomason's Findings and Judgment, Sentence and Order, and Hearing Transcript, Mar. 16, 1955, pp. 40–52 ("to try and undo," 43; Thomason quotations, 50), box 10, file 9, Matusow Papers; *New York Times,* Mar. 17, 1955 ("Matusow Receives 3-Year Term").

42. Kahn, *Matusow Affair,* 204 (Stone quotation); *New York Times,* Mar. 17, 1955 ("Eastland Praises Judge") (Eastland quotation).

43. *New York Times,* Mar. 20, 1955 ("Sentence for Matusow"), Apr. 5, 1955 ("Matusow Freed on Bond"), Apr. 20, 1955 ("Woman Who Furnished Matusow Bail Calls Him Symbol of a National Blight"); Kahn, *Matusow Affair,* 211–19; Sylvia Matusow to Harvey Matusow, Mar. 21 and 25, 1957, box 22, file 5, Matusow Papers; Matusow to Kahn, Mar. 30, 1955, Matusow-Kahn Correspondence, 1955–57, and Chuck [Allen] interview, 1976–77, 22–23 ("recanted his recanting"), Kahn Papers. Kahn believed that the union "double-crossed" Matusow and "failed to keep their word" when it declined to provide funds for his bail (ibid.).

44. *Jencks v. United States,* 226 F. 2d 553, 556 (5th Cir. 1955).

45. *Jencks v. United States,* 226 F. 2d 540, 552 (5th Cir. 1955), *rev'd* 353 U.S. 657 (1957). A year prior to the Supreme Court's decision, the Mine-Mill union had requested and obtained Jencks's resignation. (C. Jencks interview, July 26, 1977, 55, Kahn Papers.)

46. *Matusow v. United States,* 229 F. 2d 335, 341, 346–47 (5th Cir. 1956). The decision turned substantially on technical contempt law: only acts of contempt in the presence of the judge can be punished summarily; but in Matusow's case the only such act was perjury, and perjury alone did not support a contempt conviction.

47. Kahn, *Matusow Affair,* 164–66, 205.

48. Ibid., 205–6; *New York Times,* Mar. 27, 1955, Sunday Book Review ("Double Switch"), Apr. 17, 1955, Sunday Book Review (advertisement), 31; Jencks motion transcript, 444–45; Matusow interview, Dec. 23–24, 1996. The book sold for $1.25 in paperback and $3.00 in hardback.

49. Kahn, *Matusow Affair,* 208–10 (quotation from *Winston-Salem Journal and Sentinel*); *Herald Tribune Book Review,* May 8, 1955 ("Is It Perjury or Overpublicized Piffle?"); *New York Times,* Mar. 27, 1955, Sunday Book Review ("Double Switch").

50. *New York Times,* Feb. 24, 1955 ("M'Carthy Scores Matusow Queries"), Feb. 27, 1955 ("Matusow Called 'Just a Stooge'"), Mar. 8, 1955 ("Matusow Publisher Invokes the Fifth"), Mar. 9, 1955 ("Matusow's Book Drew Union Cash"), Mar. 10, 1955 ("Publisher Bars Red Tie Queries"); Matusow Hearings, 525–641 (Kahn), 641–47 (Tank), 691–95 (Cameron); Kahn, *Matusow Affair,* 179–91.

51. Matusow Hearings, 747–802; *New York Times,* Apr. 19, 1955 ("Aid for Matusow on Book Depicted"); SISS Matusow Report, 84. Witt did deny bizarre testimony at the hearings by informer John Lautner that, while a Communist Party member, he was directed by Witt to arrange the delivery of a bouquet of white lilies to Whittaker Chambers as "a very subtle form of intimidation" (Matusow Hearings, 800–801, 893–94).

52. Matusow Hearings, 829–44; *New York Times,* July 12, 1955 ("Senate Group Cites Three in Contempt"), July 29, 1955 ("Senate Cites Sacher"), Dec. 22, 1955 (U.S. Jury Indicts Unionist, Sacher"), Feb. 1, 1958 ("Contempt Ruling on Sacher Upheld"), May 20, 1958 ("Court Reverses Sacher Decision"). Sacher's objections appear at Matusow Hearings, 836–39. The Supreme Court's per curiam opinion is reported at 356 U.S. 576 (1958).

53. Matusow Hearings, 845–90; *New York Times,* Apr. 20, 1955 ("Woman Who Furnished Matusow Bail Calls Him Symbol of a National Blight"). Willcox's "symbol of a sickness" comment appears in a prepared statement on p. 890 of the published hearings.

54. Matusow Hearings, 969, 995–96, 1139.

55. Kahn, *Matusow Affair,* 175 (Stone quotation); Kempton, "Achievement of Harvey Matusow," 10.

56. *New York Times,* Mar. 22, 1955 ("Brownell Accuses Reds on Matusow"). See text of speech in *U.S. News and World Report,* Apr. 1, 1955 ("Attorney General Says: Reds Are Trying to Wreck Informant System of FBI"), 68–71.

57. *U.S. News and World Report,* Mar. 4, 1955 ("Can Informers Be Trusted? How Agents Planted by FBI Convicted Red Leaders"), 47, and Feb. 18, 1955 ("Paid Informers in U.S.— They're Used All the Time"); *New York Times,* Mar. 13, 1955 ("Recanters Pose a Problem for Government").

58. *New York Times,* Apr. 16, 1955 ("Brownell Drops Informant Plan"); *New York Post,* Apr. 16, 1955 ("Red 'Consultants' Paid by the Job: Brownell"). Earlier the same week, in House committee hearings, INS commissioner Joseph M. Swing disclosed that his agency had dropped Matusow from its list of witnesses in April 1954 (*New York Times,* Apr. 11, 1955 ["U.S. Knew in 1952 Matusow Was Ill"]).

59. *New York Times,* Apr. 16, 1955 ("Brownell Drops Informant Plan"); Rovere, "Kept Witnesses," 117–20.

60. *New York Times,* Aug. 24, 1955 ("U.S. Bureau Lists Informants' Fees").

61. Mario Noto, memorandum for file, Apr. 7, 1955, DOJ DCSW minutes. The committee's materials were classified; now released under FOIA, they are heavily redacted, with many pages withheld entirely.

62. Minutes for meetings, Apr. 6 and 12, 1955, in DOJ DCSW minutes.

63. Minutes for meetings, Apr. 21 ("unless in a specific case"), May 5 ("not be used in the future"), and June 30, 1955, "Progress Report April 5–May, 31, 1955," Tompkins to DCSW, June 30, 1955, Commissioner of INS to DCSW, June 29, 1955, and Thomas K. Hall to Tompkins, June 30, 1955, in DOJ DCSW minutes. See Leab, *I Was a Communist for the FBI,* 101. In the case of Paul Crouch, Tompkins had recommended to Brownell at the end

of February that he not be used "unless his testimony is essential to successful prosecution and your prior approval has been obtained" (Tompkins to Attorney General, Feb. 28, 1955, 4, in DOJ DCSW minutes).

64. *New York Times*, Mar. 9, 1955 ("Jury Studies Matusow"), Mar. 13, 1955 ("Recanters Pose a Problem for Government" ["plans to have a go"] and "The False Witnesses"); Murray Kempton, *New York Post*, Apr. 29, 1955, quoted in *The Nation*, July 23, 1955 ("The Nation and Mr. Brownell's 'Justice'"), 68.

65. *New York Times*, Apr. 28, 1955 ("2d Top Red Seeks Right to Quit U.S."); Matusow to Kahn, Feb. 5, 1957, Matusow-Kahn Correspondence, 1955–57, Kahn Papers; Kahn, *Matusow Affair*, 227–28.

66. *New York Times*, May 5, 1955 ("Republican Club Ousts Matusow").

Chapter 10: Paying the Piper

1. Kahn, *Matusow Affair*, 236–39 (quotation, 239); *New York Times*, June 11, 1955 ("Matusow to Wed Artist"). Matusow later had a different version of meeting Raskin: that they met on a sunny day in Washington Square Park, after a policeman complained about Raskin's daughter playing in a wading pool without clothes ("Cockyboo," chap. 12, p. 6).

2. Indictment, filed July 13, 1955, *United States v. Harvey M. Matusow*, C147-345 (S.D.N.Y.); *New York Times*, July 14, 1955 ("U.S. Lays Perjury to Matusow Here").

3. Dufty telephone conversation, Dec. 21, 1999.

4. One can understand Brownell's support at the time for proposed legislation that would make the "willful giving" of conflicting testimony a crime and relieve the government of the obligation of proving which of two conflicting statements was false. See *New York Times*, Mar. 7, 1955 ("Stiffer Perjury Law Sought by Brownell").

5. See *United States v. Flynn*, 130 F. Supp. at 420. John McTernan, lead defense counsel in the Jencks case who had participated in the Smith Act trial, believed that defense counsel in the latter case used poor judgment in allowing Matusow to testify that Cohn suborned his perjury, a charge for which he had no corroboration (McTernan interview, Nov. 14, 2002).

6. *New York Times*, July 30, 1955 ("Matusow Goes to Jail"), Aug. 4, 1955 ("Matusow Freed in Bail"), Aug. 5, 1955 ("Matusow Bail Is $3,000").

7. Order, Apr. 19, 1956, Judge Sylvester J. Ryan; *New York Times*, May 1, 1956 ("Novel Jury Tests Used in Red Trial").

8. Matusow to Kahn, June 11, 1955, and Kahn to Matusow, July 24, 1955, Matusow-Kahn Correspondence, 1955–57, Kahn Papers; Kahn, *Matusow Affair*, 238.

9. Kahn, *Matusow Affair*, 247–48; Matusow, "Cockyboo," chap. 12, pp. 8–9. The legal costs of simultaneously appealing his contempt conviction and preparing to defend against the perjury charge aggravated Matusow's poor financial situation. His lawyer, Stanley Faulkner, wrote that "Harvey is completely without any funds whatsoever. Truthfully, the situation is rather desperate with him" (S. Faulkner to J. Calamia, Oct. 14, 1955, box 18, file 2, Matusow Papers).

10. *New York Times*, July 14, 1955 ("U.S. Lays Perjury to Matusow Here") (quotation); *The Nation*, July 23, 1955 ("The Nation and Mr. Brownell's 'Justice'"), 65–68. A separate indictment, also handed down the same day, accused Martin Solow, an assistant to the

publisher of *The Nation*, with obstruction of justice in destroying four letters relating to meetings between *The Nation* employees and Matusow, which the magazine said were written "in his individual capacity and in no way in behalf of *The Nation*" (ibid., 65). See *United States v. Solow*, 138 F. Supp. 812 (S.D.N.Y. 1956). The article referred to is Donner, "Informer."

11. *United States v. Siegel*, 263 F. 2d 530, 531–32 (2d Cir. 1959). Judge McGohey had been the lead prosecutor in the 1949 Foley Square Smith Act trial. See chap. 3, p. 49.

12. *New York Times*, Sept. 15, 1955 ("Another Accused in Matusow Case"); John Earl Haynes, "The 'Spy' on Joe McCarthy's Staff: The Forgotten Case of Paul H. Hughes," *Continuity: A Journal of History* 14 (Spring/Fall 1990): 21–38; Oshinsky, *Conspiracy So Immense*, 311–13 (states "a superb con artist"); Herman, *Joseph McCarthy*, 236–37 ("a skilled, if slightly deranged, amateur confidence man"); Laughlin to Director, Feb. 9, 1955, FBI 100-375988-465; Laughlin to Director, Feb. 10, 1955, FBI 100-375988-481; Torrillo to Belmont, Feb. 20, 1955, FBI 100-375988-650 (quotation).

13. Haynes, "'Spy' on Joe McCarthy's Staff," 38–61. To William F. Buckley Jr., who covered the trial for the newly established *National Review*, and other McCarthy partisans, the Hughes affair has been an unending source of satisfaction and amusement—proof to them of the hypocrisy of liberals who complained of McCarthy's methods. Buckley, according to John Earl Haynes's inventory, "published eight *National Review* articles on the Hughes case [and] twice reproduced a chart showing the liberal personae involved" (ibid., 48 and 48 n. 78). Buckley also included the tale in his *Up from Liberalism* (New York: McDowell, Obolensky, 1959), 70–85, in a *New York Post* column (cited by Haynes) on March 5, 1977 ("Joe McCarthy's Foes"), and again in 1996 when his book *McCarthy and His Enemies* was reprinted. See William F. Buckley Jr. and L. Brent Bozell, *McCarthy and His Enemies: The Record and Its Meaning* (reprint, Washington, D.C.: Regnery Publishing, 1996), xiv n and appendix G ("The Liberal in Action"), 393–404.

14. SISS press release, Dec. 29, 1955 (Eastland quotation); SISS Matusow Report, 88–90 (other quotations); *New York Times*, Dec. 31, 1955 ("Matusow Switch Tied to Red Plot").

15. SISS Matusow Report, 91.

16. Ibid., 28 and 28 n. 8. The subcommittee was criticized sharply in the press for quoting selectively and misleadingly from Matusow's affidavit. See *New York Times*, Jan. 6, 1956 ("Strategist for Inquiry").

17. *Communist Party v. Subversive Activities Control Board*, 351 U.S. 115, 121, 124–25 (1956); *New York Times*, May 1, 1956 ("High Court Sees Taint in Red Case"), May 2, 1956 ("Ruling Holds Up Subversion Cases"), May 6, 1956, sec. 4 ("Court and S.A.C.B."); *The Supreme Court in Conference (1940–1985): The Private Discussions behind Nearly 300 Supreme Court Decisions*, ed. Del Dickson (New York: Oxford University Press, 2001), 294 (Warren quote). The SACB wasted little time in expunging the testimony of the three witnesses from the record, after which it again concluded that the Communist Party must register. See *New York Times*, Aug. 12, 1956 ("Evidence Erased in Red Party Case"), and Dec. 19, 1956 ("Reds in U.S. Ruled Tools of Moscow").

18. *Mesarosh v. United States*, 352 U.S. at 9, 10. The government dropped the case less than a year later, reportedly after another prosecution witness (not Mazzei) recanted (Caute, *Great Fear*, 222).

19. Trial transcript in *United States v. Harvey M. Matusow*, C147-345 (hereafter, Matu-

sow trial transcript), 1–735; *New York Times,* Sept. 19, 1956 ("Matusow's Trial on Perjury Opens").

20. Testimony of Asst. U.S. Attorneys David L. Marks (Matusow trial transcript, 118–63), John M. Foley (ibid., 163–98), Albert A. Blinder (ibid., 199–305), Robert M. Reagan (ibid., 479–527), and James V. Ryan (ibid., 527–47) and FBI agent James F. McCarthy (ibid., 62–117a); *New York Times,* Sept. 19, 1956 ("Matusow's Trial on Perjury Opens"), Sept. 20, 1956 ("Cohn Repudiates Matusow Story").

21. *New York Times,* Sept. 20, 1956 ("Cohn Repudiates Matusow Story") ("Matusow, now a slight 148"), Sept. 21, 1956 ("'Tampering' Role Is Denied by Cohn") ("calm and confident"). Cohn's testimony appears at Matusow trial transcript, 305–478.

22. Matusow trial transcript, 319.

23. Matusow's testimony appears in ibid., 556–735; his direct examination in ibid., 556–66; the portion of his cross-examination quoted in the text in ibid., 567–68; *New York Times,* Sept. 22, 1956 ("Matusow Admits to 'Vicious' Lying").

24. Matusow trial transcript, 576–77, 592–96; *New York Times,* Sept. 25, 1956 ("Matusow's Trial Nearing Verdict").

25. *New York Times,* Sept. 26, 1956 ("Discredit of U.S. Laid to Matusow").

26. *New York Times,* Sept. 27, 1956 ("Matusow Guilty in Perjury Case").

27. Order, Judge McGohey, Sept. 27, 1956, fixing bail (C147-345); Judgment and Commitment, filed Sept. 28, 1956 (ibid.); *New York Times,* Sept. 28, 1956 ("Matusow Surrenders to U.S."), Sept. 29, 1956 ("Matusow Sentenced to 5 Years for Perjury in Communist Case").

28. *New York Times,* Sept. 29, 1956 ("Matusow Sentenced to 5 Years for Perjury in Communist Case") (Matusow quotation), Sept. 30, 1956, sec. 4 ("Matusow Guilty") ("theatrical").

29. Order, 2d Circuit, Dec. 31, 1956, filed in Dist. Ct., Jan. 8, 1957 (C147-345); Bail Certificate, Jan. 4, 1957, signed by Sylvia Matusow (ibid).

30. Matusow to Kahn, Jan. 9 and 25, 1957, Matusow-Kahn Correspondence, 1955–57, Kahn Papers; Kahn, *Matusow Affair,* 259–60.

31. Matusow to Kahn, Feb. 26 ("It meant a lot"), Mar. 8, 15, 20 ("Ellen refuses"), and 28, 1957, Matusow-Kahn Correspondence, 1955–57; Kahn, *Matusow Affair,* 260–61. Matusow's March 8, 1957, letter to Ellen's parents (who lived in Los Angeles) advised, "I've held off writing so as to give Ellen a chance to break the news to you" (box 22, file 8, Matusow Papers).

32. Matusow to Kahn, Apr. 20, 1957, Matusow-Kahn Correspondence, 1955–57.

33. *United States v. Matusow,* 244 F. 2d 532, 533 (2d Cir. 1957); *New York Times,* May 11, 1957 ("Matusow Conviction Upheld").

34. *New York Times,* June 11, 1957 ("Matusow Begins Five-Year Sentence"); Matusow interview, ca. 1976, 11/83–13/85 (quotations), Kahn Papers; Matusow, "Cockyboo," chap. 15, pp. 8–10.

35. Matusow interview, ca. 1976, 13/85 (quotations), Kahn Papers; Matusow, "Cockyboo," chap. 14, pp. 1–4, chap. 15, p. 11.

36. Oshinsky, *Conspiracy So Immense,* 495–96, 502–6. McCarthy's death unleashed an emotional outpouring of frustration and anger on the part of his followers. "They believed McCarthy had been 'hounded to death by those,' according to columnist George

Sokolsky, 'who would not forget and could not forgive.' To many, McCarthy's censure and the campaign against him had been nothing less than a form of public murder—a few on the very fringe were willing to believe that he *had* been murdered" (Herman, *Joseph McCarthy*, 306; emphasis in original).

37. *Jencks v. United States*, 353 U.S. 657 (1957); *Supreme Court in Conference (1940–1985)*, 555; McTernan interview, Nov. 14, 2002.

38. The four "Red Monday" decisions are *Watkins v. United States*, 354 U.S. 178, 200 (1957), a contempt-of-Congress case in which the Court rejected any "congressional power to expose for the sake of exposure"; *Yates v. United States*, 354 U.S. 298, 325 (1957), a Smith Act prosecution in which the Court held that the prosecution must prove advocacy that urges its audience "to *do* something, now or in the future, rather than merely *believe* in something" (emphasis in original); *Service v. Dulles*, 354 U.S. 363 (1957), a federal employee loyalty-security case in which the Court set aside the discharge of a State Department China expert due to the department's failure to adhere to its own procedural rules; and *Sweezy v. State of New Hampshire*, 354 U.S. 235 (1957), a state contempt case in which the Court reversed the conviction of a college professor who refused to answer questions concerning the Progressive Party in New Hampshire. See, generally, Arthur J. Sabin, *In Calmer Times: The Supreme Court and Red Monday* (Philadelphia: University of Pennsylvania Press, 1999).

Chapter 11: Four Decades of Aftermath

1. On his prison release date see Kahn, *Matusow Affair*, 265.

2. Alverson, "I Led Twelve Lives," 22; Matusow, "Cockyboo," chap. 12A, pp. 1–7, chap. 16, p. 9, chap. 17, pp. 1–2; Matusow interview, Dec. 23–24, 1996, and telephone conversation with Lichtman, Aug. 30, 2000; Kahn, *Matusow Affair*, 265.

3. Matusow interview, Dec. 23–24, 1996; Alverson, "I Led Twelve Lives," 22.

4. Alverson, "I Led Twelve Lives," 22; Matusow, "Cockyboo," chap. 22, p. 1 (quotations); Matusow interview, ca. 1976, 10/112, Kahn Papers.

5. Matusow, "Cockyboo," chap. 22, p. 1 ("not knowing a soul"); Matusow interview, ca. 1976, 10/112, Kahn Papers; Alverson, "I Led Twelve Lives," 20.

6. Alverson, "I Led Twelve Lives," 20, 22; Matusow interview, ca. 1976, 29/101, Kahn Papers; Kahn, *Matusow Affair*, 265.

7. Harvey Matusow, comp. and ed., *The Beast of Business: A Record of Computer Atrocities* (London: Wolfe, 1968; German translation, Oldenburg: Stulling, 1969); Alverson, "I Led Twelve Lives," 22; Matusow interview, Dec. 23–24, 1996; Caute, *Great Fear*, 621.

8. Carman Moore, "International Carnival of Experimental Sound," *Saturday Review [of the Arts]*, Nov. 4, 1972, 64; Alverson, "I Led Twelve Lives," 22; Jay Landesman, *Jaywalking* (London: Weidenfeld and Nicolson, 1992), 104.

9. Moore, "International Carnival of Experimental Sound," 64–65; Alverson, "I Led Twelve Lives," 22; Landesman, *Jaywalking*, 105–6.

10. Moore, "International Carnival of Experimental Sound," 64–66; Landesman, *Jaywalking*, 106–7.

11. Matusow interview, ca. 1976, 9/111–11/113, 14/116, Kahn Papers.

12. Ibid., 2/74–3/79, 14/116 (quotation), 18/120, 22/124.

13. Ibid., 1/73–7/79 ("vows of poverty," 2/74), 14/116–16/118 ("freer in all," "This so-called psychic thing"), 21/123 ("very basic lifestyle," "Using wood").

14. Ibid., 8/80–9/81, 28/100, 24/126; Matusow interview, Dec. 23–24, 1996, and telephone conversation with Lichtman, Dec. 30, 1996; "Job Matusow" (radio broadcast).

15. Matusow interview, ca. 1976, 2/104, 5/107, Kahn Papers.

16. Matusow interview with Lichtman, Dec. 23–24, 1996.

17. *Tucson Citizen,* Mar. 20, 1980 ("There's Lots of Love in Job Matusow's Magic Mouse Show" and "Magic Mouse a Joy for Kids and Actors"); *New York Times,* Sept. 20, 1981 ("Figure from McCarthy Days Pleases People with Puppets"); *San Francisco Sunday Examiner and Chronicle,* Sept. 20, 1981 ("A Mouse Born in the Dungeons of McCarthyism," AP dispatch).

18. *Arizona Daily Star,* Nov. 8, 1982 ("Cafe Owner Fights Critics to Feed 'Hobos'"), Nov. 14, 1982 ("America's 'Most Hated Man'"); *Arizona Republic,* Nov. 22, 1982 ("Trials of Job"); *National Catholic Reporter,* Jan. 14, 1983 ("Transients Blamed for Mass Cancellation"); Matusow interview, Dec. 23–24, 1996.

19. *Bangor (Me.) Daily News,* Feb. 20, 1987 ("Boston-Based Christian Group Provides Clothing Donation for Needy Penobscots"); *Daily Hampshire Gazette,* Dec. 17, 1987 ("Ringing Bells for Joy, Peace"); Matusow interview, Dec. 23–24, 1996.

20. *Arizona Daily Star,* Sept. 27, 1994 ("Tucson's Lovable Clown"); Matusow interview, Dec. 23–24, 1996.

21. Matusow telephone conversations with Lichtman, Dec. 30, 1996, June 9, Aug. 30, 2000, and Dec. 4, 2001. According to his obituary in the *New York Times* (Feb. 4, 2002 ["Harvey Matusow, 75, an Anti-Communist Informer, Dies"]), he had "around a dozen wives."

22. Matusow interview, Dec. 23–24, 1996; *Salt Lake Tribune,* Jan. 12, 1997 ("The World of Job Matusow"); *Deseret News,* Mar. 27, 1999 ("'Job' Turns His Trials into Blessings").

23. Matusow interview, Dec. 23–24, 1996; "World of Job Matusow."

24. "World of Job Matusow."

25. Matusow telephone conversations, Sept. 7 and Dec. 4, 2001.

26. Irene Gibson, telephone conversation with Lichtman, May 29, 2002; *New York Times,* Feb. 4, 2002 ("Harvey Matusow, 75, an Anti-Communist Informer, Dies"); *Washington Post,* Jan. 28, 2002 ("Anti-Communist Witness Harvey Matusow, 75, Dies").

27. "Harvey Matusow, 75, an Anti-Communist Informer, Dies."

Epilogue

1. On the continuing debate, see Michael J. Heale, "Beyond the 'Age of McCarthy': Anticommunism and the Historians," in *The State of U.S. History,* ed. Melvyn Stokes (Oxford, Eng.: Berg, 2002), 131 ("there is probably at the moment less agreement than there has ever been on how to interpret domestic anticommunism"); and *New York Times,* Oct. 18, 1998, sec. 4 ("Witching Hour: Rethinking McCarthyism, if Not McCarthy") ("It is no surprise that, given the ferocity of the political struggle at the time, the scholarly struggle over the new data is raw and impassioned"). On the degree of culpability issue, Ellen Schrecker wrote that those who gave information to the Soviets "did so for political, not pecuniary, reasons," "thought they were 'building . . . a better world for the masses,' not

betraying their country," and acted mostly during World War II "when the United States and the Soviet Union were on the same side" (*Many Are the Crimes,* 181). But Harvey Klehr terms Schrecker's views and those of historians who agree with her "lies, evasions, and morally obtuse views . . . the desperate flailings of a doomed viewpoint . . . vile efforts to rewrite history" ("Reflections on Anti-Anticommunism," *Continuity: A Journal of History* 26 [Spring 2003]: 36–37). See also John Earl Haynes and Harvey Klehr, "The Historiography of American Communism: An Unsettled Field," *Labour History Review* 68 (Apr. 2003): 61–78; Haynes and Klehr, *In Denial: Historians, Communism, and Espionage* (San Francisco: Encounter Books, 2003).

2. Cook, *Nightmare Decade,* 11–12, 382–83; Navasky, *Naming Names,* xxii, 40–41, 342–43; Schrecker, *Many Are the Crimes,* 188, 311–13, 342, 344–46; Caute, *Great Fear,* 133–38.

3. Powers, *Not without Honor;* Tanenhaus, *Whittaker Chambers;* Klehr and Haynes, *American Communist Movement;* Harvey Klehr, John Earl Haynes, and Fridrikh Igorevich Firsov, *The Secret World of American Communism* (New Haven, Conn.: Yale University Press, 1995); Klehr, Haynes, and Anderson, *Soviet World of American Communism;* John E. Haynes, *Red Scare or Red Menace? American Communism and Anticommunism in the Cold War* (Chicago: Ivan R. Dee, 1996), 182–83.

4. Herman, *Joseph McCarthy,* 312–13.

5. Olmsted, *Red Spy Queen,* 6, 68, 181–85, 193–94. See chap. 5, n. 4.

6. Leab, *I Was a Communist for the FBI.*

7. See, generally, Powers, *Secrecy and Power;* Theoharis and Cox, *Boss;* David J. Garrow, *The FBI and Martin Luther King Jr.: From "Solo" to Memphis* (New York: W. W. Norton, 1981); Gentry, *J. Edgar Hoover;* and Theoharis, *Chasing Spies.*

Index

ROBERT M. LICHTMAN, a Washington, D.C., lawyer for nearly thirty years, has practiced in San Francisco since 1986. He has argued frequently in federal appellate courts and in 1967 served as counsel to the special U.S. House committee assigned to report on the Adam Clayton Powell seating controversy.

RONALD D. COHEN, a professor of history at Indiana University Northwest, is the author of numerous articles and books, including *Children of the Mill* (1990) and *Rainbow Quest: Folk Music and American Society, 1940–1970* (2001). He is a former president of the History of Education Society and past president of the Historians of American Communism.

The University of Illinois Press
is a founding member of the
Association of American University Presses.

Composed in 10.5/13 Minion
by Jim Proefrock
at the University of Illinois Press
Manufactured by Thomson-Shore, Inc.

University of Illinois Press
1325 South Oak Street
Champaign, IL 61820-6903
www.press.uillinois.edu